Also by the authors

THE ONLY RETIREMENT GUIDE YOU'LL EVER NEED

THE ONLY JOB-HUNTING GUIDE YOU'LL EVER NEED

JOBS '90

JOBS '91

JOBS '92

JOBS '93

THE

OVER -40

JOB

GUIDE

KATHRYN & ROSS PETRAS

POSEIDON PRESS

NEW YORK LONDON TORONTO SYDNEY TOKYO SINGAPORE

POSEIDON PRESS
Simon & Schuster Building
Rockefeller Center
1230 Avenue of the Americas
New York, New York 10020

POSEIDON PRESS is a registered trademark of
Simon & Schuster Inc.

DESIGNED BY BARBARA MARKS & LYNNE KOPCIK
Manufactured in the United States of America

10 9 8 7 6 5 4 3 2 1

Library of Congress Cataloging-in-Publication Data

Petras, Kathryn.
   The over-40 job guide/Kathryn & Ross Petras
      p. cm.
   Includes bibliographical references and index.
   1. Job hunting. 2. Middle-aged persons—
Employment. I. Petras, Ross. 2. Title.
HF5382.7.P483   1993
650.14′084′4—dc20   93-3846
                                                     CIP

ISBN: 0-671-78078-6

Contents

Introduction

▶ **You're over 40, you're looking for a new job—and you're facing a rapidly changing job market.**

You know it—it's not an easy job market out there, especially if you're over 40.

This book isn't designed to mince words and pretend otherwise. It's designed as a down-to-earth, practical handbook for over-40 job hunters who want a detailed but user-friendly guide to finding out what they *need* to know. It is based on interviews and research with recruiters, employers, and, most importantly, with over-40 job hunters themselves. It's packed with sources, tips, examples, and ideas—all tailored for your situation as a middle-aged job hunter who needs to find a new or better job now.

▶ **First, one very important fact to keep in mind: You're not getting older, you're getting better. The problem is, not many employers acknowledge that fact.**

You've probably noticed it yourself—you're actually *more* efficient on the job now than when you were younger. You're less inclined to make errors out of ignorance, you've got more street smarts, you *know* your job, you know how to work well, and you want to work well.

Several studies bear out this gut feeling that, in the job world, older actually *is* better. On-the-job productivity actually increases as you get older, according to a study done at the State University of

New York at Binghamton, for both white- and blue-collar workers. Other studies show less absenteeism with older workers, and that they are easier and cheaper to train. Older employees are just as flexible in their working arrangements as younger employees, and can be as easily or more easily trained in new technologies. In other words, as you know well, there's no magical cutoff point after which computers and new management techniques become too new to learn, and there's always the added benefit of age bringing experience to the job.

The bottom line: All things being equal, hiring older workers is more cost effective than hiring younger workers, in most white- and blue-collar professions.

So why isn't the world beating a path to your door?

▶ **Like it or not, this is a youth-oriented culture, at least for the short term—and your job is to face that fact and get a job anyway.**

Let's not pretend that by reciting a few facts about reduced absenteeism you're going to convince a prejudiced employer to hire you.

All things being equal, employers prefer to hire younger workers. Study after study, survey after survey bears this out, even though few employers will admit it openly due to the possibility of age-bias suits, and even though age discrimination has been illegal for 26 years. Euphemisms abound—you're overqualified. "We're re-examining the requirements of the position," etc., etc. But age discrimination exists and is a problem to be faced, even if the reasons for it are based not on fact, but on the myths that older employees are less innovative, more expensive, and less productive than younger employees. The goal of this book is to face this problem squarely and help you work *around* inevitable age bias—to show how you can counter the age question, or avoid it, or, in some cases, hide your age until the hiring decision has been made.

▶ **Now for some good news: The way the job trends are going, age bias will *eventually* diminish.**

It's not going to make you feel better now, but as the economy improves and as corporations reposition themselves after the great downsizings of the late 1980s and the early to mid-1990s, the need for skilled employees will increase, and with it, so will demand for skilled workers over 40. In short, age bias will decrease in the future. But what about *now?* What are your prospects for finding a job in *today's* market?

▶ **The old rule of thumb: A job hunt will take you one month for every $10,000 you earned—more if you're over 40. The new rule of thumb: There is no rule.**

The job market has changed radically—and become so fragmented that generalizations are far more difficult to make. How long your job hunt will take depends on what specific set of skills you have to offer, and what the market is for them. While it may take five months for you to find a job as a lending officer, your neighbor may find a job as a highly paid environmental engineer in five days—and someone else might not find a job at all. Age as a factor in hiring now varies more widely than it did several years ago.

▶ *The bottom line:* **The changes in the job market have forced employees and job hunters to change as well.**

In the past ten years, over two million jobs have been lost by middle managers, blue-collar workers have found entire factories moved south of the border, and entire professions or managerial specialties have disappeared. To say these shifts have been difficult is an understatement—and to say that they're over is simply wrong.

The pace of corporate downsizings will diminish, the great industry shifts will slow—but the changes are permanent, and they will have a profound impact on the job market in the next five years.

Key: As corporations continue to downsize, they'll hire in a much more discriminating manner. This puts the burden on you, the job hunter, to show how useful you can be to the company. And it requires you to be more flexible, nimble, and ready for change. *You must be independent, not dependent.* You must think of yourself as an independent contractor, not an employee.

No longer can you count on staying in one job for five or ten years, no longer can you expect the company to "take care of you."

▶ **Here are some general guidelines to today's job market.**

Whatever your specific job situation, there are some *general* guidelines you'll have to follow to be successful in the years ahead. You'll have to:

- *Be flexible:* Business and the job market are changing so quickly you must always be ready for change. You'll have to take and accept responsibility for your career, and not entrust it to your superiors at work. You must learn to think and plan ahead at all times.

  What to do: Train yourself to welcome change, keep up with current events, keep current with your industry (read the appropriate trade journals), and cultivate friendships both inside and outside your career area.

- *Be innovative:* Think creatively—the rest of the century will reward those who use their brains and streamline procedures and cut costs. The rate of change will continue, and those who can *spot* innovation can keep ahead in the job game. Pay particular attention to major innovations that change entire industries. For example, the personal computer was a nice electronic toy in 1979 —and a multibillion-dollar business five years later. Job switchers who noticed this developed computer skills and knowledge early—and many had a key hiring advantage. They could get in on the ground floor at companies with tremendous futures, and they had knowledge that distinguished them from the rest and was salable.

- *Get in-demand skills:* Seek to continually broaden your base of specific and general skills, both inside and outside your area of expertise. *Remember:* Executives in the 1990s will not be as interested in who you are as in what you can do. Key general skills for the 1990s: languages (as business and government go international); computers (as they become ubiquitous); mathematics (as scientific innovation comes to the workplace); and, of course, communications skills (writing, speaking, making presentations, etc.).

  How to broaden your skill mix: Go to night school; moonlight in a skill-building area; ask your superiors for extra work or a transfer into an area where you can develop more salable skills; continually seek new assignments.

- *Get credentials:* If you've got skills—prove it. It's always best to have rock-solid credentials that prove you're skilled.

  What to do: Collect diplomas or certificates from training programs and courses. Mention certification on your resume and during interviews. If your company offers in-house courses and programs, take them.

- *Network:* With downsizing so prevalent, you can't afford to be complacent. Get into networks—formal or informal—now. Contacts will be the prime way of getting jobs for the rest of this century, as rapid change makes other avenues more difficult.

  What to do: Maintain a high profile—let others see how well you work. Get into networking groups; maintain a broad and informal group of contacts. Help others who are seeking jobs—they could help you out later. Read more about networks on page 72.

- *Be on top of the job market—always:* Whether the job market is good or bad, those who keep their informal networks strong, who know who's hiring, are ready when the unexpected happens. *Key:* As change accelerates, companies and jobs will come and go more rapidly—and those who stay on top of the job market will be ready if the ax falls.

- *Know how to job hunt effectively:* And that's what the rest of this book is about.

▶ **A brief note on how to use this book.**

This book was designed with a modular approach—it can be read from cover to cover, but individual chapters, sections, and subsections are designed to be easily accessible as well. You can refer to what you need when you need it, without having to flip through page after page of extraneous material.

The book covers the entire spectrum of the job hunt for over-40 job hunters—it's a complete, step-by-step approach to getting a job.

It begins with setting a job objective, then goes on to discuss researching jobs and companies, networking your way into job opportunities, writing an ageproof resume, writing cover letters and other letters that sell you, tactics to land interviews, interviewing well, answering sample interview questions, following up effectively, and, finally, assessing job offers.

In addition, we've included special sections on dealing with being fired or laid off, dealing with age discrimination, and self-employment.

At the end there is a list of sources—but we've made a point of including sources throughout the book. Our rationale is based on our own experience—the best way to remember and use sources is to have them mentioned when you need them. And that's part of the rationale behind the whole book—to make your job hunt as efficient as possible.

1

SETTING A JOB OBJECTIVE

INTRODUCTION

▶ **Assessing yourself and then setting clear goals: the *key* to an effective job hunt.**

An effective job hunt begins with a long, cold, hard look at yourself, your career goals, your personal goals, and the job market you face. Only once you've done this can you plan a focused campaign to meet your goals.

Obvious, but too many job hunters gloss over these very important beginning steps. They jump in without taking more than a perfunctory look ahead. They answer the classifieds, send out resumes, and go to interviews before answering the following questions:

- Where am I really going?
- How do I plan to get there?
- Am I doing the right thing?

259 0800 0618863

The result: unfocused resumes, poor research, a confused job hunt—and much wasted time.

Key: Just because you're over 40 and very probably saddled with responsibilities ranging from mortgages to children doesn't mean you can avoid these very essential steps in the interests of saving time and money. *It is even more important now.* Self-assessment and hard-headed goal setting focus your job hunt—and get you to the right job more quickly.

SELF-ASSESSMENT

▶ **Setting job goals begins with self-assessment.**

Chances are you've been so busy working over the past 20 or more years that you haven't had time for a *focused* look at yourself, at what motivates you beyond getting a paycheck—or even if getting a good paycheck is what matters most. You may have felt a vague dissatisfaction—"What I *really* should have done is . . ."—but you probably haven't gone beyond that to ask yourself: Do I want to change? How can I do it?

Key: A transitional period like the one you're probably in now gives you much to worry about. But it also gives you an opportunity to change things for the better, and to finally obtain the right job. At the very least, you may approach your job hunt more realistically.

▶ **For some, the impetus to change jobs and careers comes from hard economic realities—they've been laid off, or they're stuck in declining industries with little hope of a good future.**

The economic changes sweeping America have brought bad news to many. Many employees have been literally forced out of careers they had been planning to stay in until retirement. They're involuntary career changers. According to the Bureau of the Census, two-thirds of those switching careers who are 55 years and older do so involuntarily.

If you're in this position, the question may not be "Should I change careers?" but "Where can I go?" Self-assessment can help by pointing you toward the right areas; then comes job assessment and answers to the other key questions: Are my prospects better there? If not, what else should I consider?

▶ **Self-assessment begins with stopping for a moment and taking an honest look at yourself.**

There are many complex methods of getting at the real you—but the bottom line is that you must answer as honestly as possible a few key questions. For a (brief) moment, forget about money, forget about your responsibilities, forget practicality, forget "what I should be doing." Ask yourself:

- What interests me?

- What makes me angry?

- What hobbies do I enjoy?

- What have I accomplished in my life—and what do I want to accomplish?

- What areas of my job have I enjoyed the most, the least?

- Have I met my career and life goals?

- What kind of lifestyle do I have—and what kind do I want?

- What type of people do I enjoy working with?

- Where do I want to be 10 or 20 years from now?

Key: Get past the quickie definitions and labels—"I'm a banker," "I'm an employee of Chemical Bank," etc. Work at finding your underlying characteristics—"I love convincing people, being with people, showing people how to use things."

▶ **Another quick method of self-assessment: Write a brief autobiography.**

Go all the way back, paying special attention to the transition points in your life. Did you make the right decisions or do you feel a lingering regret at roads not taken?

Think back to where and when you have felt the most satisfied. What jobs and what job elements made you the happiest and most productive?

Assess your personality as honestly as possible. Forget how you *want* to be regarded—think of who you really are. How would your spouse, your friends describe you?

When you're done, read what you've written and see what conclusions you can make. Almost always, you'll find one or two jobs or job areas where you were the happiest. Focus on these. Do they point to different careers?

TIP: **A quick way of getting a feel for your interests is to flip through a college catalogue, particularly a night-school catalogue that includes job-related courses. Note which course descriptions you stop to read, which interest you enough to actually consider taking the course. If you have the time and money, take the course. And check the US Bureau of Labor Statistics'** *Occupational Outlook.* **It lists hundreds of careers, with descriptions and sources. Available at U.S. Government Bookstores, or order via telephone: 202-783-3238.**

▶ **Before deciding you're ready for a new career, ask yourself: Is it the career I'm unhappy with or is it the job?**

In today's stressful environment, it's easy to confuse career dissatisfaction with job dissatisfaction.

Ask yourself:

- *Would a vacation change my attitude?* Sometimes temporary burnout makes you unduly negative.

- *Do I have a personal problem with my superiors or with the corporate culture?* In other words, is it the specific company or job, and not the career?

- *Would more (or less) of a work load ease my problems?*

- *Would a lateral move be better?* This is important. A lateral move—if possible—may be the real answer to your problems. You may be bored with your present position, and a lateral move may energize you—and give you more skills.

- *Is the industry or profession declining or downsizing?* This raises questions of economics. And it forces you to decide: Is there any *practical* and *reasonable* hope for my staying in this career—or should I seek an alternative?

▶ **Self-assessment is difficult: at times you may need professional help.**

The problem with self-assessment is that it's easy to lie to yourself, to hide your real wants and needs behind a fog of self-justification. It can also be difficult to weigh alternatives on your own, and decide upon a course of action. Sometimes, professionals can help. You may wish to consider:

- Career counseling. See pages 29–34 for a full discussion of where to go, what to look for, what to look out for, and how counseling can help.

- Testing. See pages 30–32 for a full discussion of what psychological and career testing can tell you.

- Computer programs. See pages 34–35.

- Books. Many books offer detailed methods of self-examination and ideas for discussion. Some of the best:

SOURCE: *Wishcraft,* by Barbara Sher with Ann Gottlieb (New York: Ballantine Books, 1983).

SOURCE: *Where Do I Go from Here with My Life?,* by John C. Crystal and Richard Nelson Bolles (Berkeley: Ten Speed Press, 1974).

SOURCE: *What Color Is Your Parachute?,* by Richard Nelson Bolles (Berkeley: Ten Speed Press, 1987).

▶ **Don't get caught in the self-assessment trap.**

Overquestioning your motivations can be as bad as underquestioning. It's not too common, but some over-40 job hunters turn self-assessment into mental paralysis. They waste severance pay and valuable time delving deeper and deeper into their psyches, considering option after option. They avoid the neccesity for action, for decision making.

The bottom line

Discipline yourself, as you would at work. Recognize the need for educated decisions based upon active questioning and research —and then a plan of action. If you get stuck, consider seeking professional help.

CAREER ASSESSMENT

▶ **Self-assessment determines if you're content with your career and points out areas for you to consider. Job and career assessment deals with the specifics, the actions you can take—and the economic realities you must face.**

Essentially, you come out of self-assessment with one of two realizations—either you are content with your career path or you are not. If you are not, *now* is the time to consider a new career. Your discontentment may have arisen out of economic realities—there may simply be very little gainful employment in your field or very little hope for upward movement. Or it may have arisen out of deep-rooted dissatisfaction with the very nature of your career. Either way, you must now decide what to *do*.

▶ **You have several options to consider.**

Career changing is difficult; but so is staying put if you're emotionally dissatisfied, underemployed, or unemployed in a career facing economic difficulties. It might be more practical to change careers now, or at least work toward that eventual goal. Essentially, if you've come out of self-assessment with the feeling that you're in the wrong career area, you have three options:

1. Worst case: *You stay in your current career or look for a job in your current career area.* Even here, you might be able to make some adjustments—for example, search for a better job, a job in a different locale, etc.

2. Middle case: *You change careers now.* This might *feel* or sound like the best option, but by changing immediately, you forgo time researching and planning—which can make your career move better and easier. Of course, unemployment and poor employment prospects may force this option on you.

3. Best case: *You stay in your current career but plan on taking interim steps to move into another career.* This is usually the best option, because you give yourself time to plan.

▶ *Key:* **Before you make any final decision, take the time to research and consider all your options.**

Many times, dissatisfied over-40 job hunters play the rationale game—"I'm too old for a change, the job market is terrible, I don't have time," etc. And so they go on and search for a job in their old unsatisfying or weak career area. Or, worse, they jump into a new career without researching it. A franchise may look like the answer to your dreams—but be forewarned that one-third of all franchises fail.

Key point

Don't give up and don't jump before you know what you're talking about. Take the time to do some initial research into a new career area if you're dissatisfied—even if money concerns force you to keep on searching for a job in your field or accept an interim job.

▶ **Here's how to research new careers effectively.**

The best place to start: The career section of your local library —or better yet, try a nearby college library. See Chapter 2 "Research," for details on how to research effectively.

The key to effective career research is to start with a very large focus—and then narrow down, based upon in-depth research into the careers or opportunities that interest you. With each career area that does interest you, assess the:

- *True nature of the career, not the ideal:* For example, many idealistic and imaginative types of people (and there are many in even the most practical of professions) start out with unrealistic ideas of how wonderful "glamour" fields like restaurant entrepreneurship are, only to find that the hard work, cutthroat competition, insecurity, and high failure rate make it far from glamorous. Others will say: *So what? It's worth the chance.*

- *Training required:* If training to enter the new field is extensive and you're in your early 40s, you may consider the time well spent—but what if you're in your 50s . . . or 60s?

- *How much you can bring to the career now:* The easiest and often the best career changes are those where you already have a lot to offer. From the train hobbyist who opens a model train store, to the environmental engineer who opens a consultancy, to the banker who now runs the financial side of a museum, those who already have something to offer tend to find their moves easier —and more lucrative more quickly.

- *Personality fit:* Will you fit in? This is particularly important in entrepreneurial fields. Downsizing and large retirement checks have made it easier for many middle managers to decide to embark upon a new entrepreneurial career. Going out on your own may sound wonderful, but think about the loneliness, lack of corporate support (you'll have to manage everything yourself, from buying paper clips to ad time), insecurity, long hours. Some people thrive on such regimens; others realize they're happiest in nice, "safe" corporate environments. For more on self-employment, see page 299.

- *Job and advancement potential:* As an older entrant, getting into a new area may be tougher, and advancement may be slower or more difficult.

- *Subfields within your target career area:* Look for *specific* areas that interest you the most. Write them down and research thoroughly.

- *Your interest level:* Now that you know more about it—does it still really interest you?

- *Finances and feasibility:* For the time being, don't overworry about these—that's the next step.

Work at eliminating areas that don't seem right. When you're down to one or two, move on to the next step.

TIP: Call your stockbroker for industry research reports and corporate reports—you'll get an up-to-date feel for the business and job-hunting climate.

SOURCE: *Second Careers: New Ways to Work After 50,* by Caroline Bird (Boston: Little, Brown, 1992).

▶ **Network and interview to get the inside scoop on a new career area.**

Books and library research are one thing—but to get the real "feel" for a new career, industry, or position you must talk to people in the business or profession.

How can you find the right people to talk with?

The answer is found in the overused word *networking*. Even today, with *everyone* talking about it, it can still be quite effective, particularly if your enthusiasm and knowledge levels are high. Also, in hard times many contacts may be willing to talk just in case they need you to return the favor later. A persistent, polite, and focused network campaign can still work. See page 72 for details on how to network.

▶ **This is what to ask your network contacts.**

The key is to get an *honest* assessment of the career and job. Watch out for the natural human tendency to gloss over the bad and tell you only the good. And realize that just because *they* like it, this doesn't mean that you will too. Ask negative as well as positive questions—find out the downside before you make a jump.

Essentially, you'll be asking questions in two broad categories—about the career itself, and then, if you're still interested, about your possibilities to enter the career. Below are some of the major areas to cover.

Career Assessment

- What kind of person fits in well?

- Would you work in this profession if you could do it all over again?

- What are the best and worst points about the career?

- What do you enjoy about the career?

- What does the future hold for the field?

Job Assessment

- Are there job opportunities available? If so, where? At what level?

- What kind of training or education is required? Where would you go about getting it?

- Would your age be a significant problem? (Be careful—sometimes the answer is yes, when the reality is no. If your informant thinks age is a problem, ask for details and examples.)

- Do you know of other career changers in this career area?

- Considering your background, what problems or advantages would you have that might affect your performance or ability to find employment?

- What kind of advancement potential is there?

- What kind of monetary potential is there?

WEIGHING CAREER ALTERNATIVES

▶ **This is the toughest part: weighing what you've found out and answering the question** *Now what do I do?*

It may take you only a week or two to decide what you *want* to do, but many prudent career changers take upward of six months to focus, and then, often, several years of planning and fine-tuning before they actually reach a long-term goal.

You have several key criteria to weigh:

- *Psychological:* Do you really want to change careers after all? How strongly do you wish to do so?

- *Ease of entry:* How much training or education is necessary, and can you—and do you want to—do it? How difficult will it be to find a job later? *Key point:* You probably won't start at the absolute bottom in a new career. Chances are your accumulated experience will count for something.

- *Time:* Are you willing to take time out of your life now to start over?

- *Trade-offs:* Nothing is perfect. What will you have to give up in your new career—and what will you gain? Is the new balance worth it?

- *Financial aspects:* Often the key criterion. Can you afford to? How? Think this over carefully. Is it worth it, and can you afford to draw on your savings? Can your spouse support you temporarily? Is there a part-time way you can obtain initial training? Can you make a lateral move and not lose salary? Are there skills on your resume that might make a lateral move likely? And on the other hand, can you afford *not* to? Is it better to take a risk now or in a few years than to plan on "waiting it out" in a declining field?

TIP: **Go over the financial aspects with a *trusted* financial planner. There may be some you haven't thought of.**

- *Family:* How will all this affect your family? Even beyond the financial aspects, a new career can mean much more time spent away from your family.

For all the above, remember one thing: Often your subconscious mind has weighed all these factors and has already made your decision for you. If in your gut you know it's right—listen to your gut feelings.

▶ **The worse the job market or economic climate is, the easier it is to postpone decision making.**

But that doesn't mean you can't or shouldn't do anything. If you've reviewed the above and are telling yourself you should eventually make a switch, plan now on your interim steps.

Key: Go back and ask your network contacts how to plan a long-term switch into this new career—and ask for advice based upon your current job or career. Are there areas through which it might be easier to move into the new career? If so, prioritize your job search accordingly. In other words, you might normally view job A as a worse position than your present one, but if it gets you closer to your ultimate goal of switching careers, put emphasis on it during your job hunt.

▶ **Develop a plan of action.**

Prepare, preferably in conjunction with some of your network contacts, a plan of action that includes the following:

- *Further research:* Fill in knowledge gaps on your chosen career. Work on finding and targeting the most feasible and specific areas within your new career.

- *Training or education:* Research the best schools or training areas, entry requirements (including financial), and duration of training. List and weigh the different training alternatives.

- *Job-search information:* Find out now what you should emphasize during training and research to make you employable, and work now to develop a network of contacts. Find out how long it will take and how hard it will be to find a position. See if there are any part-time or full-time positions available now where you may learn on the job.

- *Financial aspects:* Develop a plan to support your switch. See below for details.

▶ **Financial aspects of a job or career switch must be looked at carefully.**

Finances are often the key criterion in deciding if, when, and how to make a switch. Here's a brief outline of what to do:

- *Check with your company about your pension, insurance, and severance pay.* (See pages 27–28 for specifics.)

- *Prepare a cash-flow statement* of current income and expenses.

- *Estimate income and outflow if a change is made;* include educational expenses (if any); job-hunting expenses; insurance payments you may have to assume; lack of income from current job, etc. *Rule of thumb:* Plan to have at least six months' cash on hand to support yourself if you're switching careers—more if the economic outlook is poor in your field or if you're starting a business on your own.

- *If there are problems, tinker with your statement.* See if you can reasonably increase income or reduce expenses. For example, are there expenses you can cut? Can you go for part-time rather than full-time training?

SOURCE: The Business and Professional Women's Foundation (2012 Massachusetts Ave. NW, Washington, DC, 20036) has information on scholarship and loan programs for adult students.

TIP: **If you are a career changer considering entrepreneurship, check various sources of capital, including the National Association for Female Executives, which now has a venture capital program (page 311), and the Small Business Association; also, see pages 299–309 for more detailed information.**

▶ **What to check when you're considering leaving your company.**

If you've decided to take the plunge into a new career, there are a number of practical steps to take:

- *Find out the terms of your retirement plan(s).* Terms vary according to your specific pension plan. Talk to your company's pension administrator or human resources manager to determine the parameters of your plan. If you're a participant in a defined benefit plan (a plan under which you receive a guaranteed amount of money upon retirement), your plan probably isn't portable—that is, you typically cannot switch your pension over to your new company. If, on the other hand, you're covered by a defined contribution plan (in which the company contributes a set amount to the company pension fund in your name), your plan is probably portable and can be rolled over into your new employer's plan. In this case, you also have the option to leave the plan with the company. If you feel the plan has been well administered, leave it. However, given recent problems with pensions, your best bet may be to take the money and roll it over into your new company plan or into an IRA you set up for this purpose. (For more information on this, see pages 282–84.)

- *If you're an upper-level executive, be sure to find out if your retirement plan is a SERP* (Supplementary Employee Retirement Plan). If you earn upward of $200,000, chances are all or part of your retirement benefits isn't in a qualified pension plan, but in a SERP. If this is the case, you may lose your entire benefit amount if you leave the company prior to retirement.

- *Determine whether you will take benefits from company plans in a lump sum or roll them into another tax-deferred plan* (either your new employer's or a segregated IRA you set up). Obviously, if you choose to receive your benefits from such company plans as pension plans, profit sharing, and 401(k)s, you face a tax bite and a 10% penalty if you're under 59½. However, if you need the money to fund your job hunt, this is an option to consider.

Otherwise, you'll probably roll your benefits into another tax-deferred plan. (Remember, you must complete your roll-over within 60 days of withdrawing the money. In addition, if you don't arrange a trustee-to-trustee transfer, you'll pay 20% withholding. See pages 282–84 for more information.)

TIP: There is one way you can receive your money from a company plan before the age of 59½ and avoid paying a penalty—receive your payout in a series of scheduled payments over your life expectancy (or joint expectancy of you and your designated survivor). These payments must be relatively equal, must be paid at least annually, and must cover at least 5 years.

If you're over 59½, you may face a choice between receiving your payment either as a lump sum or as an annuity. In this case, you should weigh the options and choose accordingly.

- *Recognize what will happen to your various company-covered insurance policies.* Here is a quick rundown of the different types of insurance.

Health insurance: Under COBRA laws, you have the option of picking up the bill for your health coverage and can be fully covered for up to 18 months. The drawback, however, is that these costs are usually very high. You may be better off seeking health insurance on your own.

TIP: If you have few medical needs, consider opting for a low-cost, high-deductible major medical insurance policy to cover you only until you've landed another job. This will take care of your bills if you're hit with a major illness or catastrophic accident, but it won't cost you a high premium.

Disability insurance: This will cease upon your leaving the company. As such, you may want to consider getting your own policy to fill the gap.

TIP: If you do want to continue disability coverage, get an individual policy guaranteed renewable (which means there will be no rate fluctuation) *before* you quit your company. Costs that often rise for the self-employed are lower this way, and you won't be refused coverage—a common problem for the unemployed.

Life insurance: Although you can usually switch your company policy over into an individual one under the same insurance carrier, you're usually better off not doing so. Reason? As with medical insurance, costs for these policies are usually higher than what you can get on your own.

TIP: **If you belong to a trade or professional association, check to see if it offers any insurance coverage. Many groups offer competitive or better rates on all forms of insurance—health, life, etc. For example, the National Association for Female Executives offers competitive term life rates.**

- *Look into and weigh the terms of your severance pay*—lump sum or weekly paycheck? It's an important point. In some cases, if you opt for the weekly paycheck, you'll also continue being covered on your employer's medical insurance policy, and will continue having your employer contribute to your 401(k). But if you opt for the lump sum, you get nothing but that lump sum.

- *If you've taken loans from your 401(k) plan, pay them back.* Remember —these loans are due upon your leaving the company. If you don't pay, they are considered early distribution, which means you owe a 10% early-distribution penalty, as well as tax on the money received.

CAREER COUNSELING AND TESTING

▶ **Career counselors can help you in several ways—but make certain you pick the right counselor.**

Career counselors can be useful for the busy over-40 job hunter. They can speed the self-assessment process, they can give you an objective and clear picture of your career potentials and problems, and they can help you move into the right job more quickly. Sometimes, they can help with the job search itself, counseling you on interviewing or resume writing. Or they may provide you with access to career data banks, and other educational information and sources. Note that career counselors are not employment agencies or headhunters—and beware of those who claim they can find you a job.

▶ **Career counseling is normally a three- or four-step process.**

Step 1: A good career counselor will interview you in depth, discussing your background, education, work experience, and specific career problems or goals.

Step 2: You'll probably take tests to determine your career aptitudes and skills.

Step 3: You'll discuss the test results and work at putting them together with the results of further in-depth discussions to determine career goals. You'll also discuss the steps you need to take to meet those goals—either job related or educational.

Step 4: You'll be given a summary of the results.

▶ **Career testing is one way of identifying your career goals and skills.**

Many people hope to find all the answers with a simple test—and therein lies the danger. Career tests are guides—and you'll most often need the skills of a good counselor to interpret them correctly.

▶ **There are three basic types of career tests: interest inventory tests, personality tests, and aptitude tests. All are designed to help you arrive at answers to questions you may have difficulty answering on your own:** *What do I like to do? Are there other fields or careers I've overlooked where I might be happier or more productive? What kind of employee am I? What do I value in my work?*

Interest inventory tests are tests that measure your basic preferences in hundreds of categories—and make career suggestions based on your answers.

The Strong Interest Inventory is one of the most frequently used. It's a multiple-choice test of over 300 questions that focuses on specific types of work and general interests, as well as the individual characteristics that make up one's personality. Essentially, the test is a series of lists: lists of professions, school subjects, activities, and so on. As a test taker, you rapidly fill in your likes and dislikes in each category, or your preferences—for example, whether you would prefer being a stockbroker or a warehouse manager, are indifferent to the choice, or can't decide. Your scores are analyzed and matched against the scores of others who have taken the test. Certain conclusions are drawn. For instance, you may currently be a logistics engineer, but your responses may be found to largely match those of salespeople. This could prompt you to look more closely at sales or related careers, and consider such options as selling logistics services instead of providing them.

Other commonly used tests similar to this are the Kuder Occupational Interest Survey and the Jackson Vocational Survey.

Personality tests: Whereas the Strong Interest Inventory is primarily concerned with careers, the Meyers-Brigg Type Indicator test and others like it concentrate on personality. The Meyers-Brigg test is a three-section test of 126 questions that give choices between activities and attitudes, and between different words. It can tell you how you behave, how you want to be perceived, and how you view yourself. One question might ask if you would rather be considered a tough person or a gentle person; another might ask you to decide which of two words appeals to you more: "innovative" or "traditional."

When the test is scored, you are designated as one of sixteen personality types, based on four scales: extroversion-introversion; sensing-intuition; judgment-perception; thinking-feeling.

The Meyers-Brigg test has many satisfied customers, including top executives. The premise behind the test is that certain personality types do best in certain types of careers. Many people have found that the test has accurately predicted or assessed their "unscientific" gut-level preferences in careers, or in specific jobs within careers. It is particularly valuable in conjunction with the Strong Interest Inventory.

Aptitude tests: By the time you're 40 or older, you're probably fairly certain of your talents and skills. But for those thinking about switching careers, aptitude tests like the ones administered by the Johnson O'Conner Research Foundation can be valuable. They are also used by some career counselors.

On-your-own testing: the Holland Self-Directed Search is a combined interest and ability test that is available at many community centers, colleges, etc. One advantage: It's much cheaper than the others.

Key: These tests are guides, and are best taken under the auspices of a trained counselor. Evaluate their results with a large degree of flexibility and creativity. For example, a stockbroker might find he or she scores highest in the Strong test as a research scientist, and very low in most sales categories. Quite obviously, instead of suggesting the stockbroker pursue a Ph.D. in chemistry, one might best interpret the results by suggesting that this person explore a career as a stock analyst, or work as a non-sales staff member or in a management position with a brokerage house.

▶ **Choose a career counselor carefully.**

In today's difficult job market, there are many charlatans who seek to exploit the unwary. Here are some rules of thumb to keep in mind when choosing a counselor:

- *Check the counselor's credentials.* In most states, career counselors are unregulated, but there are certifying boards. While certification is no guarantee, it does indicate that the counselor has met certain standards, at least on paper. To find counselors with proper credentials, check for certification from:

SOURCE: **The National Board of Certified Counselors (NBCC)** and **The National Career Development Association (NCDA)** (Both are divisions of the American Association for Counseling and Development, 5999 Stevenson Ave., Alexandria, VA 22304.) The NBCC is the major certifying agency for career counselors. Certified counselors have an accredited graduate degree in an appropriate field, supervised experience, and endorsements, and they have passed a certification examination.

Also check listings in:

SOURCE: **Catalyst National Network of Career Resource Centers,** 250 Park Avenue South, New York, NY 10003. Tel.: 212-777-8900. Lists reputable member counselors in its nationwide listing of career centers for women.

SOURCE: *Directory of Outplacement Firms,* Kennedy & Kennedy, Inc., Templeton Rd., Fitzwilliam, NH 03447. Tel.: 603-585-2200. Lists names and addresses of outplacement firms.

SOURCE: *Executive Employment Guide,* American Management Association, 135 W. Fiftieth St., New York, NY 10020. Tel.: 212-586-8100. Lists career counselors; provides general employment listings.

SOURCE: **Other listings:** Check state and local offices. For listings of counselors, network groups, church groups, and others may be helpful.

- *Check the counselor's references.* Is the counselor affiliated with any groups, such as a university, a corporation, or a nonprofit group? Ask for a listing of previous clients, and call these people or groups.

- *Beware of any counselor who offers job placement or demands a large up-front fee.* Counselors who do this, or who promise miraculous results, are usually frauds. Don't necessarily be impressed by a large well-appointed office—high fees may generate luxurious offices . . . and bad service.

- *Research the background of your counselor.* Call your state or local department of consumer affairs to see if any complaints have been registered.

- *Interview the counselor to make certain his or her general approach is agreeable with you.* This is an important step in your life, and you should feel comfortable with your counselor. Some people prefer a trained psychologist, others an outplacement specialist. Ask about testing, research facilities, his or her definition of success, and anything else important to you.

- *Ask about the price per session.* Shop and compare—prices may vary enormously. Again, beware of high fees, particularly high up-front fees. You can get excellent service for low prices. The average range is $50–100 per session. Most counselors require a minimum of five sessions, so the total cost with testing should be about $250–$500, more for specialized or in-depth sessions. Some nonprofit organizations have a sliding scale, based on your ability to pay.

- *Get it in writing.* Ask for a written statement of what services you will receive and the costs for these services.

▶ **Other types of career counseling.**

Some university night schools offer courses on career changing, which usually include group counseling and exercises. The value of these courses varies, but the price is usually low, and it is often easier, and sometimes more useful, to contemplate a career change with others in the same boat. Another option is to sign up with:

SOURCE: **The Crystal-Barkley Corporation,** Headquarters: 111 E. Thirty-first Street, New York, NY 10016. Tel.: 212-889-8500.

The Crystal-Barkley Corporation offers an interpersonal approach to counseling, based upon the experience of the founder, John C. Crystal, an ex-OSS officer and businessman, and co-author, along with Richard Bolles (*What Color Is Your Parachute?*) of the bestseller *Where Do I Go from Here with My Life?*

In groups or as individuals, clients are led through a unique series of in-depth exercises and counseling sessions designed to help them discover who they are, what they want to do—and, most important, how to go about accomplishing it. A network listing of successful job and career changers is maintained, and the centers offer lectures by businessmen, entrepreneurs, and experts in career-changing and motivation.

COMPUTER PROGRAMS FOR FINDING CAREERS

▶ **More and better computer programs are coming on the market to guide you through career decisions.**

Most of these are computerized substitutes for career counselors, with an interactive format that guides you, through a series of questions and answers, to a focused career decision.

Below are listed a few good programs currently on the market —call or check at your local computer software store for current prices and compatibility with your computer system. Also: ask for a demonstration or a demonstration version to make certain the program will actually be useful for your purposes. (Local libraries and colleges may have these or other programs available for use for a nominal fee.)

SOURCE: *Career Design:* Sophisticated question-answer format. In a series of modules you gradually focus on your underlying career desires. Stresses self-motivated action rather than just passive analysis. For more information: Career Design Software; PO Box 95624; Atlanta, GA 30347. Tel.: 800-346-8007; 404-321-6100; $99.

SOURCE: *Peterson's Career Options:* Question-and-answer format. Leads you to various career options, with brief general descriptions of the careers. For more information: Peterson's; PO Box 2123; Princeton, NJ 08543-2123. Tel.: 800-338-3282; $295.

SOURCE: ***Career Opportunities:*** Not a career-assessment program but a computerized career bank, which includes the texts of *The Federal Career Guide, The Occupational Outlook Quarterly,* and *Your Military Today* (which lists civilian employment opportunities in the military). Useful for browsing, and computerized searching and information. For more information: Quanta Press, Inc.; 1313 Fifth St. SE, #208C; Minneapolis, MN 55414. Tel.: 612-379-3956; $129.

SOURCE: ***The Ultimate Job Finder:*** A computerized listing of sources of job vacancies; includes all sources listed in *Professional's Job Finder, Non-Profits' Job Finder,* and *Government Job Finder.* Helpful in tracking down information for your job hunt. For more information: Planning/Communications, 7215 Oak Ave., River Forest, IL 60305-1935. Tel.: 708-366-5200, 800-859-5220; $59.95 + $3.95 shipping.

2

RESEARCH

INTRODUCTION

▶ **Everyone knows research is a vital part of job hunting—but what everyone *doesn't* seem to know is the smart way to do research.**

It's a damn shame. So many job hunters put in their time researching, spending hours in the library, poring over directories and magazines . . . but they're spending more time than they have to. Or they're not getting the payoff they could.

The problem? They're not researching as efficiently or effectively as possible. They're not taking advantage of the information explosion going on around them.

When you research the smart way, you can:

• Research on company time, using the corporate library as a job-hunting headquarters.

- Use CD-ROMs to access information in seconds.

- Use your personal computer to pull together a targeted list of companies that meet certain criteria.

- Plan and carry out a long-distance job search without ever leaving town.

Smart research is especially important in these tough times—when more people are falling victim to downsizing or feeling concerned about a shrinking industry.

EXAMPLE: **Marilyn S., a director of human resources for a large department store chain, began thinking about looking for a new job when her company filed for bankruptcy. Recognizing that the retail industry in general was going through a rough period, she first used research to choose a growing industry. By reading general business magazines and going through financial statistics and industry forecasts, she chose the health care field. Next, she used research to narrow in on target companies—large health services chains that could use her human resources skills in setting up training programs, screening applicants, and the like. She read through trade journals to learn which large chains were expanding and which incorporated extensive human resources programs. Finally, she chose fifteen companies—and used research to tailor her letters *specifically* for each company. The outcome? Offers for interviews from three of the companies—and offers for jobs from two of those three.**

Convinced that there's a better way of researching? Read on, and we'll run down the specific research tools to use and tips on how to get the most out of them.

One note: Smart doesn't necessarily mean new. Some old, tried, and true methods are still viable—and still the best way. *The bottom line,* as always, is getting the information you need in the least amount of time. The following methods and tips will help you meet this goal.

BASIC RESEARCH TOOLS: WHAT TO USE TO GET THE INFORMATION YOU NEED—AND WHAT TO DO WITH THE INFORMATION YOU GET.

▶ **Let's start with the basics in a quick rundown of the research tools you'll be using: directories, trade publications and other** business periodicals, computer data bases, company material (annual reports, media kits, etc.), and others.

Directories

▶ **Directories are probably the most widely used reference tool— easily available, straightforward, and comprehensive. Use them for a quick-and-easy way of finding the basic information you'll need in different phases of your job hunt.**

Most of you have used directories at one point or another in your work life—perhaps to locate sales prospects, get competitive information, or target possible acquisitions. You'll use them in your job hunt in a similar way.

As a job hunter, you can use directories to:

- Find target company names and addresses for a direct-mail campaign.

- Get background information on companies and leads to *other* sources of information on companies.

- Find biographical information on top executives in a company that will be interviewing you.

If you don't know the specific directory you need, your first stop will be a directory of directories. One of the best:

Directories in Print
Gale Research, Inc.
PO Box 33477
Detroit, MI 48232-5477
800-877-GALE
Fax: 313-961-6083
This is an old standby, available at virtually every public library, as well as in many corporate libraries. It lists thousands of directories. But be aware that information is often outdated; be sure to check when the directory referred to was printed—you generally don't want to use anything over a year old. Also, in this publication, books that include lists are considered directories—and for your purposes, they're really not. Read the descriptive material carefully.

▶ **To pull together names of companies to compile a mailing list for a direct-mail campaign, use one or more of the following** *corporate directories.*

These all list thousands of companies, typically including company name, address, phone and fax numbers, and some general information: the company's line of business, branch offices, key executives, financial statistics, number of employees, and the like. Most offer indexing by industry categories according to SIC (Standard Industry Classification) codes (listed in the front of most directories), and by geographic location (state or zip code). Some also include lists of companies in the same industry ranked by sales or by number of employees.

Note: Many of these directories are on computerized CD-ROM lists at the library. For more information on computerized research, see page 61.

TIP: Some of the following directories offer their listings on mailing labels—but *don't be tempted.* Yes, you don't have to type addresses, but you still *will* have to type the name of the person to whom you're sending your letter and resume. The outcome? Your envelope looks sloppy, and you're advertising the fact that you're doing a large mailing. Not a great way of making a first impression.

TIP: Whenever possible, double-check directory information—names, addresses, and telephone numbers. Even in a directory marked 1993, the information is already a year old. Companies change addresses, merge with other companies, even go belly up.

TIP: Many directories offer their data on computer disks. This may be a help if you're planning to do your direct-mail campaign on computer. You can import names and addresses from the disk into your word processing program and do a mail merge.

The following directories are general business directories—not trade or state specific. (In most cases, costs are steep—often hovering around the $1,000 range. So you may be better off using them at your local library than buying them.)

Dun's Million-Dollar Directory
Dun's Marketing Services
3 Sylvan Way
Parsippany, NJ 07054
800-526-0651

Available at virtually every library and also on-line on CD-ROM, *Dun's Million-Dollar Directory* lists over 160,000 businesses—including name, address, phone number, key executives, and financial statistics. Often more useful than *Standard & Poor's Register* (see below), because it includes smaller companies, subsidiaries of companies, etc. One problem—corporate names are often abbreviated. If you use *Dun's,* always call for the complete name of the company.

Standard & Poor's Register of Corporations, Directors, and Executives

Standard & Poor's Corporation
25 Broadway
New York, NY 10004
212-208-8702

Another library staple, *S & P* consists of three volumes, covering over 50,000 firms. Listings include brief financial profiles, and names and addresses of major executives, directors, new firms, etc. The key problems with using this to put together a resume mailing list— *S & P* often lists only headquarters addresses, contains only major incorporated companies, and *doesn't* contain listings for subsidiaries or private companies.

Ward's Business Directory of U.S. Private and Public Companies

Gale Research, Inc.
PO Box 33477
Detroit, MI 48232-5477
800-877-GALE
Fax: 313-961-6083

Not at every library, but one of the best guides for job hunters, this covers over 107,000 businesses, listed alphabetically, and includes ranked listings with addresses—making it very handy to quickly pull together a mailing list.

Corporate Yellow Pages

Monitor Publishing Company
104 Fifth Ave., Second Floor
New York, NY 10011
212-627-4140
Fax: 212-645-0931

A good choice if you're targeting major public corporations and are thinking about buying a directory—this cost only $185 in 1992. It lists over 38,000 executives—and includes their *direct-dial phone numbers*—a nice time saver, and a great way of contacting prospective employers.

Standard Directory of Advertisers: Classified Edition
Standard Rate & Data Service
3004 Glenview Road
Wilmette, IL 60091
708-256-6067

The "Red Book," as it is usually called, lists companies that spend $75,000 or more a year on advertising. In keeping with this slant, it includes names of advertising, marketing, and sales executives, as well as an index of brand names.

TIP: If you're planning a resume mailing to chiefly well-known companies, you may want to use a less expensive method of getting addresses. The *National Directory of Addresses and Telephone Numbers* (Gale Research, Inc., PO Box 33477, Detroit, MI 48232-5477. Tel.: 800-877-GALE, Fax: 313-961-6083) has addresses and phone numbers of thousands of companies. At only $49.95 (1992 price), it's a great inexpensive source of information.

Find often hard-to-locate private companies in:

Macmillan Directory of Leading Private Companies
Reed Reference Publishing
PO Box 31
New Providence, NJ 07974
800-323-6772

Directory of Leading Private Companies
Reed Reference Publishing
PO Box 31
New Providence, NJ 07974
800-323-6772

If you're targeting manufacturing companies, your best bets are:

Moody's Industrial Manual
Moody's Investor Service
99 Church St.
New York, NY 10007
212-533-0300

This lists about 3,000 publicly traded US and international companies. (Moody's also puts out manuals for: Bank & Finance, Public Utilities, Transportation, Municipals.)

Thomas Register of American Manufacturers

Thomas Publishing Co.
1 Pennsylvania Plaza
New York, NY 10110
212-695-0500

A 12-volume directory that lists virtually all US manufacturers—not only those publicly traded. A plus: It also lists products and product lines.

American Manufacturers Directory

American Business Directories
5711 S. 86th Circle
PO Box 27347
Omaha, NE 68127
402-593-4600
Fax: 402-331-5481

Not typically in the library, this may be a good choice for home use since it's relatively inexpensive—$545 in 1992. It lists 120,000 manufacturers and includes up to four executives in each listing.

On the other hand, if you're after a job in the service industries, check:

Dun's Directory of Service Companies

Dun's Marketing Services
3 Sylvan Way
Parsippany, NJ 07054
800-526-0651

This directory covers a range of service industries, including management consulting, executive search services, public relations, engineering and architecture, accounting, auditing and bookkeeping, health services, legal and social services, research, hospitality, and motion picture, amusement, and recreational services.

If you're thinking about casting your job-search net overseas, check the following:

America's Corporate Families and International Affiliates

Dun's Marketing Services
3 Sylvan Way
Parsippany, NJ 07054
800-526-0651
201-455-0900

This directory covers 1,700 US companies and their 13,000 foreign subsidiaries, as well as 6,000 US subsidiaries of international companies.

International Corporate 1000 Yellow Book
Monitor Publishing Co.
104 Fifth Ave., Second Floor
New York, NY 10011
212-627-4140
Fax: 212-645-0931

Covering the world's top 1,000 companies, this directory lists names of executives, direct-dial phone numbers, etc.

International Directory of Corporate Affiliations
Reed Reference Publishing
PO Box 31
New Providence, NJ 07974
800-323-6772

This directory includes listings of US-based subsidiaries of foreign companies and international subsidiaries of US companies.

If you're targeting smaller companies, check:

Dun's Million-Dollar Directory
(listed above)

Dun's Middle Market Directory
Dun's Marketing Services
3 Sylvan Way
Parsippany, NJ 07054
800-526-0651

Some other fairly general directories that may fit into your job hunt:

Directory of Corporate Affiliations
Reed Reference Publishing
PO Box 31
New Providence, NJ 07974
800-323-6772

This directory covers divisions and subsidiaries of more than 4,000 companies. Listings include financial statistics, officers, and—a plus for putting together a mailing list—names of officers at the divisions and subsidiaries.

Dun's Business Rankings

Dun's Marketing Services
3 Sylvan Way
Parsippany, NJ 07054
800-526-0651

This is a compilation of ranked lists, by industry. The top 7,500 companies (both public and private) are ranked by sales and by number of employees. Includes address, phone, etc., but doesn't include executives.

Dun's Career Guide

Dun's Marketing Services
3 Sylvan Way
Parsippany, NJ 07054
800-526-0651

Another of Dun's guides, this lists employers, hiring areas, contact names, etc., arranged by state. A key problem—information is often overly general. For example, when listing the areas in which a company hires, this guide names virtually every general business category—from accounting to administration to sales—which makes it not as helpful as one would like. In addition, many large employers aren't included—making the state listings incomplete. Even so, it's worth a quick look if you've got the time.

▶ **If you're planning a direct-mail campaign in specific geographic regions—or if you're considering relocating—use specific *state directories* to narrow down your job search.**

As you'd expect, state directories are helpful in putting together mailing lists for a particular state. They're especially handy if you're planning to relocate to another state and need to pull together an extensive list of companies there, if you're targeting certain regions, or if the companies you are intending to contact *aren't* large enough to be included in the standard Dun's or Standard & Poor's type of directory.

You'll find state directories in the business sections of larger public libraries. If you're planning a very large mailing and would save time by owning a state directory, you can buy one—prices are relatively low, typically from $45 to $200, depending upon the state and the number of companies listed. To make this simpler for you, we've listed most state directories in the Sources, page 313.

One problem: Many state directories list only manufacturing companies, an obvious drawback if you're targeting service companies. However, a number of directory companies put out service directories as well as manufacturing.

Some of the larger directories offer regional breakdowns or geographic indexing. In addition, some of them put out regional directories. One of these, at many libraries, is:

Dun's Regional Business Directory
Dun's Marketing Services
3 Sylvan Way
Parsippany, NJ 07054
800-526-0651
This directory consists of several volumes, covering different regions of the United States. It's a handy guide for quick regional information.

To find state directories, you can check:

City & State Directories in Print
Gale Research, Inc.
PO Box 33477
Detroit, MI 48232-5477
800-877-GALE
Fax: 313-961-6083
Available at many libraries.

Note: For more information on regional job hunts, see "Researching Long-Distance," page 69.

▶ *Industry-specific directories* **make your life easier—in one volume, you get the names and addresses of thousands of companies in your field.**

It's yet another way of targeting your research. Industry-specific directories are available for virtually every field—from advertising to biotech, from candy manufacturers to wholesale drugstores, and so on.

In addition to using these directories to put together a list of target companies, you can use them to get the names of contacts and to find out basic information about an industry or target company—financial statistics, number of employees, etc.

Another plus: Industry-specific directories often contain general information about the field, sometimes forecasts or analyses that can help you understand where the industry is headed, information and listings on related industries, and associations.

As with most other directories, you can find many leading industry directories in the business section of the library; or you can check the *Directories in Print* (listed above), the *Encyclopedia of Business Information Sources,* or other directories of directories.

TIP: **Many trade publications put out an annual directory or data book that lists top companies (sometimes with addresses). These are especially helpful because of the text that often accompanies these lists—roundup articles that discuss the different companies, sidebar articles about up-and-comers, etc. You can usually buy these directories direct from the publisher at a fairly low cost. Call the specific trade publications for information.**

TIP: **Use industry-specific directories to find fields and areas *related* to your target industry—suppliers, companies that service the industry, etc. These may give you employment targets you hadn't thought of.**

▶ *Biographical directories*—**which contain brief bios of corporate executives—are good sources of information on higher-level executives who will be interviewing you.**

It's a painless way of getting inside information on your interviewers—if they are fairly highly placed in the company.

What can you expect to learn? Place and date of birth, education, club and other memberships, charitable and other activities, and the like. It gives you some insight into the person who'll be interviewing you—and possible hints on what to include or leave out of your resume or interview. For example, if you learn that your interviewer is an active member of the local Republican Party, perhaps it's best not to mention that you're an avid Democrat. Conversely, you may learn that your interviewer-to-be is active in local arts-related charities. You can play up your similar interest (or get involved on the double!).

Such information also gives you a picture of the type of management preferred by a target company, and insight into the corporate culture. Check other company officers and executives—did most of them go to the same or similar schools? Are they members of the same groups? You can use what you learn to better position yourself in your letter or in interviews with the company.

The bottom line? Biographical directories give you inside intelligence that can help you sell yourself.

Two of the most commonly found:

Dun & Bradstreet Reference Book of Corporate Managements
Dun's Marketing Services
3 Sylvan Way
Parsippany, NJ 07054
800-526-0651

A directory completely devoted to bios, this covers executives from the vice-president level on up—a wider range than in other directories. Profiles are fairly comprehensive, including address, phone, education, employment history, place of birth, memberships, civic and political activities—useful information for writing your resume or preparing for an interview.

Volume 2 of Standard & Poor's Register of Corporations, Directors, and Executives
Standard & Poor's Corporation
25 Broadway
New York, NY 10004
212-208-8702

The second volume of S & P includes background information on over 75,000 key executives and directors at firms covered in the other volumes—business and home addresses, date and place of birth, memberships. One plus: This is often more widely available at public libraries than the Dun & Bradstreet directory.

▶ **To begin gathering information on an industry or company, you can use directories that compile industry statistics, include company profiles, etc.**

This may be particularly helpful for those of you considering career switches. The reason—these directories are quick ways of tracking industries. Which ones seem to be growing and why? Which are heading downhill? Of course, you should augment this very general research with more specific reading—in business magazines and trade journals, for example. Nevertheless, these industrial directories often provide you with a real feel for an industry and help steer you away from dead ends, toward flourishing fields.

Some of them:

Manufacturing USA

Gale Research, Inc.
PO Box 33477
Detroit, MI 48232-5477
800-877-GALE
Fax: 313-961-6083

Covering over 300 manufacturing industries, this directory includes such information as: industry statistics (people employed, number of companies, etc.), market trend analysis, product share information, state and regional analysis, occupations employed by each industry, leading companies in each industry, and employment trends. A good place to get a quick overview of a particular manufacturing industry—and relatively inexpensive ($159 in 1992).

Service Industries USA

Gale Research, Inc.
PO Box 33477
Detroit, MI 48232-5477
800-877-GALE
Fax: 313-961-6083

This directory includes analyses of over 300 service industries—including advertising, hotels, restaurants, sports, entertainment, and more. Industry analyses include: statistics, product share information, geographic analysis, occupations employed, employment, leading companies, etc. Also included is information on over 15,000 companies. Like *Manufacturing USA,* it's relatively inexpensive ($170 in 1992) and is a good source of quick industry overviews.

If you need a source for a range of information on different industries try the *Encyclopedia of Business Information* (same address and phone as above). This one-volume directory is a convenient one-stop source—containing magazines, newsletters, data bases, associations, books, etc. on a wide range of industries. One potential problem: Information is often outdated. Sometimes associations listed are defunct or have moved; magazines and newsletters have folded. But aside from this, it's a decent starting point for quick research.

Trade Publications

▶ **You're probably already reading the trade publications that apply to your field. (If you're not, start now!) Now's the time to read *creatively*—with an eye to finding information that can help you land a job.**

Read properly, trade publications and other business periodicals can:

- *Give you strategic background information on companies*—information you can use to target a direct-mail campaign or prepare for an interview.

- *Help you identify industry targets*—a real help if you're in an industry that's going through tough times and downsizings, and are considering a career change.

- *Clue you in on job opportunities that haven't hit the recruiters or want ads yet*—hints and patterns that, added together, can show you hidden job opportunities that other people don't know about.

- *Learn about job opportunities and more through help-wanted ads*—the most obvious reason of all, and a strong argument for reading trade journals. While classifieds in general aren't the greatest job leads, those in trade journals are often a better bet. Plus, you can get information on salaries, job areas that seem to be heating up, etc.

If you're unsure what the specific trade publications for your area of interest are, check one of the following: *Business Publication Rates & Data* (Standard Rate & Data Service, Inc., 3004 Glenview Rd., Wilmette, IL 60091, 708-256-6067), which lists business, trade, and technical publications both in the US and abroad; or *Source Directory* (Predicasts, 1101 Cedar Ave., Cleveland, OH 44106, 216-795-3000), which lists technical, financial, business, and trade publications.

TIP: **Read more than one publication in your industry—you want to get as much news as possible. One publication may overlook something that another doesn't. Of course, you should pay special attention to the "industry bible"—that publication that everyone in the industry reads. One compelling reason: It usually has the best classified sections.**

TIP: **Get the publication put out by the leading trade/professional association in your field. While these publications are often sketchy, they offer you more than the articles: (1) Contacts: Check to see who wrote the articles in the journal. The authors are often well connected in the field and may be great contacts.**

(2) Upcoming events: Check the listings of conventions, meetings, or seminars. These may be good networking opportunities.

▶ **Following are tricks and hints that can help you get the most out of trade publications.**

- *Do the obvious—use trade journals to keep abreast of your industry and to keep track of how well companies are doing.*

    This is the primary use of trade journals in your job hunt—and the one you're probably already aware of. See what specific companies are doing—read about their new business, earnings, policies, failures, and successes. You can use this information to target companies you may approach, to skew your direct mailing, and in interviews, to show you have done your homework and know what a company is about.

TIP: **Read about competing companies as well—this can give you a better idea of the general market, and also may lead you to ideas on how your target company can beat the competition—ideas which you can incorporate in your pitch.**

    On a less obvious note, also check for specific *individuals* in trade journals. The person to whom you're writing, or who is going to interview you, may have been prominently featured in an article or may have written one. When possible, mention this in your letter or interview. Honest flattery never hurts—and may help.

- *To scope out hidden employment opportunities, read between the lines.*

    You have to dig a bit to come up with insights in the hidden job market. The trick—to determine what companies or industries may be hiring on the basis of often oblique stories or inferences.
    To do this, look for stories on:

    · *Expansion plans*—companies that are planning to expand often add new staff.

    · *Corporate relocations*—when a company moves, staffers often don't move with it. This may mean job openings in the new location.

· *New products/areas of business*—new business can mean new staff. This is an especially good tactic for those with expertise in the specific area that a company is entering or in new product rollouts.

TIP: Some of you may do best if you're contrarians—i.e. if you're a troubleshooter—or, in some cases, even if you're not—companies that are doing *badly* may be employment prospects. Maybe they're intending to cut staff members or want to replace a failing management team. Think creatively! (The drawback: If you do land a job at a struggling company, it's clearly a risky proposition. But it is a job. . . .)

TIP: The "People" or "Executive Changes/Promotions" columns can be very useful. Take note of people in companies you're targeting. Can you detect any trends? Promotions in a particular department or area? New managers being added? This may point out potential job opportunities.

If you know the person who was promoted/hired, call or write congratulations. It's a great way of keeping in touch—and of finding out what's happening at the company.

If you don't know him or her, you still may want to drop a congratulations note—especially if you have something in common (same schooling, same hometown, etc.). Touch on your common ground, say congratulations . . . and drop it there. You're not after anything (yet). You just want someone on staff to know who you are.

• *Read* everything *in the publication. (Well, almost everything.)*

You'd be surprised how much helpful information and how many potential sources you can dig out of a trade publication.

Some are obvious: For example, you should always check the upcoming "Events and Conventions" column. A meeting, seminar, or convention in your area can be a good networking opportunity.

The "New Business" or "Business Digest" column can give you a quick sense of what specific companies are doing—expanding, adding staff, moving, etc.

Columns on advertising or media expenditures let you know about new products/services a company is offering or give you a feel for their financial standing.

Even the masthead—which lists reporters, bureau chiefs, ad sales reps, etc.—can be exploited for your job hunt. You may want to call or write to see if the reporter who covers your specific industry or specialty can give you any insight into the field. One word of warning: Many reporters won't want to be bothered. If you run into this, don't be a pest.

- *Along the same lines, always read the want ads—even if you aren't planning to reply to any of them.*

Want ads aren't useful only as job leads. They're also great intelligence. By scanning them regularly, you can determine trends—the hiring activity in your industry, the standard salaries being paid, the types of positions that are available more often than others, the regions of the country that seem hottest in terms of opportunity.

TIP: **Before interviewing for a position, check to see if there's an ad for a similar position at a similar company—you may find tips on what to say during your interview, points to highlight, and the likely salary/benefits package.**

- *For a cram course in an industry—especially helpful for career changers —read "Year in Review" and "Forecast" issues.* It's the simplest way of hitting the ground running where understanding an industry is concerned.

"Year in Review" issues, as you'd expect, usually come out in December or January, and run down the most important events of the year in an industry: What companies folded? Who merged with whom? What new product rollouts took off or bombed? What executives were big news? And the like. It's a great way of getting a thumbnail history of an industry's recent past—and of pinpointing companies that are on the move (or headed downward).

- *Get your hands on special issues.*

Most helpful for you—the Corporate Scoreboard, Top 100 Companies, or directory issues. These handy quick references show you which companies are doing well, which aren't, general financial stats, industry standings, etc.

Also find out about special issues that concentrate on a specific industry segment. (For example, *Advertising Age* puts out special "Direct Marketing," "Marketing to Minorities," and other issues.) These can give you a more in-depth look at that segment —and classifieds in these issues are often more targeted as well.

Other Periodicals: Business Magazines and Newspapers

▶ **Reading basic business magazines can help give you a general view of what's going on—where industries are heading, what's hot and what's not, and so on.**

It's a simple way of keeping up with what's happening in American business. Read the business sections of newspapers for the same reason.

In addition, you should check both these sources for information on the specific companies you're targeting. Often, even smaller companies are covered. Check the pertinent periodicals index—the *Business Periodicals Index* for major business magazines, *New York Times Index, Wall Street Journal Index,* etc. for newspapers or (even better) *Predicasts*—which indexes and abstracts from over 1,000 trade journals, business and financial magazines, newspapers, and government reports—at the library, to zero in on specific stories.

The following business periodicals are especially good sources:

Barron's
Dow Jones & Co.
200 Liberty St.
New York, NY 10281
212-416-2759
Chiefly an investment tool, *Barron's* is useful for determining the financial stability of a company, and getting a feel for industry forecasts.

BusinessWeek
McGraw-Hill, Inc.
1221 Avenue of the Americas
New York, NY 10020
609-426-7500
A good all-around business source for tracking industries, up-and-coming companies, etc.

TIP: **The annual directory *The BusinessWeek 1,000* is handy if you're planning a mailing to top companies in an industry. Unlike *Fortune 500, BW* lists addresses and phone numbers. A nice, cheap directory.**

Forbes

Forbes, Inc.
60 Fifth Ave.
New York, NY 10011
212-620-2200

Another great source for keeping up with business in general, tracking industries, etc.

TIP: **If you're planning a direct-mail campaign, get your hands on *Forbes' 400 Largest U.S. Private Companies* issue (it generally comes out in December). It's a help when putting together a mailing list: Many of the companies listed aren't included in typical directories, and Forbes lists addresses, telephone numbers, etc.**

TIP: **A great source if you're pinpointing up-and-comers (which often offer better employment prospects): *Forbes' 200 Best Small Companies* issue (generally comes out in November), which, like the above, includes names, addresses, and telephone numbers—very handy.**

Fortune

The Time, Inc., Magazine Company
Time & Life Building
New York, NY 10020-1393
212-522-1212

Yet another good all-around source of information on different industries, companies, etc.

TIP: **There's useful information on up-and-coming companies in each week's "Companies to Watch" feature.**

Inc.

38 Commercial Wharf
Boston, MA 02110
617-248-8000

Invaluable for targeting the fast-moving corporations that tend to do the most hiring.

TIP: **Inc.'s special issues on the fastest growing small companies in the US are great sources of names for a mailing list.**

Industry Week

1100 Superior Ave.
Cleveland, OH 44114
216-696-7000

This semi-monthly covers industrial management. As such, it's best for those involved in industry.

Nation's Business

US Chamber of Commerce
1615 H St. NW
Washington, DC 20062
202-463-5650

National Business Employment Weekly

420 Lexington Ave.
New York, NY 10170
212-808-6791

The text offers job-hunting tips and strategies, but this newspaper is chiefly useful because each issue contains a week's worth of *Wall Street Journal* help-wanted ads. In addition, it offers weekly special sections, including "Engineering Weekly," "Computer," and "High Technology."

Wall Street Journal

200 Liberty St.
New York, NY 10281
212-416-2000

A business standby, the *Journal* is great for quick updates on industries and businesses. Another plus: It often has good job-hunting articles aimed at upper managers.

▶ **Some general tips and hints on using magazines and newspapers effectively in your job hunt.**

- *As with trade publications, seek out special issues of business magazines.*
  These may give you more focused information. Many of the general business magazines put out special issues in which they cover a specific industry more closely, or a professional group (such as managers). To find out about special issues, call the publication and ask for an editorial calendar or check the *Business Periodicals Rate & Data* directory at your library.

- *Where newspapers are concerned, think geographically.*

    First, keep in mind that certain areas of the country are centers of specific industries. The major newspaper in such an area will often offer comprehensive coverage of that industry. For example, if you're aiming at banking, check the *New York Times;* the film and entertainment industry, *Los Angeles Times;* the automotive industry, *Detroit Free Press,* and so on.

    Second, if you are considering relocating, start reading newspapers from the areas of the country you're thinking about. A big plus: Often the business sections of papers outside your current area can give you a better feel for employment and industry conditions in other regions. Even more practically, you can scan the want ads for different areas.

- *Along these lines, once you've homed in on several target companies, begin reading the local newspapers of the areas in which they're headquartered.*

    Even if you're not relocating, you should do this. Newspapers will often do in-depth coverage of a locally headquartered business because it's such an important presence in the community. For example, if the company you're targeting is headquartered in Atlanta, the *Atlanta Constitution* will probably have more stories on the company than the *Wall Street Journal.*

- *Also look into state business publications.*

    Publications such as *Crain's New York Business* for the New York area, *Warfield's* for the Baltimore area, etc. cover business matters for a specific region—and often offer information unavailable in other sources. For more on these, see "Researching Long-Distance," page 69.

High-Tech Research: Computer Databases

▶ **You can use a PC to tap into many of the sources listed above.**

It's a good way to make your life and job hunt simpler. If you subscribe to an on-line information service (or if your library does), you can access much of the preceding information on computer.

Among the information available on-line: directories, articles from newspapers, magazines and trade journals, company reports, industry analyses. In other words, virtually everything you can find in hard copy at the library, you can get in seconds on your computer screen.

Some brief tips on how to use computers in your job hunt:

- *To generate a list of potential employers based on specific criteria:* You can quickly and easily compile a list of target companies based on such factors as product, geographic location, sales, number of employees, etc. An added time-saver: Once you've down-loaded this list, you can import it into your word processing program for use in a mail merge of letters and envelopes. It's quite a time-saver—you can pull a list of job leads via computer more quickly than it would take you to physically flip through a directory and copy the appropriate pages, and you won't have to type in all the addresses.

- *To get specific information on a company or companies to use in an interview or a direct-mail campaign:* By using precise search terms (dates, company names, specific department names, etc.), you can get your hands on those articles in major magazines and smaller newspapers and trade journals that will help you posi-tion yourself in your interview or direct-mail letter.

- *To get financial information on a company or companies:* Most on-line services offer investment and business databanks that include recent financial statistics, sales figures, corporate plans, forecasts for companies, and complete industry categories. You can search SEC reports, brokerage analyses, corporate financial statements, and more. This is a help not only in choosing what companies are good prospects, but also for career changers who are trying to determine a strong industry category to move into.

Some leading on-line services and what they offer:

BRS Information Technologies
8000 Westpark Dr.
McLean, VA 22102
703-442-0900, 800-289-4277, 800-955-0906
Offers a wide range of databases, including Business Periodicals Index, DISCLOSURE Database, National Newspaper Index, PTS F&S Indexes, PTS PROMT, Trade & Industry ASAP.

CompuServe Information Service
5000 Arlington Centre Blvd.
PO Box 20212
Columbus, OH 43220
614-457-8600, 800-848-8990

Offers wide range of databases, including Businesswire, DISCLOSURE, Magazine ASAP, Value Line Annual Reports, Value Line DataFile, and Washington Post.

DIALOG Information Services, Inc.
3460 Hillview Ave.
Palo Alto, CA 94304
415-858-3785, 800-334-2564

Offers extremely wide range of databases, including ABI/INFORM, American Banker (full text), Business Dateline, Businesswire, Career Placement Registry, Chemical Business Newsbase, Los Angeles Daily News, Detroit Free Press, DISCLOSURE, Dun's Electronic Business Directory, Dun's Financial Records Plus, Dun's Million-Dollar Directory, Encyclopedia of Associations, Financial Times Company Abstracts, Gale Database of Publications and Broadcast Media, ICC Directory of Companies, ICC Full Text Company Reports, Industry Data Sources, Los Angeles Times, Magazine ASAP, Moody's Corporate News (International and US).

Dow Jones News/Retrieval
PO Box 300
Princeton, NJ 08543-0300
609-520-4000

Range of business-oriented databases, including Advertising Age, Automotive News, Asian Wall Street Journal, Aviation/Aerospace Newswire, Business Insurance, Business Marketing, Businesswire, DISCLOSURE, Dow Jones Business and Finance Report, Modern Healthcare, Pensions & Investment Age, PR Newswire, Wall Street Journal.

Genie (General Electric Network for Information Exchange)
401 N. Washington Blvd.
Rockville, MD 20850
301-340-4000

In addition to general-interest databases, financial databases, and more, offers Dr. Job, an interactive question-and-answer column on job hunting.

NEXIS
Mead Data Central, Inc.
9443 Springboro Pike
PO Box 933
Dayton, OH 45401-9964
513-865-6800, 800-227-4908

Wide range of databases; especially useful for its business magazines, regional magazine/newspaper and trade journals available on-line—among them ABA Banking Journal, Advertising Age, Adweek, Aerospace Daily, American Banker Full Text, American Lawyer, Arizona Business Gazette, Atlanta Constitution/Atlanta Journal, Automotive News, Aviation Week & Space Technology, Beverage World, Boston Globe, BusinessWeek, Chemical Engineering, Chemical Week, Chicago Tribune, Coal Week, Computerworld, Crain's Chicago Business, Crain's Cleveland Business, Crain's Detroit Business, Crain's New York Business, Data Channels, Data Communications, Denver Post, Engineering & Mining Journal, ENR: Engineering News-Record, FINIS: Financial Industry Information Service, Forbes, Fortune, Georgia Trend, Greensboro News & Record, Houston Chronicle, Industry Week, Institutional Investor, Jack O'Dwyer's Newsletter, Kansas City Business Journal, Mining Journal, New York Times, Newsday/New York Newsday, Oil & Gas Journal, Pensions & Investment Age, Platt's Oilgram News, Sacramento Bee, San Francisco Chronicle, Seattle Times, Washington Post, Washington Times.

NewsNet, Inc.
945 Haverford Rd.
Bryn Mawr, PA 19010
215-527-8030, 800-345-1301

Particularly useful for those in technical, scientific, and related industries. Databases include: Aerospace Daily, Aerospace Electronics Business, American Banker Full Text, Biotech Business, Communications Daily, CommunicationsWeek, Commuter/Regional Airline News, Corporate Jobs Outlook, Defense Week, Electronic Engineering Times, Health Business, Health Manager's Update, HealthWeek, Online Libraries and Microcomputers, Plastics Business News, PR Newswire, Regional Aviation Weekly, Telephone Industry Directory, Television News, Television Digest, U.S. Oil Week.

To find the names of specific databases that may help you, check:

Directory of Online Databases
Gale Research, Inc.
PO Box 33477
Detroit, MI 48232-5477
800-877-GALE
Fax: 313-961-6083
    Lists nearly 5,000 databases that are accessible via many common on-line information services companies. Available at most major libraries, and includes explanations of what each database offers, as well as the on-line services that carry them.

TIP: **For a quick mailing list: On some databases, first type in the industry you're interested in. Then choose the !Directory heading under the industry name. This will give you a list of top companies in the industry. (Note: This is only available on certain databases, and even then available only with certain industries.)**

▶ **The key asset to going on-line? Speed and accuracy. The drawback? Price.**

Computerized searches can save you a lot of time—but cost a fair amount of money. It's a trade-off, yes, but one you should consider.

The beauty of searching on-line is its specificity. For example, if you want only those articles over the past year that discuss the sales and marketing department of Procter & Gamble, that's all you'll get. Not general articles on sales and marketing and not general articles on P&G. On-line searching does all the focusing for you and weeds out the unnecessary information. Of course, the problem is your on-line searches are only as efficient as your search instructions are. Your best bet? Practice. The more searching you do, the more precise you'll get. And don't give up.

TIP: **A costly option, but a time-saver—a clipping service offered by many databases. It's a simple setup—you tell them the search terms, they do the search and either download the information to you or send you the hard copy. Prices vary, but are generally higher than if you did the search yourself. Even so, if you're in a rush or lack the time, this may be an option to consider. Check with your on-line company or database.**

TIP: **Many libraries now offer special searching services—you tell them what you're after, they'll do the search for you. In some cases, there's a fee. In others, the** service is free. If you're strapped for time or if you're uncomfortable working on computers, this may be a good option for you. Ask your reference librarian.

▶ **If your computer is equipped with a CD-ROM reader, keep in mind that you can buy most of the previously mentioned directories and many other sources on CD-ROM.**

This option makes sense only if you're planning a major mailing —say, of 500 to 1,000 letters—to companies that will be included in these directories, as CD-ROMs are fairly expensive.

In general, much of the information available on CD-ROM is that which is available on-line—directories, business information (SEC reports, financial statements, brokerage information, etc.), and periodical indexes.

As with on-line searching, you use CD-ROMs to streamline your research, typing in search criteria and generating lists based upon those parameters. The only drawback: Because CD-ROMs are disks, the information on them isn't necessarily as current as that which you'll get on-line. However, many vendors (such as DISCLOSURE, mentioned below) send updates periodically.

Some leading CD-ROM vendors:

Dun's Marketing Services
3 Sylvan Way
Parsippany, NJ 07054
800-526-0651

DISCLOSURE, Inc.
5161 River Rd.
Bethesda, MD 20816
301-951-1300, 800-843-7747

Standard & Poor's
Standard & Poor's Corporation
25 Broadway
New York, NY 10004
212-208-8702

▶ **Another type of computerized research that can save you time in your job hunt: using computerized CD-ROM indexes, such as ABI/Inform or Business Periodicals Index.**

These are available at most libraries. The premise is extremely simple. You type in your search terms at the first screen (typically a company name or an industry name). The computer comes up with any articles on the subject. In some cases, you'll have access only to the basic index information (article name, periodical name, date, page length, etc.). In others, you can see an abstract. And in still others, you can get the entire article off the computer.

The most commonly available indexes: ABI/Inform (covers numerous magazines—trade journals and other business publications), Business Periodicals Index (covers major business publications, leading trade journals, etc.), UMI Newspaper Index (covers leading newspapers—*Boston Globe, New York Times, Los Angeles Times,* etc.), Management Contents, Trade and Industry Index, PTS T&S Indexes, and PTS Promt.

Trade and Professional Organizations

▶ **Obviously, trade and professional associations are valuable for networking. But you can also use them as a source of research tools and other job-hunting aids.**

For the networking opportunities alone, if you aren't already a member of the leading associations in your field, you should join. (For more on the role of trade and professional associations in networking, see "Networking," page 76.)

Networking aside, you can take advantage of associations in other ways. Where research is concerned, they can offer you a number of handy tools:

- *Membership lists or directories*—which you can use to find new contacts.

- *Journals/magazines*—which sometimes include help-wanted ads, keep you abreast of industry news, and may lead you to new contacts (people who've written the articles, etc.).

- *Job services*—many associations run job banks, resume services, job-hunting workshops, and more for their members. Some are even available to nonmembers.

To find the names of associations, check:

Encyclopedia of Associations
Gale Research, Inc.
PO Box 33477
Detroit, MI 48232-5477
800-877-GALE
Fax: 313-961-6083

This is the most common directory of associations, available at virtually every library. One tip in using this: Be sure to check under multiple headings, or check the Key Word index—some of the industry headings are vague. For example, computer associations are listed under data processing.

Other sources:

Association Yellow Book
Monitor Publishing Co.
104 Fifth Ave., Second Floor
New York, NY 10011
212-627-4140

Business Organizations, Agencies, and Publications Directory
Gale Research, Inc.
PO Box 33477
Detroit, MI 48232-5477
800-877-GALE
Fax: 313-961-6083

National Trade and Professional Associations
Columbia Books
1212 New York Ave. NW, Suite 330
Washington, DC 2005
202-898-0662

This is a good choice if you want to buy a directory. It's inexpensive—$65 in 1992—and lists thousands of associations.

▶ **Don't limit yourself to associations in your specific field.**

Many more general professional associations (such as the National Association for Female Executives or the American Management Association) offer a wide range of helpful material.

In some cases, they offer more career assistance or job services than the smaller associations.

Some examples:

AMA's Executive Employment Guide

Eileen Monahan, Editor
American Management Association
135 W. Fiftieth Street
New York, NY 10020
212-586-8100
Fax: 212-903-8163

This guide, free to AMA members, lists search firms, job registries, etc.

AMBAs MBA Employment Guide

Association of MBA Executives
227 Commerce St.
East Haven, CT 06512
203-467-8870

The AMBA will send you a listing of corporations in three states of choice for one functional area for only $10 each. A helpful source, especially if you're relocating.

For other associations, see Sources, page 311.

RESEARCH METHODS YOU MAY NOT HAVE THOUGHT OF: LESS COMMON (BUT HIGHLY USEFUL) TECHNIQUES

Using Target Companies as Sources

▶ **If you've narrowed down your search to certain companies, call them for media kits, annual reports, and the like.**

It's a simple and effective way of ascertaining the company's financial health, and of seeing how the company promotes itself. By reading through company material, you can obtain facts that will help you market yourself better to the company, information that will help you decide whether the company is a good employment prospect or not, and more.

More specifically:

- *Annual reports:* These, obviously, give you an idea of how well the company has been faring financially—a necessity in today's competitive corporate world.

TIP: **A good idea—check annual reports for the past few years to get a better feel for the company's performance and to see how well the company has forecast its own performance. This should give you a better idea of how much to believe in the current annual report.**

Generally, when reading annual reports to determine the financial health of a company, you must read beyond the numbers. Be on the lookout for tip-offs that things aren't as rosy as they seem—overblown puffery about the future, phrases like "challenges ahead," overemphasis of less-than-important achievements.

TIP: **An annual report that *looks* inexpensive to produce—black-and-white photos only, no multicolor cover, etc.—may signal economic tough times for a company.**

But there's more to find in annual reports than just the bare financial facts. You can learn about subsidiaries that will be formed, expansion plans, new business, etc.—any of which could point to employment opportunities and give you incentive to contact the company.

Annual reports also can give you a true feel for the company—a look at its corporate style. Look at the photographs—what type of shots are they? Posed and formal? Casual? Are there women and minorities pictured? If so, do they appear to be in upper-level positions or lower? Does the CEO dominate all the pages—both in photographs and in text? Or is the emphasis on teamwork? The answers to these questions can help you come up with the best way to target yourself to the company.

TIP: **Women—read the list of corporate directors and officers. See any women's names? This can give you a quick tip-off on how far women have advanced in the company.**

- *Proxy statements and 10-Ks:* These will give you hard information on the benefits you can expect from the company—statistics about pension plans, profit-sharing plans, 401(k)s, stock options, and other employee financial plans. You can also learn about executive salaries from the proxy statements—helpful if you're going for a top position or if you want to get a feel for executive compensation in general.

• *Media or press kits:* These typically consist of recent press releases, annual reports, or other financial statements, and often also include reprints of articles favorable to the company and pamphlets or reports on the company's business, products, or services. Read them to see what achievements the company is stressing, what (if any) new projects, products, or business the company has. Pay special attention to the press releases, as these show you what the company thinks is important enough to publicize to the press. You can use this information to target your direct-mail cover letter more precisely to the needs of the company, or in an interview.

In addition, you can see what type of image the company is trying to create—is the media kit modern in appearance and tone, or more conservative? Is the writing technical or zippy? Is the emphasis on past traditions or on future innovations? This type of information can help you determine how to present yourself to the company.

TIP: As with other forms of research, you should read between the lines when you look at media kits. Is the company talking about expansion? Or does there seem to be an emphasis (even inferred) on cost cutting? This can give you clues as to potential employment opportunities. For example, a great deal on new products, business, etc. may translate into new management staffing. A bottom-line focus may mean you can position yourself as a cost-cutting specialist, and so on.

For annual reports and other financial statements, call the investor relations department. For media kits, call press relations or corporate communications. In both cases, you should meet with little resistance.

TIP: If you're going to be interviewing at one company, also take a look at the annual reports and press kits for competitors. These may give you ideas of what the competition is planning—and thus give you ideas to present to your interviewer.

▶ **Another source of company information—clients and customers, ex-employees.**

This is by no means a failproof research method, but it is one that bears trying. Seek out customers and clients of your target company. Be honest—no "I'm writing an article" line. Explain that you've targeted the company as a prospective employer and are interested in learning more about it—how they work with clients, the corporate culture, etc. Yes, there's a good chance that whoever you've called will hang up on you. But there's a chance (slim, maybe, but a chance) that the customer will speak with you. And you'll have even more insight into the company you want to work for, and more ammunition to use when you make your formal approach to it.

Similarly, talk to people who have worked at the company. They have an insider's view that can't be equaled. Ask them to be frank with you—what was the company like? The management style? In what direction is the company headed? Any new business plans? Of course, if they were laid off or fired, you'll have to take their negatives with a grain of salt. Even so, this is an opportunity to learn what you probably couldn't learn elsewhere.

TIP: **Make your conversations with clients and ex-employees even more profitable by learning about the people who do the hiring at the company—names, attitudes, etc. You may even take this a step further and ask for an introduction, if it seems appropriate and if the client is on good terms with the individual in question. The latter point is crucial. Be *sure* that you're not going to get an introduction or recommendation from someone who's considered a pain in the neck. It will kill your campaign before you've even started.**

Researching on Company Time

▶ **If you're currently in a job, take advantage of your corporate library to start your job-hunt researching. Discreetly, of course.**

This is yet another way of maximizing your time and streamlining your research. If you have access to a corporate library, by all means use it to help you seek a new job.

A key asset of using a corporate library: Most are equipped with CD-ROMs and other high-tech equipment that you can use free of charge, saving both time and money.

Ask the corporate librarian to do searches for you as you would on your own. Give him or her your general search criteria—geographic location, company size, sales, etc.; the librarian can generate a list of prospects. Or ask for articles and information on companies you've already targeted.

TIP: **This is, of course, risky if you're trying to keep your job hunt under wraps. If, however, your company is planning layoffs or downsizings, it's unlikely you'll run into any trouble. But in all cases, stress the need for discretion to the librarian. Why advertise your job hunt?**

If you'd rather handle the search yourself, use the library on off hours—during lunch and before or after work. You probably won't be interrupted.

Using Your Broker for More Than Investments

▶ **Think about it—your broker has access to corporate reports, industry analyses, forecasts, and more . . . all of which can be used in your job hunt.**

You're already paying a commission—so why not get the most out of your broker?
Ask for:

- *Research reports on companies:* These can give you brief background on the company, information on their business, forecasts for the future—all of which can help you pinpoint companies and, once you've chosen a company as a potential target, give you information on how to present yourself in your letter and interview.

- *Industry segment reports:* Helpful for career changers in particular, these can help you determine which major industries are good prospects and which aren't.

▶ **Similarly, take a second look at investment materials—such as** *Value Line.*

Again, investment information can be easily translated into job-hunting intelligence. Investor guides such as *Value Line* give you background information on companies, a look at their performance over the past year, important developments that have affected the company, forecasts, etc. Updates come out weekly, rotating through different industries, so that each company is updated quarterly. Plus there's industry information—examining trends and summarizing the general climate—especially helpful if you're considering moving to another industry.

As such, investor guides like *Value Line* are great one-stop sources of corporate information. Use them to get a quick feel for a company, or (especially useful) just before an interview to brush up on the basics.

TIP: **These are also excellent sources if you're offered a job—and a stock option plan. Use them to determine the worth of the stock option you're being offered.**

Researching Long-Distance

▶ **If you're considering relocating and seeking work in other cities or states, you can begin your job hunt by researching job opportunities while still at home.**

Many of you are probably considering relocation as an option. Act on your thoughts by beginning a long-distance job search.

Your first step: pinpointing target companies in the new area. You can use the geographic indexes of many of the directories listed previously or, if you're researching on computer, narrow your search according to geography.

As mentioned previously, you can also pinpoint prospects by using state and local directories. For listings of the most widely used ones, see Sources, page 313.

▶ **Start reading the newspapers from the area you're considering.**

They're helpful for a number of reasons—as a source of want ads, but also to give you a feel for the area, housing costs, events, etc.—the elements that will help you realize whether you'd be happy relocating there. Business sections will cover local companies closely, giving you inside information on who's expanding, who's going into new businesses, etc.—all of which can unveil employment targets for you.

And don't overlook local business magazines and journals. While these are sometimes small, they're still good sources of general information on business in the geographic area you're targeting. You'll learn about local movers and shakers, businesses that are growing, and more.

TIP: It doesn't always work, but try calling the business journalists at the local paper or reporters for the local business publication. Because their job is to track local business trends, they're often fonts of information regarding strong prospects, the types of expertise needed, etc.

To find the names of out-of-state newspaper and business publications, check:

Gale Directory of Publications and Broadcast Media

Gale Research, Inc.
PO Box 33477
Detroit, MI 48232-5477
800-877-GALE
Fax: 313-961-6083

Available at many libraries, this directory lists newspapers, magazines, and other periodicals by state and city—which makes it a quick and easy way to locate the pertinent newspapers and magazines for your target region.

Ulrich's Directory of Periodicals

R.R. Bowker/Div. of Reed Publishing
121 Chanlan Road
New Providence, NJ 07974
800-346-6049

A library standby, *Ulrich's* is a good source of state business periodicals—check listings under the "business" heading; state business magazines and newspapers are listed there alphabetically by title.

TIP: Many state business publications put out an annual directory issue that lists top companies in the state, or a yearly book of lists that breaks it down further and lists the top ad agencies, top manufacturers, top real estate companies, etc. Both of these are helpful in planning a long-distance job search—you can easily pull together the names of top companies, often with addresses and phone numbers, sales figures, and employee figures. Call the magazine's circulation or editorial offices—single-copy sales are common.

▶ **Another often-overlooked source when planning to relocate: the state and local chambers of commerce.**

While information from chambers of commerce is sometimes sketchy, it can be helpful, and is certainly worth the phone call.

Most chambers of commerce will send you information on local businesses—addresses, phone numbers, key executives' names, general financial statistics, etc.—all of which can help you add to your list of target companies.

3 ▼

Networking

INTRODUCTION

▶ **In today's difficult job market, focused networking is particularly important for the over-40 job hunter.**

Networking is simply another word for using friends, colleagues, and business acquaintances to get you the contacts that will give you a job. Focused networking is doing so in a goal-oriented, organized manner—to get you to your goal faster and more effectively.

Key: The job market of the 1990s is flexible, fast-moving, and difficult, particularly if you're over 40. Jobs may open up and be filled before a company has time to advertise a position or use the services of a recruiter. And, of course, when firms do use executive recruiters, the recruiters themselves often rely on recommendations to obtain the name of candidates for positions.

The bottom line: Upward of 90% of all jobs are filled by word of mouth. In other words, if you don't network, you'll miss out on the so-called hidden job market—and miss a substantial number of good positions.

Networking has another key advantage for the over-40 job hunter. By getting in and talking directly with executives who are hiring you'll be better able to avoid age discrimination. You'll be able to sell yourself *before* resumes and cover letters come into the picture—and before you're automatically disqualified because of your age.

So the better your job network, the more and the better your contacts, the greater the odds of your finding a job.

▶ **There are four basic steps to setting up a strong job-hunting network:**

1. Planning

2. Building a base of contacts—friends, business associates, and formal networking groups

3. Expanding the base by getting and using referrals

4. Following up

STEP ONE: PLANNING

▶ **Before you open your mouth, decide what you want.**

Networking is popular—too popular, perhaps—and many executives are deluged with requests for meetings and help. Don't waste their time or yours by being vague. Write down your objective—to find out more about a *specific* area of a *specific* industry and to make contacts within. If you want to explore several different areas, write down several specific objectives. If, while networking, you find other avenues opening up or looking interesting, don't hesitate to add them to the list.

Key: The more focused your objectives, the more easily your contacts will be able to help you. They will remember you as someone with skills or interests in a certain area, not as a desperate individual who "wants a job."

▶ **Plan on initially asking your network contacts for** *information* **and** *referrals***, not a job or a job lead.**

The primary objective of networking is to build a base of referrals so that eventually:

- You'll see an opening and will be able to present yourself as *the* person to fill the position, tailoring a very focused resume for the job.

- One of your referrals will tell you of a position opening up, and you'll be able to contact the hiring executive with a focused approach.

- Your referrals will ask you to work for them.

- After several meetings, you will know your contact's "hot buttons" and be able to sell yourself into a job.

Almost never ask for a job or hand over your resume in the initial phases of networking. A resume can be used to screen you out of a job. Also, the odds are your early contacts won't have a job available, and if you've asked and gotten a "no" answer about a job, the chances are strong your contact will answer other requests from you with that same answer—"No."

▶ **Track your networking process.**

Keep a networking log—whether on computer, on 3″ x 5″ cards, or in a notebook. List each contact's name, place of work, phone number, and key information and names he or she has given you. Each time you're given the name of a new contact, write down the name of the person who referred him or her.

This will keep you up to date and allow you to call your contacts back and refer accurately to your prior conversations with them.

Update continually—even after you've landed a new job.

▶ **Today networking is so common that you should try to have something to offer that will differentiate you from the rest of the pack of networking job hunters.**

The key is to present yourself as a high-profile, successful, well-connected individual who will be able to provide help for your contacts and referrals in the future. During your networking, if you find information—an article, a contact, etc.—that may be of help to someone you've met, by all means pass it on. In fact, actively *look* for information, articles, etc. to pass on. You'll be remembered.

And, more important, while you're working and while you're networking, concentrate on maintaining a high profile in your career: Volunteer for high-profile assignments, become known as someone who helps others, offer your help with outside activities, take outside courses. If you have time, write articles for publications in your field. For more, see page 77.

STEP TWO: BUILDING A BASE OF CONTACTS

▶ **Start networking where you're most comfortable—among your close business associates and friends.**

Even if they're not in your target industry or field, friends or associates may know someone who is. Don't hesitate to call acquaintances from the past as well.

With each individual, *briefly* explain your situation, and let him or her know you'd appreciate advice, suggestions, ideas. The key question: *Do you know anyone appropriate I can talk to?*

Make it clear to your contacts that you're asking not only for names of people who could hire you, but for anyone who knows the field and people in it. This includes those working in the industry or for the companies that interest you and those in the type of position you want. Someone who isn't in a hiring position can often lead you to someone who is.

TIP: With very close friends, be honest about your concerns and any shortcomings that might hinder your employability. They might be able to offer you insider's suggestions you won't hear from others later during your networking, when you need to impress and "make a sale."

▶ **Don't overlook formal networking groups.**

These can range from networks of displaced executives who meet in a local high school to giant groups with branches nationwide.

Key advantage: Everyone is in the same boat—or has been. Members are apt to be more anxious to help you (in the hopes that you'll help them later), you'll get inside information on your target industry or companies, you'll gain the advantage of leverage (as members network themselves they may give you contacts who didn't work out for them but might for you), and last but not least, you'll gain valuable moral support during this difficult phase of your life.

And remember: If there is no network in your area, you might consider starting one, either locally or as a local affiliate of a national group. Some national groups, such as the National Association of Female Executives (NAFE), provide information and support to those who wish to form local network chapters.

SOURCE: **NAFE Network**, 280 Blacks Mill Valley, Dawsonville, GA 30534. Or call: Pat Poole Newsome, National Network Coordinator, Atlanta, GA. Tel.: 706-216-1650, 212-645-0770 (for information on existing networks). The National Association for Executive Women (NAFE) supports a number of geographically diverse network groups (from Stockton, CA, to Naugatuck, CT), industry and career specific, as well as general, both formal and loosely structured.

TIP: **Support groups for the unemployed may also be a place to meet contacts—and practice job-hunting skills. Check your local church or synagogue, or send $1 and a self-addressed stamped envelope to the National Self-Help Clearinghouse, 25 W. Forty-third St., Room 620, New York, NY 10036, for a listing that includes various unemployed support groups and more.**

▶ **If you're still employed, get exposure by maintaining a high-profile career and get contacts by being in the thick of things.**

There are many ways to get yourself out there and get noticed —and find contacts for networking. If you let people see what you can do, they'll be more apt to remember you, recommend you to recruiters, and help you with referrals. Here are some ways to make yourself more visible.

▶ **Join trade and professional associations.**

Trade associations are a built-in, prefabricated network of industry sources. Use them.

When you research your job hunt, you should compile a list of associations related to your fields of interest. Check the *Encyclopedia of Associations,* found in most libraries, for the names, addresses, and phone numbers of the associations you need. Call or write the national offices for *local* chapters nearest you.

Most associations sponsor meetings, seminars, trade shows, and conventions. Of the most value to you is the membership roster or directory—it can be a gold mine of contacts. However, keep in mind that associations can be overused; many members resent the large number of networkers who use them to seek jobs.

Key: The best way to use associations for networking is to belong before your job hunt, and to cultivate contacts before you need them to help you. If you're not a member of an association, join now if you can. If you are a member, take a higher profile position and try to become better known.

TIP: **Join the membership committee of your association. This will give you a good reason to contact new people in your field at different companies or organizations.**

▶ **Join volunteer groups.**

Identify and join those professional or civic groups that can aid your job hunt—or a future job hunt. For example, many corporations sponsor charities or benefits—if you don't know which, just call the PR office of your target company and ask. Then call the organization and volunteer. This way you can gain business contacts in a friendly, social setting. As with associations, work at obtaining a high-profile position or job within the organization.

▶ **If you can write—or know someone who can help you—gain a higher profile by writing and submitting articles for trade magazines or local newspapers.**

Trade journals are sometimes starved for timely, knowledgeable articles on interesting aspects of the business they cover. Even if they're not, if you're persistent and read the journal carefully, you'll notice gaps in coverage, where a well-written query letter (in which you propose an article, explaining why your idea is important and pertinent) could produce results. Before proposing an article, determine what types of articles the publisher prints and the usual length, and tailor your approach accordingly. Check *The Writer's Market* (found in local bookstores) or other general books on getting published for information on how to write a query letter to a magazine publisher.

The payoff: The more you are published, the better your name will be known and the bigger your pool of potential contacts. Bonus: Other news people may notice you as well, and perhaps call on you for information and quotations, further increasing your exposure. Moreover, journalists are often the first to know of impending changes in an industry, and helping them may help you later. And of course, authorship of articles on your industry always looks good on your resume.

▶ **Don't stop with the obvious—contacts can be found virtually anywhere.**

As long as you're focused on a clear, coherent objective, you may find useful contacts virtually anywhere. Don't be a one-note bore, but casually mention your search for information to people you meet. Consider taking night-school courses related to your field. The casual atmosphere can be congenial to informal networking—and result in a job lead, or at least a valuable contact.

STEP THREE: EXPANDING YOUR CONTACT BASE BY GETTING AND USING REFERRALS

▶ **You should now have gotten used to the basic idea of net-working, and you should have a list of people to talk to.**

With any luck, your friends and close business associates have given you a few names to contact. Now is the time to expand your networking base and call your referrals. For some, this is the most difficult part of the entire process.

But remember that this second circle of contacts—or referrals, the people you must call—is often the most useful in your job hunt. Go through your card file of contacts, and begin with the names of those who have the most potential to help you. Networking with referrals can be time-consuming and stressful, so get the best pay-out by starting with the best names.

▶ **You can either cold-call referrals yourself or have your initial contact pave the way for you by making an introductory call or writing a letter.**

For those with a non-sales personality, cold-calling can be stressful. Follow these rules of thumb to make the calling easier:

- *To ease the stress, think of and treat the call as you would any other routine business call.*
- *Dress as if for work before you phone*—studies have shown that the appropriate clothing mentally prepares you to speak and act professionally.
- *Call from an office* or another quiet place with some privacy.
- *Best times to call: early in the morning, in the middle of the week.* For very important or busy people, very early in the morning, before regular work hours. Worst times to call: Monday, Friday, lunch hours, or late afternoon.

▶ **When you have your referral on the phone, remember to get to the point quickly.**

You have three objectives:

- To introduce yourself.
- To briefly explain why you're calling.
- To arrange for a meeting.

Mention to your referral as soon as possible your mutual friend or acquaintance to legitimize your call and your request for time. If the referral sounds busy, acknowledge this and say you won't take much time.

EXAMPLE: **"This is Tom Jones. Mary Everson from ABC Company tells me that you're the person I should speak to about [a profession, a company, or an industry]. She suggested I call you and see if we could get together. Would coffee on Wednesday morning be convenient for you?"**

Don't ask for a job over the phone, nor for specific advice. You want a meeting, not a five-minute telephone chat. And aim to set a specific time for a meeting (as in the example above). It's harder for your referral to refuse a meeting. If the referral suggests that you come to his or her office, choose a time outside of working hours if possible, to allow for an uninterrupted discussion.

▶ **Of course you want a job, but the best approach in networking is an indirect one.**

At your meeting with your referral, remember that this isn't the time for a hard sell. Take a tip from top sales pros, who know that one of the best ways to make a sale is to listen, ask intelligent questions, and learn all you can *before* you make your pitch. Get the referrals interested in you first.

A few pointers:

- *Do your homework.* Call back your initial contact and thank him or her for the referral, and mention your upcoming meeting. Find out what you can about your referral. Research the industry, the company, and the person you're meeting before you go in.

- *Be brief.* State your objective and questions concisely.

- *Listen.* Listening is the most important aspect of good networking. People (even busy people) like the sound of their own voices and, not surprisingly, are more apt to be impressed by people who are good listeners than good talkers. And the more you listen, the more you'll learn.

- *Ask questions.* Work on formulating intelligent questions about the industry or field. Build on what you learn; jot down new questions to ask after each interview.

- *Be an active participant.* Don't just ask one question after another like a test examiner—keep up your end of the conversation by responding and trying to make the meeting more of a dialogue than an interview.

- *Personalize your questions and conversation.* Mention specific features of your referral's career or company; impress him or her with your knowledge.

- *Avoid giving away too much information.* We already mentioned that giving away your resume at the wrong time can hurt you by disqualifying you for a job. For the same reason, and particularly with early referrals, don't give away too much in conversation.

- *Don't leave without asking for two or three or more names to call.* Remember your main goal—to build on your contacts until you hear of a job.

▶ **Just because this isn't an interview doesn't mean you shouldn't treat it like one.**

You—and most probably your referral—know you want a job. Therefore, you must act as if you were being interviewed for a job, by maintaining a positive and professional demeanor, dressing appropriately, not bad-mouthing your previous employer or career, and above all, showing a genuine interest in the career you are exploring and the individual you are meeting. (For more tips on handling interview situations, see page 194.)

STEP FOUR: FOLLOWING UP

▶ **Follow-up is essential—your goal is to keep you and your situation in your referral's mind.**

Meeting with your referral isn't an end—it should be a beginning. Strive to remain in contact, even if your referral has answered all the questions you have for now. Obviously, if your referrals keep you in mind, they're more apt to recommend you or tell you of opportunities to pursue.

What you should do:

▶ **Before you leave, ask if you can call again at a later date.**

Better yet, if it seems appropriate, give the person a definite time when you will call.

The best way: *Set a concrete reason for calling back later.* This makes it easier to suggest, and easier for your contact to agree.

EXAMPLE: "John, I appreciate the suggestions that you've given me on researching the different opportunities available in purchasing. I'll call you next Thursday to let you know how they've worked out.

▶ **After each meeting with a valuable contact, send a thank-you note.**

It's common courtesy, but also very helpful. The letter should be more than just a thank-you; it should help sell you. Keep things low key. Don't write a hard-sell resume letter, but do try to highlight skills that relate to the new job you're looking for. Or you might mention something he or she said that was particularly interesting. Be certain to personalize your letter; avoid stilted, overly formal language.

▶ **Don't stop with a phone call or follow-up letter. Re-contact your referral periodically—but not too frequently.**

There's a definite line between being persistent and being a nuisance. Most people make the mistake of not calling enough; but others make pests of themselves and turn off potentially valuable contacts.

So how do you call your referral back without seeming pushy? Establish a reason for the call. Two of the best justifications:

1. You have a *specific* question, which relates to your past discussion.

2. You are giving your contact an update on how his or her advice is working out.

EXAMPLE: **"The articles you mentioned were terrific. I've written to the people who were interviewed, and I've already received an answer and arranged for a meeting."**

Don't keep calling referrals with the same news. Keep your approaches fresh—and let your contacts know that you're not sitting still.

Some more suggestions to keep your referrals interested in you:

• *Send clippings of newspaper or magazine articles that might interest your contacts, along with a short note.*

• *Use other people to follow up for you.* Have your initial contacts speak to the referrals they gave you. Ask them for feedback.

▶ **Keep your network strong.**

Weed your network periodically; get rid of those contacts who have been unhelpful and don't hold much promise of changing. It makes your network smaller but stronger. And you won't waste your valuable time.

If you have contacts who can't help you but may be able to help others, pass along their names. They may reciprocate the favor.

4

THE AGEPROOF RESUME

INTRODUCTION

▶ **Let's get one thing straight—at some point during your job hunt, you'll need a resume.**

You're not off the hook just because you're no longer after entry-level jobs. Yet many older job seekers, especially those in the upper levels, automatically assume they're beyond resumes. They're wrong. *Whether you're a CEO, a mid-level manager, or a lower-level employee, if you want to land a new job, you're probably going to need an updated resume.*

▶ **Why? Because a resume is a *selling* tool.**

The product? You and your expertise. A resume is the means by which you can position yourself as a valuable commodity and sell yourself into an interview or a job.

Of course, whenever possible, a face-to-face sales meeting is best. But that doesn't mean a resume isn't an important part of the over-40 job hunter's campaign. Simply put, you can't expect to sell yourself in person at all times. You're going to need to do some selling on paper at various stages in your job hunt:

- *In direct-mail campaigns:* Direct mail of a resume and cover letter is still one of the best methods of landing a job. Many of you will be using this job-hunting tactic. You're going to need a strong resume, which sells you into an interview by convincing recipients that you have a background their companies can use.

- *With executive recruiters:* If you're planning a mailing to executive recruiters in hopes of getting one interested in you, again you'll need a resume as part of your direct mailing to clearly lay out your experience, achievements, and objectives. And if a recruiter has already contacted you about possible openings, you *still* need a resume, to ensure that the recruiter has all the pertinent information about your background to pass on to employers. Yes, recruiters will typically put together a resume on you following their firm's format. But by supplying your resume to them, you can be sure they have all the details that you want them to include.

- *After interviews:* Like a salesperson's leave-behind, a resume is a memory tickler that can reinforce the points you covered in an interview. It enables the interviewer to easily recall you, your background, and what you can do for his or her company.

▶ **But remember the flip side: Even while you are using a resume to sell yourself, potential employers are using it to screen *out* the candidates they don't want.**

This is what makes resume writing such a tricky business. It's one thing to just list your background, another thing to put together an effective sales document. The trick, of course, is to know what the red flags are and devise ways to either remove or downplay any potential drawbacks. At the same time, you have to select the specific achievements from your background that best highlight your skills and will make the reader want to meet you—and hire you.

The bottom line: To maximize your chances of landing the job you want, you must write a strong resume . . . an ageproof resume.

THE AGEPROOF RESUME: WHAT IT IS

▶ **An ageproof resume is, simply, one that downplays your age and draws the reader's attention to where it *should* be—your abilities.**

Obvious, yes. But not as simple as it sounds.

An ageproof resume must cover the basics—your work experience, achievements and accomplishments, and educational background—in a compelling enough way that the reader doesn't *care* how old you are. In other words, it must be a carefully targeted, strongly written document . . . the best resume you've ever written. A tall order? Maybe. But it's do-able, and it's necessary.

▶ **First, the basics: As you plan and write your resume, keep these two facts in mind:**

Fact #1: You have one chance to make your resume sell you—and that's the first time someone reads it.

There are no second chances where resumes are concerned. If the resume doesn't grab the reader's attention the first time it's read, it's destined for the round file.

Fact #2: You have to grab the reader's interest in 15 to 30 seconds.

That's the average amount of time that headhunters and prospective employers spend on resumes before deciding whether to continue reading or not.

Your first goal, then, is to write a resume that grabs and holds people's attention—one that encourages them to read on.

▶ **How do you go about doing this in a time when resumes have become the corporate equivalent of junk mail?**

By thinking like a direct-mail salesperson and recognizing what appeals to your target audience of prospective employers, recruiters, and referrals.

They have hundreds of other resumes on their desks. They don't want to work to read yours; they want to be able to scan it and, in the 15 to 30 seconds they've allotted to it, learn enough to determine whether they're interested in you.

Under circumstances like these, the style, format, and layout of your resume are crucial. You want to ensure that readers can quickly see your strong selling points, and that the points are simple to digest but also explicit enough to give the reader a distinct impression of you.

▶ **If you've gotten the recipient to read on, your second goal is to convince the reader that you are worth getting to know better.**

A face-to-face meeting is usually what you're after—whether it's with a potential employer, an executive recruiter, or someone who has been referred to you by a networking contact. To get you to this meeting, your resume must contain information that makes the reader want to meet you in person.

To do this, make your resume targeted—in the following two ways:

1. *Skew your resume to your audience.* The people reading your resume aren't interested in *you*. They're interested in how well you can fill their needs. So the information on your resume should always be answering their question: What can this person do for me?

2. *Have a clear idea of the job you're after.* Remember, you're trying to sell yourself into a job. And you won't make the sale if you're at all vague about your goal. In other words, the more clearly you mentally define your objective, the more effectively you can target your resume. The key is *focus*. The information in your resume must all add up to one thing: you have the background that makes you right for a job. If you don't know what that job is, you won't convince the reader of your resume. Keep in mind: This applies even if you aren't using your resume as part of a direct-mail campaign. Whatever your use of a resume (after an interview, while networking, with an executive recruiter), it still must be positioned for a specific job.

TIP: If you have more than one job objective or are trying for jobs in different industries, you may be best off writing a different resume for each situation. This way you can tailor them to the particular needs of each target employer or industry. Yes, in many cases the information you include will be substantially the same, but the *emphasis* will differ.

▶ **To meet these goals, you must engineer your resume in three main areas: (1) Format and style, or how you package yourself. (2) Contents, the information about yourself you choose to include. (3) Presentation, the actual words you use and the appearance of your resume.**

THE TWO BEST RESUME STYLES FOR THE OVER-40 JOB SEEKER: WHAT THEY ARE AND WHEN TO USE THEM

▶ **There are many different resume styles, but at this point in your career, there are only two that you should use.**

Resume guides go on at length about different styles: functional resumes, achievement resumes, letter resumes, and so on. To be perfectly blunt, most of these hotshot new variations are absolutely useless.

Don't get caught in the "flavor of the month" trap and write your resume according to the popular style of the moment. Job hunting, like anything else, succumbs to fads. And the hot resume style everyone is raving about today is bound to be replaced by a hot new one tomorrow. But there is one part of job hunting that never succumbs to fads—and that's the ultimate goal, a job. One way to get that job is to write the most *effective* resume possible, not the most fashionable.

This is why you should restrict yourself to using the two resume styles described here. These have proved to be the most effective formats for the over-40 job seeker: the reverse chronological, in which work experience is listed, as you would expect, in reverse chronological order; and the combination (or achievement/chronological), in which work experience is presented in terms of achievements, followed by a brief chronology.

▶ **The simple truth: Most employers and recruiters prefer the old, tried-and-true reverse chronological resume.**

It's probably the type of resume you've always used. Chronological resumes have been around as long as people have hunted for jobs. And for good reason: They work.

They're easy to read. They cut to the chase. The reader can immediately see what you've been doing, what you've accomplished, and whether you're the right person for the job.

What it is:

- *A reverse chronological resume is, exactly as it sounds, a resume in which your experience is arranged in chronological order,* starting with the most recent position you've held and going back in time.

Your first heading should be "Work Experience," "Professional Experience," "Experience and Achievements," simply "Experience," or the like. Under this heading, you will list your various jobs, duties, and achievements.

More specifically: For each work experience entry, list your job title, the company name, and the years you held the job. Under this, briefly describe your duties and list several of your most impressive accomplishments and achievements.

After the work experience section, include such information as: education, any trade/professional organizations (optional), technical skills (for those in high-tech fields—engineers, scientists, etc.), and anything else of relevance.

Who this is best for:

- *Virtually anyone.* As mentioned before, this is a common format, and one that recruiters and corporate officers say they prefer. It is concise—the reader can see precisely what you have done, where you've worked, and for how long.

- *Best bet:* This format is especially effective for people with impressive credentials (tenures at blue-chip companies, etc.), since position title and company name are emphasized, and for people with strong advancement and achievement records in a single field, since upward growth is immediately noticeable.

TIP: **While you probably will use this format at all times anyway, do note that it should *always* be used when preparing a resume for executive recruiters or when the human resources or personnel department of a prospective employer requests a resume. In both instances, a clear rundown of your employment history is required, and no other resume format meets these needs.**

Potential problems:

- *Any gaps in your employment history or short tenures are immediately noticeable.* Short of lying, you can't hide job hopping or periods of unemployment. In these cases, you may want to consider using the combination format, explained on page 92.

- *If your experience isn't directly related to the job you're aiming for, it will be apparent.* Tackle this issue head on in your cover letter or interview.

SAMPLE CHRONOLOGICAL RESUME

ALEXANDRA CORY
100 Main St.
New Rochelle, NY 10802
516-555-1111

SUMMARY

Results-oriented public relations professional with track record in both print and broadcast media. Extensive background developing and supervising innovative programs designed to attract and win media and consumer attention.

EXPERIENCE

Director of Public Relations
Blaine Communications, Inc., New York, NY   (1987–present)
Coordinate all public relations and media relations for leading trade magazine publisher, reporting to Executive Vice President. Supervise staff of 15.
- Spearhead coordinated public relations program for 15 publications. Designed and oversaw production of new media kit, all corporate literature.
- Established extensive media relations program—including setting up panel of experts available for television and print interviews. Media coverage of publications has leaped 41%.
- Introduced successful publicity campaign revolving around editorial roundtable forums and tie-ins with major industry events.
- Conceived and oversaw development of special product spin-offs—videotapes, books. In one year, new product line generated sales of $300K.

Public Relations Manager
Advertising Era Magazine, New York, NY   (1980–1987)
Developed and supervised promotion and public relations activities for top trade publication.
- Created and designed brochures as part of comprehensive direct-mail campaign designed to win new subscribers.
- Devised all promotion activities for publication—sponsored trade workshop—resulting in heavier media coverage and 28% increase in attendance.
- Wrote press releases, flyers.

Senior Account Executive
Buxton-McAllister, Inc., New York, NY   (1971–1980)
Handled national account responsible for $2 million in agency billings. Supervised staff of 4.
- Directed multiphase public relations campaign for Penton Drug Co., including swift damage control during difficult Non-Aspirin pill tampering case. Won American Women in Radio & Television "Silver Pinnacle" award for successful handling of situation.

- Conceived and directed national public relations campaign for successful introduction of Penton Drug Co.'s new painkiller—including heavy network exposure, successful 21 city tour by spokesperson.

Account Executive
Buxton-McAllister, Inc., New York, NY   (1965–1971)
Managed Hairol account during product introduction period.
- Established contacts with prominent television producers, magazine and newspaper editors through extensive phone work and
- Increased media bookings by 25% over predecessor. Promoted to second in command on account after only six months.

Associate Producer
WXYX-TV, New York, NY   (1962–1965)
Produced special taping session, feature stories and in-studio interview segments for leading independent television station.
- Developed and produced special summer replacement series, focusing on cultural activities in New York.
- Wrote news and feature copy. Coordinated talent for studio interviews.
- Produced news and feature stories requiring special production techniques.

EDUCATION

Bachelor of Arts, New York University

ACTIVITIES

Member, Public Relations Society of America
Member, American Women in Radio & Television

▶ **There are a few instances in which the chronological resume is *not* the best bet: You have a spotty employment record or you're switching careers. In these cases, you may be better off with a "combination resume."**

A combination resume (also called an achievement resume) is the only other format that fits the needs of the over-40 job hunter. While not as widely accepted as the reverse chronological resume, and for this reason not as strongly recommended, the combination resume is a good choice for people with special problems or circumstances that make the chronological resume less effective.

What it is:

• *The combination resume combines the chronological resume with a so-called functional format.* Its first section is the equivalent of the "Employment History" or "Work Experience" section of the chronological resume and should be titled "Skills," "Experience," "Achievements," "Accomplishments," or the like.

Instead of organizing your experience by particular jobs, you use broader, functional headings that cover general areas of expertise (for example, Marketing, Administration, Sales, Public Relations, and so forth).

Under each function heading, write a paragraph or series of brief paragraphs explaining your accomplishments and achievements in that area. These don't necessarily have to be work related; you can use examples from such activities as volunteer work. If you want, include company names and titles, but this isn't necessary.

Information is set forth not in chronological order, but in the order you decide makes you appear right for the position you're after.

After the functional section, list your employment history—literally. Just company names, job titles, and dates. Follow this with such basic information as education, any trade/professional organizations (optional), etc.

Who this is best for:

• *Career switchers.* You can emphasize the experience in your background that pertains to your new target career or position by focusing on the tasks, skills, or achievements in your previous employment that relate to your current objective. Because employment dates, company names, and titles are de-emphasized here, you have the chance to grab the reader's attention and convince him or her that you have the right credentials . . . before it hits him or her that your work history doesn't completely mesh with the job you're after.

- *Job hoppers.* If you've held several jobs in a short period of time, you can consolidate them under a function heading and make your background appear more stable. This downplays a spotty work record and highlights the continuity in the jobs you've had.

- *Reentry workers.* You can use this format to stress non-work achievements, such as volunteer work. This is a definite plus for those who are reentering the labor market after a hiatus and haven't had recent professional experience. (This is also a plus for career switchers who want to make their background mesh with their new target career.)

Potential problems:

- *Many recruiters and employers red-flag this type of resume,* immediately assuming the person is trying to hide something . . . which is often the case. The only way around this is to write a strong cover letter and hope for the best.

- *It's very easy to make this type of resume confusing and difficult to read,* both in content and appearance, since you never spell out specific job duties or positions you've held. As such, it's important to take special care in writing and layout.

SAMPLE COMBINATION RESUME

ALEXANDRA CORY
100 Main St.
New Rochelle, NY 10802
516-555-1111

SUMMARY

Results-oriented public relations professional with track record in both print and broadcast media. Extensive background developing and supervising innovative programs designed to attract and win media and consumer attention.

SKILLS

Management
- Supervise staff of 15 with $1 million budget.
- Established all procedures and training for newly created public relations department.
- Handled national account responsible for $2 million in agency billings. Managed all levels of administration, promotion work. Supervised staff of 4.

Public Relations
- Spearhead coordinated public relations program for 15 publications. Introduced successful publicity campaign revolving around editorial roundtable forums and tie-ins with major industry events.
- Conceived and oversaw development of special product spinoffs—videotapes, books. In one year, new product line generated sales of $300K.
- Created and designed brochures as part of comprehensive direct-mail campaign designed to win new subscribers. Devised all promotion activities for publication-sponsored trade workshop— resulting in heavier media coverage and 28% increase in attendance.
- Directed multiphase public relations campaign for Penton Drug Co., including swift damage control during difficult Non-Aspirin pill tampering case. Won American Women in Radio & Television "Silver Pinnacle" award for successful handling of situation. Conceived and directed national public relations campaign for successful introduction of Penton Drug Co.'s new painkiller—including heavy network exposure, successful 21-city tour by spokesperson.

Media Relations
- Established extensive media relations program for leading trade journal publisher—including setting up panel of experts available for television and print interviews. Designed and oversaw production of new media kit, all corporate literature. Media coverage of publications has leapt 41%.
- Established contacts with prominent television producers and magazine and newspaper editors through extensive phone work, meetings.

• As account executive on national hair-care account, increased media bookings by 25% over predecessor. Promoted to second in command on account after only six months.

EXPERIENCE

Director of Public Relations
Blaine Communications, Inc., New York, NY   1987–present

Public Relations Manager
Advertising Era Magazine, New York, NY   1980–1987

Senior Account Executive
Buxton-McAllister, Inc., New York, NY   1971–1980

Account Excutive
Buxton-McAllister, Inc., New York, NY   1965–1971

Associate Producer
WXYX-TV, New York, NY   1962–1965

EDUCATION

Bachelor of Arts, New York University

ACTIVITIES

Member, Public Relations Society of America
Member, American Women in Radio & Television

CONTENTS: WHAT TO INCLUDE (AND WHAT NOT TO INCLUDE) ON YOUR AGEPROOF RESUME

▶ **Another basic stage of resume writing is reviewing the contents and the categories you'll be including.**

Following are the typical vital parts of a resume and the information each should include. They're listed in the order in which they'd ordinarily appear in your resume, although in some cases this order may differ.

1. **Personal data:** Name, address, and telephone number at the top of your resume.

That's it. No "Health: excellent" (If you were in poor health, you wouldn't mention it, would you?), no height and weight, no other descriptive material. And absolutely no photograph.

As for date of birth—for obvious reasons, it's not recommended. Even though some experts claim that including your date of birth makes you appear forthright and avoiding it makes you look as though you're hiding something, it simply doesn't make sense to include it. Why spell out your age in black and white? All it really does is give the person reading your resume the opportunity to immediately decide you're too old for the job.

TIP: It's not recommended, but if you really want to, you can include your marital status and children on your resume. But make this a final entry at the end of your resume under a "Personal" heading. And keep it simple. For example:
  Personal
  Married (or Single, or Divorced)
  Two children (no names or ages)

2. **Biographical summary (optional):** A brief summary of your achievements, skills, and characteristics—60 words maximum.

This replaces the old-fashioned "Job Objective" you probably used in the past—that often vague one-to-two-line statement that set forth the job you wanted.

Why replace it? Because it doesn't work anymore.

Times have changed, and so has your experience. First, it has become a buyer's market out there. You don't have the luxury of choice you may have enjoyed in the past. In addition, you now have a number of strong skills and achievements, not to mention a more extensive track record, which you can use to convince prospective employers that you are a good choice for their company.

To do this, you may include a brief summary at the top of your resume, consisting of several statements that clearly demonstrate your credentials or "fit" for the position you want. Even if you open with the job title you're aiming at, the focus is on your abilities.

In other words, unlike the old "objective," you're not describing the job you want. You're describing what you can do.

You can either make your summary a condensed sales message —in effect, a showcase for your strongest selling points—or a more targeted message, in which you name the position you're after and the abilities you have that make you right for it.

Here are two different ways of using the summary statement. The first example is a condensed sales message, underscoring the resume writer's achievements in a brief biographical sketch.

EXAMPLE: **Extensive background as sales/marketing manager and as general manager, with P&L responsibility. Particular emphasis—improving cash flow and ROI, strengthening product lines, increasing inventory turns, turnaround situations, building organizations . . . and profits.**

In the next example, the same individual is taking much of the same information, but focusing it differently. He is pinpointing the position he's after and pulling up salient information from his resume to prove his credentials.

EXAMPLE:

GENERAL MANAGER Extensive background—improving cash flow and ROI, strengthening product lines, cutting costs, reducing inventory, building organizations . . . and profits.

- **General Manager—P & L responsibility 2 companies**

- **Entrepreneur—organized $3-million company**

- **Marketing Vice President—$55-million company**

As you can see, both types are, in effect, mini-resumes—allowing the reader to quickly determine whether you fit his or her needs. Which is why there is a danger to using summaries: Because you've (theoretically) put your strongest selling statement up front, the resume reader can decide whether you fit the bill *without* reading the rest of your resume. If you don't fit, you're out of luck.

The upshot? If you do write a summary, make sure it is as strong as it can be. If you're at all concerned or find you're unable to come up with a hard-hitting summary, drop it.

TIP: **When writing summaries, be specific—for example, "Proven record of increasing market share," not "Successful marketing executive." Don't fall into vague, mushy statements that make it sound like you have little to offer. Also avoid nonessentials, such as "highly motivated" or "success-oriented." What job seeker would say he wasn't?**

TIP: **Because the summary is such a concentrated sales message, maximize your limited space by using sentence fragments, not complete sentences. Strip your language down to the bare bones. Rely on action words and descriptive lines to get your message across.**

TIP: **Write the rest of your resume *first,* then go back and write your summary. Often this will help shake loose the ideas you'll want to include in your summary.**

3. **Work experience:** Past jobs and achievements (usually arranged in reverse chronological order).

This is the guts of your resume—the information that will make you or break you.

In light of this, take your time planning this section, both in terms of what you'll include and how you'll present it. Always keep your target audience and your objective in mind.

If you're writing a chronological resume, this section will consist of job title headings, company names and dates, and salient achievements and accomplishments listed beneath each heading. A combination resume will have functional headings, with related achievements beneath.

A few rules of thumb:

- *Confine your coverage to the past 15 to 20 years or so.* There's no need to go into your entire work experience since you left school. In fact, if you do, it will look as though you don't feel your recent work experience is strong enough to sell you.

- *Remember that* where *you place facts about your work history can make a huge difference in how you are perceived.* Even in a chronological resume, you have some leeway as to the order in which you present your experience. Use placement to highlight your strongest selling points. Position your most impressive achievements or the abilities and skills that directly relate to your target job at the beginning of paragraphs or at the top of bulleted lists. Don't force the reader to ferret out this pertinent information. Play it up.

TIP: **To play up your achievements, make a distinction between the duties and responsibilities of a job and what you've accomplished in that job. Write a brief statement under each job title that outlines your duties. Don't assume that your title says it all—paint as precise a picture as possible: "Supervise staff of 35," "Responsible for a budget of $250,000," etc. A line or two below, follow this with a series of achievement statements—either bulleted or in short paragraphs—that demonstrate how well you've fulfilled these duties.**

- *In a chronological resume, emphasize your most recent position more than others.* Employers are usually most interested in what you've accomplished most recently. As such, include more examples of achievements and accomplishments in your more recent jobs (a minimum of four achievements/accomplishments). The further you delve into the past, the fewer examples you need to provide.

- *In a combination or achievement resume, follow the same principle.* Pay the most attention to the skill or function that is most critical to your target position and less to the less-applicable function areas.

- *Don't include anything and everything about yourself.* Instead, stress the achievements and jobs that best underscore your ability to perform the job you're pursuing. Choose examples from your background that tie directly to your target position, and take advantage of strong achievements that *don't* directly tie in with your objective by writing them up so they relate at least indirectly.

For more specific hints and guidelines on how to write this section of your resume, see pages 105–12.

4. **Education: School(s) attended, degree(s) earned.**
Again, that's it.
You've been out of school long enough to have passed the need

to go into any greater detail. No one cares anymore what you majored in, or whether you graduated cum laude or summa cum laude.

As for dates, generally, you're best off if you don't include them. Putting down that you received your B.S. in 1949 is an immediate tip-off to your age. But don't think that you're really fooling anyone —most savvy resume readers are hip to the fact that omitting education dates means the resume writer isn't 32 anymore. (Of course, readers can't be sure how old the writer really is—a definite plus if you're over 50). Along these lines, do keep in mind that some recruiters recommend full disclosure to show how honest and open you are.

Our advice: As mentioned above, it's simplest to avoid dates. If you're 40 to 50 or so and want to include dates to prove that you're still fairly young, there's no real harm in doing so. If you're older than this, steer clear of dates.

TIP: **You're not a college graduate? Two ways of handling this—if you attended college but never graduated, simply put how many years you did attend school and the name of the school ("Three years at New York University"). If you attended more than one school, put "Three years at New York University and Columbia University," or the like. If you never attended college, don't eliminate the education section. The omission will look strange. Instead, write "self-educated." Include any work-related courses or training you have taken, and be sure to include an "Other Interests" or "Hobbies" section, which you can use to show intellectual activity—chess clubs, board membership for cultural groups, and the like, or an "Other Accomplishments" section, in which you can list articles you've written for magazines, newspapers, or professional journals, television shows on which you've appeared as an "expert," etc. The aim is to make you sound as intellectually able as possible.**

5. **Memberships (optional):** Names of trade and professional associations, civic organizations, etc.

The only time to include this section is if you have data to include that make you more salable. Good ones to include: executive committee memberships at trade associations; board memberships of cultural, charitable, or civic organizations. But be sure not to overdo this—you don't want it to appear as though you spent most of your time on nonprofessional activities and not enough on work.

TIP: *Omit* mention of religious organizations and of anything controversial or overly political—you can't be sure what the resume reader's views are, so why ask for trouble?

TIP: A sneaky idea: If you've done background research and discover that you and the person to whom you're sending the resume share a common membership, include it on your resume. People tend to like people who remind them of themselves. A sneakier idea: If you don't belong to their club or organization, but you can join it, do so. *Then* put it on your resume. What do you have to lose?

6. **Military experience (optional):** Rank, dates, etc.

Unless your military experience has direct bearing on the job you're after—that is, your skills or achievements while in service make you more employable, or if you reached a high rank that may look impressive—there's no need to include this information on your resume.

7. **Technical abilities (optional, depending upon objective):** Knowledge of using certain equipment, computer languages, etc.

Include this section if you're going for a technical job. It's self-explanatory—you list the areas in which you're an expert, including hardware, software, computer languages, and the like. If you have only a working knowledge of certain areas, differentiate them from those you have an expert knowledge of by using a heading such as "Working knowledge of."

8. **Hobbies/interests (optional):** Don't bother.

Unless (there's always an exception) you have extremely active hobbies that will make you seem younger: You're a marathoner or a rock climber.

Or (make that two exceptions), as mentioned above, you have no college background and need to establish your intellectual credibility.

9. **Languages (optional):** If you're fluent in other languages, include this information. It certainly can't hurt, and in some cases it will help.

Two final words: (1) You may notice that there is no mention of a "References" section. And for good reason—there's very rarely any need to list the names of your references on your resume. Should a prospective employer request the names of references, provide them then, separately. Or mention them in your cover letter. *Not* on your resume.

TIP: Send copies of your resume to your references, along with a brief note about the jobs for which you're trying. When and if they're called, they have background information about you right at hand.

As for the "References available upon request" line that many people persist in putting on their resumes—don't waste the space.

(2) You may want to add a last line on your resume reading "Willing to relocate," if indeed you are. This is by no means a necessity, as you can put this information in your cover letter or say it in person. However, with today's job market as tough as it is, willingness to relocate may give you an edge over other candidates.

GETTING STARTED: PLANNING AN EFFECTIVE RESUME

▶ **As with any sales and marketing project, you've got to start by planning.**

It sounds obvious, but a surprisingly large number of people don't write their resumes until the very last moment. A headhunter or networking referral says, "Can you fax me your resume? It looks as though I might have something for you." And the job hunter sits down and tries to hammer something out as quickly as possible—clearly not the optimal circumstances under which to write a document that can mean the difference between landing an interview (or maybe a job) and not.

To make your resume as strong as possible, you have to take it step by step.

▶ **The first step: Take an hour or so and list your accomplishments, the jobs you've held, and the highlights of each.**

You don't need a fancy work sheet with clever headings. All you need is a pen and paper or a computer, a little time, and a decent memory.

The simplest way to start writing your resume is to start writing it. Decide which format you'll use and jump right in.

Start with the easy part—the simple facts. List your job titles, the companies you've worked for, and your duties and responsibilities at each job. This gives you a framework upon which to build the substance of your resume, and helps you to organize your thoughts.

Next, begin fleshing out this frame by adding your specific achievements and accomplishments in each position.

TIP: **Don't be discriminating at this early stage. Write down anything and everything you can think of—there will be time to edit it down later. At the beginning, you're best off gathering as much raw material as possible.**

Always keep your target objective and target audience at the back of your mind. Focus on the specific qualities that a prospective employer would seek for the job you're after and think about how you can prove on paper that you have them.

But don't forget the *general* qualities that employers always like to see. Include examples that show:

- *Ability to contribute to the bottom line:* productivity, cost-cutting measures, turnarounds, etc.

- *Consistent upward movement/patterns of accomplishment:* promotions received within the same company or industry; increasing responsibility; stable career path or, if you are a career switcher, lateral moves into different career paths with equal responsibility.

- *Team-playing ability/"people skills":* how well you motivated your staff, your training capability, etc.

- *Communications skills:* writing ability, leading presentations/seminars, etc.

▶ **Expect to write at least two drafts.**

As mentioned above, your first draft is your work sheet. Therefore, be more concerned right now with getting information down on paper than with your writing style. Once you have gotten down everything you think you'll use, review it and begin editing. Remember, you want your resume to make the strongest possible case for someone to hire you. Edit with an eye to your reader and your target job. Keep asking yourself: Have I created a convincing case? Would *you* want to meet this person?

▶ **Once you feel you have a finished product, have friends and colleagues read and critique your resume.**

Outside opinions will give you new insight into your resume. Often, someone else will see something wrong—or right—that you have overlooked. Be sure friends and colleagues are completely frank with you. You want *them* to find errors or shortcomings, not a would-be employer.

TIP: **Often the most helpful critique comes from a person in the position you're aiming for. He or she knows what the position entails, which achievements/abilities you should stress, etc.**

Questions to ask your critics:

- *Is the resume attractively laid out and easy to read?*

- *Is it clear what type of position I'm after, or what type I would be best for?*

- *Are there enough specifics, or is the resume too general?*

- *Have I included the strongest accomplishments from my work history? Is there anything I've left out?*

- *Is there anything that can be cut?* That is, any minor position or achievement that doesn't add to my salability?

- *Is there anything in the resume that would raise questions about my background?*

- *Most important, would the reader, on the basis of my resume alone, be interested in interviewing or hiring me? If not, why not?*

▶ **A final point to keep in mind as you plan, write, and edit your resume:** *How* **you say something is as important as** *what* **you say.**

Length of sentences, the wording you choose, your resume's layout—these are all potential ammunition. Use them strategically, and make your resume as strong and effective as possible by paying attention to the little things.

TEN AGEPROOFING RULES OF THUMB: THE ESSENTIAL GUIDELINES THAT WILL MAKE YOUR AGE LESS OF AN ISSUE

▶ **The following guidelines are tested tips that *work*.**

We've collected them from successful over-40 job seekers and from resume readers on the other side of the desk. They answer common questions resume writers ask, debunk several popular myths, and help you further strengthen your resume. Follow them carefully when putting together your resume, and you'll have the type of resume that gets read—and, very often, leads to job offers.

▶ **Rule 1: *Your resume should be as long as it needs to be.***

No more, no less.

Forget all the advice you've heard about keeping your resume to one page. And while you're at it, forget all the advice you've heard about making your resume a minimum of three pages.

There is only one person who really knows how long your resume should be—and that's you.

Remember: First you want to get someone to read your resume; then you want to convince them to meet you. Neither of these goals has anything to do with length.

If you're concerned about going over one page, remember that you aren't a kid anymore. You have years of experience, you've accomplished quite a bit, you have several achievements under your belt. There's a very good chance that your strongest selling pitch simply won't fit on one page.

Of course, this isn't license for rambling on and on. To repeat, your resume should be as long as it *needs* to be. That means exactly what it says.

▶ **Rule 2: *Rule 1 notwithstanding, be brief.***

Again, think like a marketer. Demonstrate your ability to summarize and consolidate information by writing a tight resume.

Keep in mind: Clear, concise writing signals a clear, concise thinker.

Along these lines:

- *Use short words.* This isn't the place to demonstrate your ability to write like William F. Buckley. Keep it simple. Impress them with your vocabulary after you're hired, if you must.

- *Avoid bureaucratese and jargon.* This is a common pitfall of the over-40 job seeker—and as such, is an immediate age tip-off. Nothing sounds worse than slightly outdated jargon.

TIP: Especially important if you're switching careers: Don't use inside phrases to describe your experience. Many times people outside your direct field or even your specific company won't have any idea what you're talking about. Or, just as bad, you'll draw attention to the fact that you're switching careers and very possibly have no experience in your new target career.

- *Omit unnecessary words.* Cut to the chase. A few well-chosen descriptive words sell better than many vague ones. Words and phrases to drop: pronouns ("we," "you," etc.); preambles to the point, like the phrase "Responsibilities include"; mindless mush like "able to motivate workers" or "strong interpersonal skills."

- *Avoid puffery.* If you have to pad out an accomplishment, it's not a good enough achievement to include on your resume.

- *Use sentence fragments instead of complete sentences.* They read more quickly, take up less space, and force you to write tightly.

TIP: Even if you're using paragraphs under your "Experience" headings, write several short paragraphs instead of one long one, and set each paragraph off with a bullet. This breaks up the information and makes it much more readable.

▶ **Rule 3:** *Ground your experience by including background information.*

Don't assume prospective employers can read between the lines and deduce what your job truly entailed.

Give them the facts. Include background information that allows readers to understand what your duties actually were. Only when people understand the context, can your achievements and accomplishments mean anything.

A few tips:

- *As mentioned before (on page 98), it's a good idea to write a few lines describing your position*—with hard facts, such as the number of people you supervised, the budgets you were responsible for, where you stood in the chain of command, what projects you initiated, etc.

- *When appropriate, give background information on the company you worked for, or the division.* Again, you want to give the reader a context in which to understand what you've done. Lay it out in black and white. The reader may not know whether the last company you worked for was a $55-million multiproducts company or a $10-million home furnishings company. Spell it out!

▶ **Rule 4:** *Show, don't tell.*

Answer the employer's question "What can this person do for me?" by demonstrating the great things you've done for others.

Vague descriptions of your past jobs and duties won't sell you. Specific, hard-hitting examples will. Instead of bland generalities such as "Proved experience in sales/marketing," give concrete examples.

EXAMPLE: Instead of "Strong track record in new product introduction," say "Managed strategic planning and execution of successful $18-million national introductory campaign of new product line. Won 4.3% market share."

A helpful rule of thumb: Aim for a minimum of three specific achievements under each job heading, for a total of about 12 to 20 on your entire resume.

TIP: If you're going for more than one position, skew your achievements/accomplishments to fit each position. While you can use the same achievements, different wording can tailor the emphasis to the specific job.

Some guidelines:

- *The more recent the position, the more achievements you should include.* Prospective employers are most interested in what you've been doing in the recent past, not long ago.

TIP: **Whenever possible, cite examples that show how you affected the bottom line— you earned money through increasing sales or saved money by streamlining, etc. Lately, companies are extremely cost-conscious. A proven achiever in this area may have an inside track.**

- *Never say "Worked for a department that . . ." or "Held high-level position in a company that . . ."* Don't focus on what the company or department did. What did *you* do?

TIP: **For readability's sake, don't connect unrelated achievements in one paragraph. When you switch subjects, drop a line, and begin a new bulleted paragraph or statement.**

- *Use time frames when they help your case.* It makes your achievement more powerful to note that you "Doubled profits in less than two years," as opposed to just "Doubled profits."

▶ **Rule 5:** *Brag . . . a little.*

Blow your own horn. If you don't sell yourself, who will?

Excessive modesty is one of the most common mistakes job hunters make. They decide that now is the time to be humble—it isn't. Force yourself to be a self-promoter.

But don't overdo it. Some recruiters have been getting skeptical about the amazing accomplishments people include on their resumes. *The bottom line:* If you can't prove it, don't include it.

Some tips to make you sound like a winner:

- *Avoid statements like "Assisted with," "Member of a team that . . . ," "Helped with . . . ," and the like.* The immediate impression you make? You were a follower, not a leader.

- *Similarly, steer clear of words that make you sound less than sure of yourself,* wishy-washy words or phrases like "assigned to," "considerable," "competent."

- *Another offshoot of the "Be specific" rule: Take credit for the* portion of *a success that is genuinely yours.* Don't take credit for every aspect of a success. While it's smart to broadcast the part you were responsible for—you devised the plan, you designed the new campaign, etc.—if you make it sound as if you did it all single-handedly, people will start wondering, "Is anything on this resume for real?"

▶ **Rule 6:** *Whenever possible, use numbers or percentages.*

Numbers sell. They jump off a page and say "Read me." They dovetail into the modern corporate concern with the bottom line. Also, people are more inclined to believe numbers than statements.

Don't undercut the effect by writing numbers out, especially when the subject is money: Use numerals for full impact.

EXAMPLE: **Supervised staff of 78.**

Managed $2,000,000 procurement and supply budget and saved the company $250,000.

Increased productivity 23%.

TIP: **When you're including a figure you're not really sure about, use *odd* numbers. That's right. For some reason, odd numbers stand out more, and appear more precise. Better, they appear less manufactured.**

TIP: **When appropriate, include comparative figures to show just how strong your quantifiable achievements are. For example, "Increased sales from 21,000 to 38,000 units."**

▶ **Rule 7:** *Be active.*

Active words sell. Passive words don't.

Your resume should read like ad copy—succinct and strong. More important, it should be written to carry the reader through the resume, with no clunkers or dull patches to bog him or her down.

A few tips to help you achieve clean, strong copy:

- *Drop your I's*—as in "I turned around a failing department" or "I was responsible for . . ." Jump right in with the verb: "Turned around a failing department." It reads more actively. Besides, the reader already knows you're the subject of the resume. Why waste the space?

- *In line with the above, start with action.* "Saved the company $1,250,000." *Not* "Responsible for an overall company savings of $1,250,000."

- *Choose powerful action verbs.* By doing this, you subtly underscore the strength of your accomplishments. Here are a few verbs that come across in certain situations.
    To emphasize:

Analytical skills
analyzed
appraised
assessed
calculated
identified
pinpointed
questioned
surveyed
tested
tracked

Bottom-line orientation/cost-cutting ability
budgeted
centralized
cut
nullified
revamped
saved
slashed
stemmed

Creativity and innovation
built
conceived

created
designed
devised
developed
established
ignited
improvised
inaugurated
initiated
instigated
launched
originated
planned
produced
set up
sparked
started
structured

Forward thinking
anticipated
foresaw
predicted

Leadership ability
activated
administered
authorized

controlled
delegated
directed
drove
guided
instituted
led
oversaw
presided
spearheaded
supervised
trained
vitalized

Productivity/ growth contributions
broadened
doubled (tripled, etc.)
exceeded
expanded
gained
generated
increased
spurred
strengthened
stimulated
won

**Problem-solving/
troubleshooting
skills**
abolished
adapted
adjusted
alleviated
altered
amended
anticipated
detected
discovered
expedited
facilitated
improved
mobilized
modernized

quelled
rectified
reorganized
revamped
revised
simplified
solved
systemized

**And some good
all-purpose verbs**
achieved
activated
completed
conducted
coordinated
demonstrated

established
executed
excelled
heightened
implemented
maintained
operated
organized
perfected
performed
planned
prepared
proved
reinforced
showed
structured

▶ **Rule 8:** *To downplay your age, be selective.*

When in doubt, less is more.

In other words, don't feel obligated to list everything—every position, every skill, every accomplishment. Pick and choose the information that directly relates to the position you want. List only those skills or accomplishments that support your objective and prove you are the right candidate.

If you go overboard listing your experience, you immediately draw attention to the fact that you've been in the working world for a number of years. Furthermore, it detracts from the information that truly sells you.

▶ **Rule 9:** *Don't lie.*

Most people say they don't lie, but many of them do. According to a 1992 study conducted by the Certified Reference Checking Company of St. Louis, 34% of the 1,200 job applicants surveyed were lying about or coloring the facts on their resumes. More specifically: 22% lied about expertise; 12% about salary or job title; 11% about employment history; 9% about educational background, 4% about self-employment.

But lying isn't necessary. In fact, it may be downright dangerous.

The better bet? Tell the truth—but selectively and strategically. You don't need to bare your soul. You can, however, make the truth as compelling as any lie by presenting it well.

▶ **Rule 10:** *Whenever possible, include "modern" skills or accomplishments—computer ability, any technological experience or expertise, etc.*

You want to come across as a modern, vital person, not a has-been with antiquated skills who's ready for retirement.

A good way of promoting a vital image of yourself is to emphasize your facility with, knowledge of, or experience with new technologies and techniques.

There's no need to list your skills. Instead, mention the results you generated *because* of your knowledge in the statements you write about your accomplishments and achievements. What to include: recent training, updated skills—not necessarily technological, but anything that establishes you as up to date, or even cutting edge, in your field.

COMMON RESUME MISTAKES

Overemphasis on management skills:	Achievements/accomplishments revolve around managerial abilities; little or no mention of other achievements
Too crowded/poor layout:	Information crowded onto one or two pages, small type, etc.
Humor/"cutesy" lines or appearance:	One-liners, jokes, etc. in resume; resume sent in odd containers (pizza boxes, etc.)
Too much education information:	Grade-point averages, activities, etc. included, although resume subject has been out of school for years
Other extraneous information:	Months as well as years of employment included; listing of seminars attended, etc.
Job objective:	Objective listed at top of resume

THE MECHANICS: MAKING YOUR RESUME LOOK GOOD

▶ **Where appearance is concerned, you're best off playing it safe.**

Steer clear of the innovative. If you've never seen a resume with white type on black paper, it's not because no one has thought of it. It's because it doesn't work.

Stick with the basics:

- *Clear, readable typeface*—Roman, Courier, Prestige, etc. No sans-serif, script, or other nonstandard typefaces.

- *Paper: 20-pound bond in a neutral color* such as ivory, white, off-white, eggshell, gray, or buff.

- *Paper size: 8½" by 11" only.* Yes, different-size paper stands out. It's also more difficult for people to file.

- *Black print.* Or, if you feel the need to express your individuality, another dark color (such as navy, slate, or brown) that is coordinated with your paper color—but only if you're having your resume professionally typeset and printed.

TIP: **Colored paper, ornate fonts, and creative layouts are recommended for people going for creative positions *only.* But even in these cases, weigh your options carefully and be sure your prospective reader is one who will appreciate your creativity. Sometimes you're better off showing how creative you are through your strong track record and successes than through your snappily designed resume.**

As for the actual production of your resume, your best bet is to print it yourself, using a computer.

This is more efficient (and often less expensive) than having it professionally done, because you can print out as many copies as you need, when you need them, rather than being forced to order hundreds at once. Also, you can easily update and change your resume as needed. Finally, you can print out a resume precisely when you need it. This means your resume always looks fresh.

If possible, use a laser printer. A letter-quality dot matrix is acceptable, but not ideal.

TIP: If you don't own a personal computer, consider leasing or buying one. If you're planning a direct-mail campaign, and will be sending out numerous letters and resumes, it makes sense. You can target your letters and resumes more carefully, set up a mail merge, easily personalize form letters, and more.

TIP: Be sure to disable the automatic justification command if you're using one of the many popular word processing programs that has justification as a default setting. While justification, which makes the right margin even instead of ragged, works for large blocks of text, it can wreak havoc in a resume—because of the shorter sentences and fragments. The letters wind up being spaced strangely with large gaps. And even when it's spaced properly, justified text is less interesting to read.

Having your resume professionally set and printed is another option, but not as highly recommended as printing your own. It is, however, a logical choice if you have no access to a computer or are planning a very large mailing. If you do opt for professional typesetting, don't get swayed by the options—stick with conservative typeface and paper color choices.

What about photocopying a typeset (or typewritten) resume to avoid having to order more copies than you need? It's not the best method, but it can produce adequate results if you follow these guidelines. Never use copier paper—be sure to replace it with bond paper. Make sure the copy is *perfect*—no smudges on the glass, blurry lines, or scratches. Be sure that the original is aligned properly on the glass—nothing looks less professional than an ever-so-slightly slanted resume.

▶ **Pay attention to *negative* space as well as positive. (Translation: Don't fill the entire page with print.)**

This is one aspect of resume preparation that many people ignore. They spend a great deal of time selecting the ideal achievements, the perfect wording, and so forth—and then they make the resume virtually impossible to read by squeezing all the information onto one page or two.

Unbroken blocks of text look dull. Your resume is headed for the trash can if you don't lay it out as carefully as you wrote it.

Let your resume (and your reader) breathe. Leave plenty of white space—in margins, between sections, and between paragraphs within sections.

▶ **One final reminder: Proofread, proofread, proofread!**

Even the best of us make mistakes, and your resume is one of the worst places for them.

EXAMPLE: **One job hunter proofread everything over and over again—he used the spelling checker on his computer, reread his resume dozens of times to make sure nothing had slipped by, had others read it. Everything was perfect. He printed it, mailed it out, and waited for calls. They never came—and for good reason. His telephone number was wrong.**

Double- and triple-check *everything*. And we do mean everything. The spelling of your own name. Company names. Dates. (It's easy to overlook transposed digits. If you aren't careful, you may say that you worked at one company from 1890 to the present!)

Note: What about the newest innovation where resumes are concerned—video resumes? Don't waste the videotape. Recruiters and employers alike usually don't like them. Many don't have tape machines in their offices—or they simply don't want to bother watching you in action. Where resumes are concerned, a picture *isn't* worth a thousand words.

SPECIAL SITUATIONS

Certain job hunters have specific needs or problems that a resume can address—or bypass. Here are some typical special cases, and suggestions on how you can tailor your resume to give you the most possible benefit.

▶ **You're an upper-level executive—a CEO or the like.**

You're at a high enough level so that you can break the rules a bit . . . but not too much.

More specifically:

- *Write two resumes.* The first should be as described in the previous pages—a straightforward resume (probably in reverse chronological format) that covers the past 15 to 20 years of your work experience, gives examples of your achievements, includes dates of employment, etc. In truth, you may never have to use this resume. But you should have it on hand in case an executive recruiter requests one or a prospective employer's policy dictates the need for a traditional resume. Yes, it's only a formality—but it's best to be prepared anyway. Furthermore, the act of writing the resume will refresh your memory on the best sales points in your background.

- *Make resume #2 less a resume than a biography,* similar to the ones public relations departments write on their company executives. Keep it to one page—in narrative form. Cover only the salient points in your background—positions held, a few outstanding achievements, but little else.

▶ **You're reentering the work force after a hiatus.**

This is especially common with women who take leave to raise children, but it occurs in other cases, too. Whatever the reason for your hiatus, it raises a special set of problems. The key here is to convince prospective employers that your time away from the working world didn't diminish your skills, knowledge of cutting-edge developments in your field, ability to contribute to the company, and the like.

Some tricks to help you bypass potential problems:

- *First of all, if you don't have a very strong employment history, use the combination format.* If, however, your background before your leave was very strong or impressive, stick with the chronological style.

- *Think about all your recent activities in terms of how they relate to your target objective.* Turn civic, volunteer, charity, and other work into sales points. List specifics. For example, if you did fund-raising work for the hospital, how much did you raise? Did you supervise others? If so, how many? Treat these activities as you would regular work experience, that is, be specific, hard-hitting, and achievement oriented.

TIP: If possible, join the boards of local charities. This tends to signal management abilities to prospective employers.

- *If you've done volunteer work, particularly higher-level work such as consulting, list it as a regular job on your resume.*

- *If you don't belong already, join the appropriate trade or professional organization, or other work-related groups.* Not only will these provide strong networking opportunities, listing them on your resume will signal to prospective employers that you're still a professional, and part of the mainstream.

- *Include brush-up or refresher courses you've taken recently.* This is especially important if there have been changes in your field. You must prove to prospective employers that you haven't been left behind, and that you're ready to hit the ground running.

▶ **You keep being labeled as overqualified.**

This typically happens when you're going for a position lower than or equal to your most recent one. The red flag on your resume that contributes to this problem: too many positions, especially too many higher-level positions.
Ways to get around this:

- As mentioned previously, *don't list your entire work experience.* Cut it down to the essentials, the last 15 years or so.

- *List only achievements that directly support your candidacy for your target job.*

- *If you received several promotions within the same company, consolidate these under one job heading.* Listing each step makes your resume longer and more cumbersome.

- *Underplay your higher-level job titles.* Focus on skills and abilities rather than titles.

- *One final thought: If you're consistently hearing that you're overqualified, it could mean one of two things.* 1) Perhaps this is a polite brush-off. Reread your resume and rethink your job campaign. Are you selling yourself as well as you can? 2) Perhaps you're undercutting yourself by going for jobs that truly are beneath your experience level. Don't let desperation get the best of you.

▶ **You left the corporate world to start your own business . . . which failed.**

An increasingly common situation, as more people try their hand at self-employment or entrepreneurship. In this case, you have two general options: Either face the issue head on and list your self-employment as part of your experience, or completely bypass it. Clearly, the amount of time you spent on your own makes a large difference regarding which option to choose: A year or more, include it; less than a year, it's up to you (although that period of time can make you appear unemployed). The usual best bet: Include your stint as an entrepreneur on your resume.

Some guidelines on how best to do this:

- *The most important thing to remember:* The failure of your business doesn't have to mean *you* were a failure. Find the successes in your unsuccessful business bid. Did you start with nothing and increase sales? Did you develop any systems, methods, or operations? Hire and train people? Even areas that weren't totally successful can prove your business ability.

- *Good things to include:* raising capital to start the company (include the amount you raised—for example, "Secured $750,000 working capital financing . . ."); negotiation experience (if you acquired other companies, etc.); innovative strategies or systems you devised and their results.

- *If you went the nonbusiness route and became an independent—a free-lance writer or the like—here, too, you can find achievements that may make you more hireable.* Again, think salability. Were you published in major (or minor) publications? Did you increase your direct-mail experience (in writing query letters)? Who were your clients? And so forth.

SAMPLE—A WINNING AGEPROOF RESUME

PETER STARK
100 Maple Ave.
Ridgewood, NJ 07450
(201) 555-1111

SUMMARY OF ACHIEVEMENTS

Extensive background—improving cash flow and ROI, strengthening product lines, cutting costs, reducing inventory, building organizations . . . and profits.
- General Manager—P&L responsibility
- Entrepreneur—organized $3 million company
- Marketing Vice President—$55 million company

EXPERIENCE

General Manager
Nilsson Inc., Englewood Cliffs, NJ   (1987 to date)
P&L responsibility of $21 million division of U.S. subsidiary of major European multiproduct company, reporting to President. Direct 40 people through controller, sales warehouse, and service managers. *Products:* Mopeds, bicycles, accessories.
- Established new U.S. market for mopeds through comprehensive marketing and service program for the now-leading (and highest priced) moped. Increased sales from 18,000 to 32,000 units—a 34% market share and 36% rise in profit contribution.
- Positioned company as significant new factor in bicycle business; changed supply sources, developed new product line and created dealer sales programs. Sales jumped from 21,000 low-price units to 33,000 high-price units, with 31% increase in profitability.
- Decreased expenses $256,000 by cutting warehouses from 5 to 2 with no decrease in customer service; saved $110,000 in telecommunications costs.

Vice President, Marketing
American Container Corporation, New York, NY   (1982–1987)
Developed and managed marketing strategies and sales programs of $55 million multiproduct company, reporting to President. *Products:* Garden products, sporting goods, apparel, specialty chemicals.
- As acting General Manager, improved market share of sporting goods company during poor market period. Reduced excess inventories. Set up new distribution system; prepared new catalogs; secured product publicity and set up successful consumer sweepstakes.
- Increased high-profit garden products sales 18%, at lower selling expense. Repositioned product line, developed new products, redesigned packaging and revised price structure. Established new sales organization.

- Turned around earnings of apparel company $1.3 million, despite poor market. Prepared business plan, trained sales manager and developed two-tier sales organization and key discount sales program.
- Created innovative corporate-wide business planning system to enable divisions to prepare objectives-oriented action programs that could be monitored. Introduced inventory management program that cut inventory $900,000.

General Manager
E-Light, Inc., New York, NY   (1978–1981)

P&L responsibility of $5 million company, reporting to Group Vice President. Directed 90 people through 2 factory managers, controller, and 2 sales managers. *Products:* Lighting fixtures, home furnishings.

- Reversed long-term profit decline and loss, to profit. Slashed inventory 19%, cut product line 44%, with 5% sales increase from better balanced inventory. Negotiated union agreement and achieved cooperation during wage-control period.
- Repackaged profitable but slow-moving product line for first year 77% sales increase, to $870,000. Established separate organization to capitalize on this opportunity.

Vice President, Operations/Marketing
Innovation Corporation, New York, NY   (1973–1978)

As cofounder of $4 million multiproduct company, managed selected operations and all sales, reporting to President. Directed 30 people through operations manager, and 12 sales representatives through 2 sales managers. *Products:* Furniture, boats, and marine accessories.

- Stemmed losses of $1.8 million boat company, as acting General Manager. Renegotiated financing; operated company on cash flow. Improved margins 9% with smaller factory force and sales organization.
- Improved furniture company margins by redirecting shift in product mix.
- Negotiated acquisition of two companies, as principal, and secured $785,000 working capital financing.

Principal Management Consultant
Avaco Services, Inc., New York, NY   (1969–1973)

Handled management consulting projects in North America, Europe, and Middle East for leading management consulting organization. Directed four consultants. *Products:* Paints, plastics, packaged foods, construction materials, electronic components.

- Identified $10 million market for packaged food company and developed market entry plans; secured 8% share in first year at targeted profit.
- Initiated plan to establish sales effort in $400 million market for construction company; firm is a leader in this market.
- Revised paint marketing and plant expansion program, for $1.2 million savings.

EDUCATION

Master of Business Administration, New York University
Bachelor of Science, Business Administration, New York University

RESUME CHECKLIST

Questions to ask yourself when double-checking your resume:

- Have you covered your employment history for the past 15 to 20 years?

- Is it clear what type of job you're going for or suited for?

- Have you included strong achievements that demonstrate what you can do for a prospective employer?

- Is your resume scanable? Do the information and layout work together to make the resume easy to read?

- Are the tenses consistent—that is, for your current position, have you used the present tense? For all others, the past?

5

BEYOND THE RESUME: THE LETTERS THAT SELL YOU

INTRODUCTION

▶ **It's a virtual inevitability: At some point during your job hunt, you'll be contacting companies to try to convince them you're a strong employment prospect.**

Of course, under ideal circumstances companies contact *you*. Or you land a job through word of mouth and never have to bother with formal mailings of cover letters and resumes. But ideal circumstances don't always occur.

So it's up to you to seek out opportunity—by launching a direct-mail campaign, answering want ads, or following up on referrals from colleagues.

In this chapter, we discuss these and other tactics. But to put these tactics to work, you have to understand how to get your message out there through strong letters.

Face it, in most cases you're up against a lot of competition. As any advertiser will tell you, the only way to beat the competition is to first be noticed—to stand out from the clutter. Read on for general guidelines as well as specific tricks, tips, and hints that will make your sales approach even more hardhitting.

THE TARGETED SALES LETTER: THE MOST IMPORTANT LETTER YOU'LL WRITE

▶ **First, a rundown of the basics: When will you use a letter and what can it do for you?**

Letters play a major role in most over-40 job hunts. You'll use letters:

- *As the main selling tool in a direct-mail campaign* (still one of the most widely used methods of landing a job). In this case, your letter and resume package must be designed to specifically address the needs of the target company.

- *As a reply to want ads* (not the most effective tactic, but one you'd be foolish to overlook). Your letter must be designed to stand out from the hundreds of others that will be sent in response to the ad—and it must convey what is special about you.

- *As a pitch to executive recruiters* (again, a long shot, but one that may pan out). In this case, your letter won't be as specific, but will showcase your background and general assets. For tips on contacting executive recruiters, see page 172.

- *As a response to referrals* (the plus in this instance is that the path has already been smoothed by your contact, who referred you to the recipient). These letters have to build on your initial introduction and include enough new or detailed information that you'll be invited in for an interview.

Whatever the circumstances, your letter could well be the most important sales document you'll use in your job hunt.

▶ **Remember—your job hunt is a sales mission. You're the product, and prospective employers are your customers. And your**

cover letter is the sales document that should convince them you're worth getting to know further.

Your cover letter often will create the very first impression a prospective employer has of you. This is especially true in direct-mail campaigns, when you send a letter and resume, unsolicited, to target companies. Clearly, it's vital to make the right first impression.

One important point to make at the outset: Even if you'll be sending a very strong resume with it, don't make the mistake of paying less attention to your letter. A good cover letter is usually what gets your resume read. No cover letter and your resume is probably bound for the trash can. A weak cover letter, and it's probably headed for the same place.

▶ **To make your letter strong, focus on the prime goal of the letter: To convince the reader that you are worth getting to know better.**

A good letter will persuade the reader either to interview you or to read your resume . . . which, in turn, should convince him to interview you.

Either way you are trying to sell yourself into an interview.

In other words, your letter has to be compelling enough to make the reader want to meet you in person. Unfortunately, even many older job hunters, who presumably have been involved in a number of job hunts, haven't learned this. We've seen too many letters that are less direct-mail pieces as sleeping aids:

> *Dear Ms. Doe:*
>
> *I understand that Acme, Inc., is seeking a new director of planning. Enclosed please find my resume, in which you will note my extensive experience in the field. I have worked at your competitor, Nadir Co., for the past seven years as director of planning. Prior to that, I was assistant director of planning at . . .*

Yawn.

Letters like this don't do a thing for you.

But a strong sales letter can do a great deal—it can position you as a strong employment candidate . . . in fact, as the *right* candidate for a job. Exceptionally strong letters can intrigue a reader enough so that he interviews you for a job that doesn't even exist yet.

The bottom line: There's a huge difference between a bland introduction letter, like the one above, which says, in effect, "Here's my resume. Hope you like it" and one that says "Here's what I can do for your company."

▶ **The trick then is to focus your letter not on you, but on the needs of the recipient.**

It's an obvious sales tactic, and one that *works*. Play to the reader's interest by taking the emphasis off you and shifting it to the company.

A cover letter that sells is one that speaks directly to the concerns of the reader. He doesn't know you yet. Frankly, he couldn't care less if you land a job or not. What he *does* care about is his company. This is why everything you put into your letter should demonstrate not only what a great employee you'd be, but what you can do for the company.

In many cases, you can set up a *needs payoff:* Through careful research, establish a need that the company has. Then present the solution to that need—you. It's simple, straightforward, and, most important, it's usually effective. In other cases (for example, when you are doing too large a mailing to focus your letters on individual companies), you will concentrate on what you can produce for a certain *type* of company.

In *all* cases, however, you will be emphasizing one key point: I have been an asset to companies in the past, and I can be an asset to yours.

THE THREE PARTS OF A COVER LETTER

▶ **There are three vital parts of a cover letter, each with a distinct and important role in conveying your message.**

The first part, the Hook, does just what it says—hooks the reader into reading the letter by creating interest. The second part, the Sales Pitch, is where you sell yourself by demonstrating your qualifications. The third part, the Close, is both a summary and a request for an interview.

▶ **Part 1:** *The Hook*

How do you hook a reader? By offering him something he wants.

First, anticipate the reader's initial question, "Why is this person writing to me?" by jumping right in. Don't back in with unnecessary verbiage—cut to the chase. You understand the company is expanding; you were referred by a common acquaintance; you saw an ad; and so on.

When possible, set up the needs payoff here: You have a problem. I have the solution. This is a good method for two reasons—it shows that you know the company well enough to understand its needs, and it begins selling you immediately.

EXAMPLE: According to industry souces, Bigelow Toy Company is considering an expansion into the stuffed-toy market. With competition for market share so heated in this area, it's crucial that Bigelow have the toys that will win customer attention—and sales. I believe I can provide you with the designs that will do this.

(Note: By referring to an article or a recent company trend, you let the reader know this is a personalized letter, not a form letter.)

TIP: Your hook doesn't need to be catchy. Sometimes the most effective hook is to mention the person who referred you—"Jonathan Bell suggested I write . . ." Not flashy, not clever, but effective *if* the referral has clout with the recipient.

The message you're sending in Part 1: Your company could use me.

▶ **Part 2:** *The Sales Pitch*

This is the guts of your letter.

The reader's question you're answering in this portion of the letter: "What can this person do for the company?"

If you used a needs-payoff statement, this is where you support it by *proving* that you're the person who can fill the need you've pointed out. Back up your claim with pertinent experience and achievements from your background. If you used a more general opening, this is still where you prove how much the company can use you. The means are the same in either case, state clearly and precisely what you've accomplished for others.

Choose about three specific achievements or accomplishments to highlight, ones that directly relate to the job you're targeting. Make this section strong by following many of the same guidelines as in resume writing: Be specific; use numbers and facts to back up your claims; use action words; be brief.

EXAMPLE: As design director for a small toy manufacturer, I designed and oversaw production of a new stuffed toy line that was responsible for 32% of our 1992 profits. This was the first time any one toy line generated such a large margin of profitability. In addition, my "Ruggles the Bear" design won stuffed toy of the year at the Toy Fair and was the only single product in our line generating sales of over $250K.

TIP: Use bullets in this part of your letter to make the individual sales points really stand out.

An important point: Be sure this section is precisely targeted to the job for which you're trying. Don't go on and on about accomplishments that don't relate to that job. No matter how impressive such accomplishments are, they won't help sell you into the job you want.

TIP: If you're changing careers, this portion of your letter is particularly important. You must use it to demonstrate how your apparently unrelated background actually does apply to your new career choice. Carefully choose achievements that illustrate qualities and abilities important in your new target field.

The message you're sending in Part 2: I did these things for my past employers. I can generate similar results for you.

▶ Part 3: *The Wind-Up and Close*

Here's where you cement your sales pitch by briefly restating both your interest in the company *and* your ability to make a substantial contribution to it.

Don't make the common mistake of letting the letter (and the corresponding sales message) peter out by closing too weakly. These last few lines are your last chance to sell yourself. *Use them!*

In one line, restate what you can do for the company. Follow this by reiterating your interest in working for the company. Use positive language. And don't be coy—you're interested in a job with this company, let them know it.

Finally, close by angling for an interview with the reader. You have two choices here:

1. *You can use a direct approach and take charge of the follow-up:* "I will call you on Tuesday, March 11, to set up a mutually convenient time for us to meet."

TIP: If you opt for this method, it's a good idea to set a definite time to call. This makes it impossible for you to back out and keeps you on schedule.

Always use the direct approach if you're going for a sales position or other job that calls for aggressiveness. In other cases, it's up to you. Some experts claim that the direct approach is *too* aggressive —that if someone is interested in interviewing you, you'll get a call; otherwise it's a waste of your time to call him or her. On the other hand, however, it's a fact that a follow-up dramatically increases your chances of getting a positive response. *The bottom line?* Do what you feel most comfortable with.

Don't use the direct approach if you're at all uncomfortable with it, or if you think you may not call. Making a commitment you won't meet does you more harm than good and may leave a fatal impression of undependability.

2. *Your second option is the softer "I look forward to hearing from you in the near future."* Use this if you're planning a huge mailing (it's crazy to follow up on hundreds of letters); if you won't have time to follow up yourself; or if you know you may not make the follow-up phone calls.

TIP: Make this option as strong as possible: Instead of "I hope to hear from you," opt for the more positive "I look forward to hearing from you . . ." You'll come across as more of a go-getter, because you sound as though you expect a call.

EXAMPLE: I would like to have the opportunity to produce similar results for Bigelow Toys. With my hands-on experience in both product and package design and my supervisory skills, I know I can contribute a great deal to your design department. I will call you next Monday so we can set up a mutually convenient time to meet.

The message you're sending in Part 3: Now that you know some of my qualifications, let me show you more in an interview.

Note: For more information on using letters to answer classified ads, see page 164; on direct-mail campaigns, see page 148.

WRITING A STRONG LETTER: FIVE RULES OF THUMB

▶ **These tips, tricks, and guidelines will make your letter stronger.**

Some are general hints on how to sell yourself more efficiently. Others are specific ways of avoiding the "overqualified/too old" trap. All are tested and recommended.

▶ **Rule 1:** *Keep it brief—one page* **maximum.**

A cover letter shouldn't be *War and Peace*. It should be a quick overview of those qualities of yours that can win you an interview.

Your best bet: Stick with three to four paragraphs—your opening and your close should be one paragraph each, your sales pitch no more than two.

▶ **Rule 2:** *Keep your sentences sharp and snappy.*

As in Rule 1, keep your sentences tight and to the point. You just don't have room for unnecessary verbiage and empty pontifications. Also, puffed-up language only makes it appear that you're hiding something—probably that you lack the credentials to land the job you're after.

Remember—a good sales piece is active and easy to read. Make sure your letter fits the bill.

TIP: Read your letter out loud. How does it sound? Natural or stilted? Overly bureaucratic or easy to understand? Regardless of its contents, your letter should sound natural and friendly.

Some ways to maximize your letter's readability:

• *Drop the typical job-hunting phrases,* such as "Enclosed please find my resume," "As you will see in the enclosed resume," "Enclosed is a resume for your review and consideration," "I would like to take this opportunity to tell you. . . ." They don't add a thing, they make you sound like hundreds of other (probably unsuccessful) job hunters, and they take up space.

- *Similarly, cut pompous phrasings*—"Please advise me as to a time when it would be feasible to meet" and the like. Again, there's no room. Plus they're boring to read.

- *As in your resume, use action words.* (For specific suggestions of active words, see Resumes, pages 110–11.)

- *Beware of phrases and words that sound outmoded and so make you sound old.* Stilted or excessively formal language, such as "I would like to take this opportunity to thank you" or "Thanking you in advance, I remain yours truly" make you sound like a Dickens character, not a hot job candidate.

▶ **Rule 3:** *Always keep your reader in mind—literally.*

It's a trick advertising writers use—they picture a specific individual reading their copy. This way they speak to a person, not a piece of paper.
Some hints:

- *Focus on the reader's interests:* solutions to problems; profits; results.

- *Don't fall victim to the "I" syndrome*—starting each sentence with "I" or constantly referring to yourself. You come off as egotistical or simply dull, neither of which appeals to your reader.

- *Refer to specific facts about the company or, if you're planning a wide mailing, about the industry.* Not only does this make you look like an expert in the field, it also usually interests the reader.

TIP: **As mentioned previously, referring to published quotes by the letter's recipient is always a nice touch—even as an opening. It shows you've researched the company and, more important, appeals to the ego of your prospective employer. Everyone likes to know that what he or she has said has been noticed.**

- *Skew your letter indirectly:* If you know that a company or letter recipient is formal, try to avoid contractions, casual language, and the like. If the opposite is the case, or if you know the recipient, you can be more casual—but still businesslike.

▶ **Rule 4:** *Keep it focused.*

One page isn't very much room. So everything you put on that page should contribute to a single goal: presenting you as the right candidate for a particular job. You should always keep that one job objective in mind as you write.

Your sales pitch should revolve around specific examples of achievements that relate to your objective and can be backed up by your resume. This, as mentioned before, is key—hard-hitting examples of your past contributions to companies make potent sales ammunition.

Some ways to focus your letter:

- *As mentioned before, choose about three examples that show your abilities and expand upon them.*

- *Always concentrate on the "how."* You increased sales? Great. How much? How did you do it? And so on. Just because you are supposed to be pithy doesn't mean you shouldn't elaborate as needed.

- *Avoid padding your letter with achievements that don't apply to your target job, or personal qualities that mean little* ("I'm a people person," "I have strong interactive personal skills," "I'm highly motivated," and the like).

▶ **Rule 5:** *Keep it interesting.*

You've (hopefully) grabbed their attention with your hook. Keep readers interested throughout the letter. Don't let them slip away. How?

- *Vary your phrasing, sentence structure, and sentence length.*

- *Shy away from passive verbs.* Not only do active words help sell you by enhancing your achievements, they also make your letter more interesting to read.

- *Don't just repeat information that's on your resume, or merely flesh out your resume* by making complete sentences out of the fragments that appear on your resume. Your letter should *expand* on your resume, not replace or duplicate it.

- *Similarly, don't lift exact wording from your resume.* Your letter becomes redundant, you appear to have limited communication skills, and—even worse—it looks as though you have little to say about yourself. Three strikes.

TIP: **One warning: Don't confuse being interesting with being irritatingly coy or hype-y. So-called clever openings like "They thought it couldn't be done, but I did it! Increased sales by 34%, that is" aren't so much witty as annoying.**

- *Use details to create a strong image.* Remember, brief doesn't mean bland. Well-chosen details can give the reader a vivid picture of what you have done. For example, instead of a dull "I was production manager for a package goods company," write "As production manager for the second-largest package goods company in the Southwest, I oversaw a staff of 15."

- *As with a resume, use numbers whenever possible.* Numbers are attention grabbing and hard hitting.

FORMATTING YOUR LETTER

▶ **Your letter has to look right as well as read right.**

The most perfectly written letter won't sell you if it's smudged, obviously photocopied, or otherwise unprofessional in appearance. Don't ruin your sales message with poor presentation.

A quick rundown of how to make your letter look as salesworthy as it reads:

- *If you don't already have it, invest in some good-quality stationery,* with your name, address, and phone number imprinted. It's worth the money—and with reorders, the price will drop.

TIP: **If you don't have the time or money for engraved stationery, imprinted is fine (it's less expensive). If you're *really* pressed for time, typing your name and address at the top of good plain stationery will do in a pinch—but resort to this in emergencies only.**

TIP: **Never, never, *never* use company stationery, even if you're still employed. Your job hunt isn't company business. It's your business. Using company stationery** makes you look cheap and unprofessional—not the best qualities for a job hunter.

- *Paper should be 24-pound bond, with a rag content.* Limit your color choice to cream, buff, eggshell, or (if you want to get jazzy) gray or pale yellow. No colors that will make you stand out. In this case, anything that makes you stand out is a loser.

TIP: Some people swear by this one—choose letter stock in a *different* color than your resume paper. It makes your letter and resume package look less like a pre-fab product of outplacement or recruitment firms and more like an individualized mailing.

- *Keep the style simple:* a clean typeface, nothing artistic or clever; black, brown, or dark gray type, depending upon the color of your paper.

- *Use regular letter size (8¹/₂ x 11")* or, *if your letter is brief enough, Monarch size (7¹/₄ x 10¹/₂").* (A minor note: Monarch-size stationery clipped to a larger, standard-size resume looks very sharp—and refreshingly brief.)

- *As with resumes, your best bet is to compose your letters on a PC and print them on a laser or letter-quality dot matrix printer.* Photocopied or professionally offset letters are not recommended—your letters should look personalized, not like part of a mass mailing. (Even if they *are* part of a mass mailing, they still shouldn't look like it.) If you don't have access to a computer and printer, consider leasing or look into storefront office centers that allow you to use them for an hourly fee.

▶ **Check and double-check** *everything* **before you send your letter out.**

We've said it before and we'll say it again: Proofread *everything.* And then proofread it again. Nothing scuttles you more quickly than typos.

Similarly, be sure you have all the basics correct: the address, the recipient's name, his or her job title. Don't assume anything; don't ignore anything.

A few ways to make your letter letter-perfect:

- *Try an old proofreader's tip and read the letter* backward. *This way, you read not sentences but individual words, and are more likely to catch misspellings.*

- *Check everything*—especially the name and address of the recipient. Misspelling either is one of the worst mistakes you can make —and one of the most common.

TIP: Always call to double-check the spelling of names. Ask the person with whom you speak to spell out the name letter by letter. Yes, the name John Brown sounds impossible to misspell. But he might spell it Jon Browne. In other words, you can't be too careful.

EVALUATING YOUR LETTER

▶ **When you think you're done, read your letter carefully to make sure it has done everything it can.**

Your letter can (and should) accomplish a number of things that a resume cannot—many of which are especially important for those wanting to ageproof their job hunt.

A good cover letter should:

- *Draw attention away from potential liabilities, including age.* Think about possible red flags in your background—a spotty work history, long periods of unemployment, your age—and use your letter to defuse them.

  Ask yourself: Does my letter answer potential questions that my resume may raise—that is, an apparent mismatch of the job I'm going for and my background?

- *Emphasize salient achievements and accomplishments in greater depth than your resume does.* To do this, you will choose up to three accomplishments that support your needs statement and seize the sales opportunity by going into specifics to a degree that is impossible on a resume.

  Ask yourself: Does each example show how much I could contribute to the company? Are there concrete facts or numbers that can back them up?

- *Bring up new sales material that isn't included on your resume.* Just because it's not on your resume doesn't mean it's not a sales aid.

EXAMPLE: Don D. was going for a sales director position at a sporting goods importer. His resume stressed his strong sales experience. But in his letter, he also mentioned his non-work-related sporting activities—the cross-country skiing he did every winter. He got the interview—and the job—because the company felt strongly about hiring people who were as enthusiastic about their sporting products as the ultimate end-users.

Ask yourself: Is there something I haven't included on my resume that would help sell me?

- *Demonstrate your enthusiasm and knowledge.* Your resume can't show anything but the facts. A letter can express more—your sincere interest in a job or a company. It's also a great place to show off the research you've done by mentioning specifics about the company.

Ask yourself: Is my enthusiasm coming across? Do I sound interested—or does my letter sound like a flat form letter? Have I demonstrated my knowledge of the company or business by including specific information or referring to the company's unique problems or needs?

TIP: As with your resume, have friends and colleagues read your cover letter. Especially helpful will be people in the same position as your letter's recipient, or those in the area you hope to enter. Ask them how your letter comes across. Any potential weak spots? Anything that should be underscored or played down? Anything you've omitted that would help sell you?

▶ **Finally, and most important, ask yourself if the letter fulfills its primary goal: selling you into an interview.**

Your letter must answer the reader's question *"Is this person worth my taking the time to meet?"*
And the answer should always be yes.

SAMPLE COVER LETTER

Rosemarie Fallon
Executive Vice President
Barlow-Skinner Advertising, Inc.
11 West Wacker Drive
Chicago, IL 60601

Dear Ms. Fallon:

Barlow-Skinner has been making headlines lately. Winning the Athletix shoe account against competition from the heaviest hitters in the advertising community was quite a coup and testimony to the fact that Barlow-Skinner is clearly an agency on the move. As you grow beyond a primarily regional client base to national ones, you will need senior account people who can attract the major accounts that win attention—and billings. I believe I can accomplish this for you.

As you'll see by my enclosed resume, I have a proven track record of bringing in new business, supervising high-profile accounts, and developing long-term relationships with clients through superior client service. Most recently, as senior account supervisor for a mid-size New York agency, I brought in an import automobile account representing $12.3 million in billings—the first automobile account the agency has ever had. My extensive client interaction has resulted in the agency retaining the account despite outside competition from larger, full-service agencies.

This is the type of contribution I can make for Barlow-Skinner. I believe I would make a valuable addition to your team and can assist you in pursuing the high-profile national accounts your agency deserves. I will call you next Wednesday so we can set up a mutually convenient time to meet.

Sincerely,

VARIATIONS ON A THEME: DEVELOPING A MULTI-USE LETTER

▶ **You can write one basic cover letter and, with some adjustments, use it for a variety of purposes.**

It's the most time-efficient way of approaching the written part of your job hunt. For each general job objective, develop a basic framework and alter it to fit the need of the moment.

The core contents will probably remain the same. That is, you may always use the same (or a similar) opening, and the achievements you highlight in the sales pitch section will probably not vary. But, depending upon the recipient of each letter, certain elements can be added, subtracted, or skewed differently. You may choose to highlight something in one letter and play it down in another.

For example, if your letter is designed to:

- *Approach a target company or follow up on a tip from a personal contact,* you should be sure to open with or include proof that you've researched the company. In this case, a needs payoff is usually a strong hook. The rest of the letter (the sales pitch and close) would probably remain substantially the same.

- *Serve as a general broadcast letter* that will be sent to hundreds of companies, your emphasis should be on the industry, not any one company. The sales pitch would probably remain the same.

- *Contact an executive recruiter,* you can drop the opening hook and replace it with something more general about the type of job you are looking for. In addition, you should add information about your past compensation and current salary requirements.

- *Answer a blind want ad,* your opening will probably focus on the industry in which the unknown company operates. The rest of the letter will remain substantially the same, provided, of course, that any qualities or experience mentioned in the ad correspond with the sales pitch you've devised.

Whatever the circumstances, your objective is to make your letter *appear* as personalized as possible. If you can manage this, no one will be aware that you're using the same general letter for various queries.

The following sample letters will give you an idea of how the same basic letter can be re-focused to meet different needs. Note how much of the letter remains the same.

SAMPLE COVER LETTER—IN RESPONSE TO A PERSONAL CONTACT'S LEAD

120 South End Avenue
New York, NY 10280

September 19, 1993

Mr. William Avedon
Sales & Marketing Director
DataTech, Inc.
100 E. 42nd Street
New York, NY 10017

Dear Mr. Avedon:

A mutual acquaintance, Dennis Wheeler, suggested I contact you. He tells me that, with the introduction of the new DataSys operating system software, you soon will be creating the position of Northeast Regional Director. This is a position I'm very interested in—and one in which I know I can produce results.

My accomplishments speak louder than words can. More specifically: For the past seven years, I have been New York district manager for Phoenix Software. I supervise a staff of 40 sale reps who have produced the best district sales record in the company during this time period. Sales in my district have jumped 27%, for a market share increase of 11%. In addition, I have:

- established new "core values" training for regional sales reps, resulting in individual sales increases of up to 39%.

- increased customer base through prospecting—adding 17 new accounts representing $750,000 in additional sales.

- designed and implemented comprehensive dealer service program. Saw 15% increase in reorders.

Prior to this, I was a software sales representative for Phoenix and for Technology Associates. Among my key accomplishments as a sales rep:

- won company's President award given for exceeding sales quota by 100%—three years in a row.

- voluntarily took over flagging region and increased sales volume by 49% within first year.

I welcome the opportunity to deliver similar—or better—results for DataTech. I will call you next Tuesday to set up an appointment to discuss the contributions I can make.

Sincerely,

SAMPLE COVER LETTER—IN ANSWER TO A WANT AD

Box T1234
The New York Times
229 W. 43rd Street
New York, NY 10036

Your ad in the September 23rd *Sunday New York Times* seeking a National Sales Director for your computer software firm caught my attention and held it. The position you describe—setting up and supervising a national network of sales representatives and devising sales programs for a start-up computer software company—sounds like one I am tailormade for and one in which I know I can produce results. When you review the enclosed resume, I'm sure you'll agree with me.

My accomplishments speak louder than words can. For the past seven years, I have been New York district manager for Phoenix Software. I supervise a staff of 40 sale reps who have produced the best district sales record in the company during this time period. Sales in my district have jumped 27%, for a market share increase of 11%. In addition, I have:

- established new "core values" training for regional sales reps, resulting in individual sales increases of up to 39%.

- increased customer base through prospecting—adding 17 new accounts, representing $750,000 in additional sales.

- designed and implemented comprehensive dealer service program. Saw 15% increase in reorders.

Prior to this, I was a software sales representative for Phoenix and for Technology Associates. Among my key accomplishments as a sales rep:

- won company's President award given for exceeding sales quota by 100%—three years in a row.

- voluntarily took over flagging region and increased sales volume by 49% within first year.

I welcome the opportunity to deliver similar—or better—results for your organization. I can be reached during business hours at 212-555-1111 or, in evenings, at my home. I look forward to hearing from you in the near future.

Sincerely,

RESUME LETTERS

▶ **The resume letter is a cross between a cover letter and a resume.**

These aren't commonly used, but there are points in a job hunt when a resume letter might meet your needs better than any other written material.

Like a cover letter, a resume letter presents your background in a way that targets a company or a position. Like a resume, it covers more ground than a letter, and usually includes fairly comprehensive coverage of your employment history, educational background, and outside activities. *Unlike* a letter or a resume, a resume letter gives you some latitude in terms of how you can present yourself. You can avoid mentioning company names, omit employment dates, and include hobbies or other activities—all of which can make your sales message much stronger.

Under certain circumstances, your best bet will be a resume letter instead of a letter/resume package. Among these situations:

• *You don't have the right qualifications for a job*—you're changing careers, for example.

A resume letter, because it is less formal than a resume, enables you to play up the aspects of your background that make you a viable candidate for the job. And, while you can include information that usually wouldn't appear in a cover letter but that helps sell you (education, activities, etc.), you can also *exclude* information that ordinarily appears on a resume and could hurt you (dates of employment, company names, etc.).

• *You're answering an ad that lists highly specific requirements* . . . and —important—doesn't state that you should send a resume.

A resume letter works well in this instance because you can include only background information that matches, point for point, the listed qualifications.

• *You're prospecting at a company*—that is, you want to fish around for possible openings, but don't want to make a formal application.

A resume letter can help you test the waters by notifying someone of your abilities and interest without waiting to find out whether there's an opening. In this instance, your resume letter should say, in effect, here's a thumbnail sketch of my background; perhaps we could meet. The big plus: You can avoid mentioning company names (especially important if you're currently employed and don't want management to get wind of your job hunt).

- And, finally, *any other time you think sending your resume could hurt your chances.*

A RESUME THAT DOESN'T WORK

In the following resume, the job seeker is hoping to switch careers. However, you'll note that the resume doesn't convince the reader that she has the experience or background to make the switch. Instead it points out her lack of corporate experience—and keeps her from making it to the interview stage.

PHYLLIS D. SPENCER
2700 La Duela Lane, Carlsbad, CA 92008
619-555-1111

OBJECTIVE

A human-resources managerial position in the employee-counseling field, in which I can apply my superior communications skills and innovative approaches to education, motivation, and counseling.

EXPERIENCE

• Convinced superiors of necessity to revamp program of instruction and motivational strategies, and was chosen to oversee efforts of four professionals in this project, affecting over 300 people per year. Commended for ability to develop rapport and enhancement of working environment.
• Named to supervisory board of one of California's top universities. Persuaded top officers to form financial committee, to which I was appointed, to better plan budgetary matters. Resulted in a four-year wage development and review plan and a 39% cut in the employee attrition rate.
• With several others, founded local chapter of nationwide organization working against drug abuse and have given over 75 presentations on that topic at high schools, colleges and other educational and public institutions.
• Motivated over 900 people during the past five years. Received awards that reflected my ability to encourage people to achieve beyond what they believed they were capable of.

EMPLOYMENT HISTORY

Teacher in the City of San Diego school system, 1981–present
Instructor, California State University, 1969–1981
Instructor, Centenary Junior College, 1966–1969
Teacher, Immaculate Heart High School, San Diego, CA 1965–1966

EDUCATION

B.A., University of San Diego (English), 1963
M.A., University of San Diego (English), 1965

THE RESUME REWRITTEN AS A RESUME LETTER

PHYLLIS D. SPENCER
2700 La Duela Lane, Carlsbad, CA 92008
619-555-1111

January 22, 1993

Mr. Philip Downey
Executive Vice President, Human Resources
Western Bancorp
600 Broadway
San Diego, CA 92101

Dear Mr. Downey:

Western Bancorp, like so many other area companies, has been going through a period of downsizing and streamlining. In recent articles in the San Diego *Union* as well as in local television news reports, you stressed the need for offering your departing employees comprehensive outplacement services—and have mentioned your intentions to expand this area. I agree that outplacement counseling is of growing importance in today's corporate world, and endorse your view that companies must offer as all-inclusive a program as possible. And I think I could help you develop such a program.

With over twenty years in education, counseling, and administration, I have the combination of abilities and hands-on experience that would make me a valuable addition to your human resources team—specifically as an outplacement coordinator, devising and overseeing a network of services for newly retired or laid-off employees. Among my skills and qualifications:

- As a cofounder of a chapter of nationally known Narcotics Anonymous, I laid the groundwork for existing procedures, set up and implemented public affairs programs, counseled new members, and designed educational presentations for the community at large.

- My ten years' experience teaching at both the high school and college level has given me the ability to communicate with a wide variety of people. In addition, I have developed excellent organizational, presentation, and training skills.

- I also have experience organizing material and making presentations outside of the classroom. For the past three years, I have spoken to large groups—in local high schools, colleges, and universities—about drug abuse and the various programs available to them.

- Most recently, I have combined my administrative skills and counseling skills while serving as a college instructor at California State University. There, I oversaw the redesign of a business education/motivation program—a program with over 300 participants a year. The two-year project won me a commendation—both for my program design and for the working environment I fostered during its development.

- My administrative skills are not limited to devising educational programs. As an elected member of the supervisory board of CSU, I worked to establish a long-needed financial committee, and subsequently was appointed to serve on that committee. My involvement resulted in a four-year wage development and review plan and a 39% cut in the employee attrition rate.

- I hold both a Bachelor of Arts and Master of Arts from the University of San Diego.

I believe I have a great deal to offer to Western Bancorp's human resources division. The programs you are planning to put into effect sound most exciting and very similar to the projects I have implemented in the past. I would like to learn more about them from you and also discuss how I can help you expand into this vital area. I hope to hear from you in the near future.

Sincerely,

As you can see, a resume letter is usually best for long-shot situations in which your chances of landing an interview are slim to begin with. They're often a last-ditch effort. This is why there is one major drawback to their use: Resume letters often tip off the reader that something is being glossed over, hidden, or otherwise omitted.

The rule of thumb, then? When possible, stick with the traditional letter/resume. Use resume letters only when it seems necessary. And, most important, if asked specifically for a resume, send a resume—*not* a resume letter, even if you feel that it would sell you better. You'll get nowhere by breaking the rules.

▶ **A resume letter is written in much the same way as a cover letter.**

Like a cover letter, a resume letter has three basic parts: an opening hook, a sales pitch, and a close. In each part, you must include the material most likely to get you that interview.

Briefly, here are the steps to writing a resume letter:

- *Open strong*—with a hook, a needs payoff if possible, or simply by explaining your interest in the company or job.

- *Next, move into your sales pitch.* Here's where the difference between a resume letter and a typical cover letter comes into play. Your best bet is to split your sales pitch into two parts. In part one, present the highlights of your employment background, playing up, of course, the aspects that best fit your job objective. Start this portion of your letter with a broad general statement of your skills, achievements, or accomplishments, then cut to the specifics. Use bullets to make each point stand out—and make each bullet count. As with your resume, use action words, numbers, and percentages whenever possible, and detailed explanations of what you've accomplished for your employers. Because you won't be sending your resume, you can lift fragments and phrases from it wholesale.

- *In part two of your sales pitch, present the less important aspects of your background* (work experience that isn't as directly relevant to your objective) or non-work aspects of your background that will help sell you. This portion of the letter shouldn't be bulleted, but written as regular narrative text.

▶ **A key point to remember: Because you aren't including a resume with this letter, you *must* include anything and everything you believe will lend ammunition to your candidacy.**

Unlike using a cover letter, when you use a resume letter you can't count on cementing the sale with your resume. This is your only chance to win an interview.

In light of this, review your resume letter very carefully. Read it against your resume to be sure you haven't omitted anything that could help your cause.

6

JOB-HUNTING TACTICS THAT WORK FOR THE OVER-40 JOB HUNTER

(and those that don't)

INTRODUCTION

▶ **More often than not, you will be forced to create your own opportunities—by unearthing potential jobs, contacting possible employers, tracking down every possible job lead.**

Face it, you can't sit back and wait for job offers to trickle in. When you were younger, you could approach job hunting more passively. Less was at stake, and there were more jobs available. But times have changed. Now you must take charge of your own job hunt by actively pursuing prospective employers—and, in some cases, by actually creating job openings where there were none before.

To begin with, recognize that, regardless of what the pundits and experts say, *there is no one magic tactic that will land you an interview or a job.*

Yes, there's always someone espousing the tactic of the moment —one day it's networking or "job sourcing," the next it's a new twist on direct mail, and the next it's working as a contract employee.

But the truth is that there is no success-guaranteed, idiot-proof tactic. Instead, there are a *number* of tactics that *may* work—from a direct-mail campaign to using an executive recruiter. Their success depends on a combination of luck, timing, and technique.

This chapter is designed to help you with the latter. (Luck and timing, unfortunately, are out of your hands.) In it, we discuss techniques, strategies, and tips on the standard, tried-and-true approaches—direct-mail campaigns and answering want ads; the professional approach—using executive recruiters; and the "back-door" methods—executive temping, interim management, contract employment, and volunteer and part-time work.

As you'll see, each method has pros and cons. Some are more effective than others, and some work best under certain circumstances. You will probably use at least three of these tactics in *your* job hunt. The key is knowing when to use a method and how to get the most out of it. This chapter will help you do both.

DIRECT-MAIL CAMPAIGNS

▶ **Direct-mail campaigns are perhaps the most common way of seeking employment—and, in spite of the bad press they often get, they're still one of the most effective for the older job hunter.**

Direct-mail campaigns—sending an unsolicited sales pitch letter or letter/resume package to prospective companies—work. No, they don't have an incredible success rate. Yes, you will get a high percentage of turndowns. But done properly, with a strong letter and follow-up, direct-mail campaigns *can* result in a number of interviews.

They're especially effective for the over-40 job hunter for a few reasons: Unlike younger job hunters, most over-40 job hunters have more hands-on experience to draw upon for their sales pitch; most have a better idea of what a prospective employer in their field will respond to; many are going for executive jobs, which this approach works well for.

▶ **The drawback to direct-mail campaigns: A large number—in fact, the vast majority—of people who read your letter will throw it away.**

Sad, but true.

Direct-mail campaigns return at best, by most accounts, a 2% or lower response rate.

So you have to expect a certain amount of failure if you want to launch a direct-mail campaign. It's built into the system—you're soliciting job offers from companies that may have nothing to offer you.

The trick, of course, is to keep the number of throwaways as small as possible. Or, conversely, to keep the number of people who read on and decide to speak with you as high as possible.

This is where a strong letter comes into play. In the case of a targeted campaign, you can make your letter speak directly to the needs of the reader. In a resume blitz, you will focus more on the target industry or job objective. But in either case, your letter must be written with the reader in mind. (Read Chapter 5 on cover letters for general advice on letter writing; below are tips for each approach.)

▶ **The up side: Because you are sending out unsolicited material, those few people who do reply positively are good job bets.**

This is what makes the direct-mail approach ultimately worth your time. The few "yeses" you get will be from *motivated* employers. Why would they bother responding to unsolicited material if they weren't *really* interested?

▶ **Now on to the mechanics. First, there are two types of direct-mail campaigns—a *targeted direct-mail campaign*, in which you send a carefully targeted letter to a select list of companies and follow up by telephone, and the *resume blitz*, in which you send a more general broadcast letter (and sometimes a resume) to a large number of companies.**

Of the two methods, a targeted direct-mail campaign is usually the most effective. The reason? Your letter is tailored to the needs of each specific recipient. In addition, the follow-up increases your chances of nailing down an interview.

The drawback, however, is built into the notion of targeted direct mail. Obviously, the more companies you send your letter to, the higher the number of "yeses" you'll receive. But you can't target a huge mailing—it's virtually impossible for you to write individually targeted letters to hundreds of companies and then follow up on each one personally.

As for a resume blitz, the opposite holds true: The up side is the sheer number of companies you can contact; the downside is the generic quality of the letter.

▶ **The best way to proceed, then? Do a targeted direct-mail approach to 50 companies or so, and a mass-mailing resume blitz to as many other companies as time and expense will allow.**

It's the perfect compromise for most over-40 job hunters.

You get the best of both worlds—you can choose a select list of prime targets—those companies that interest you the most or seem to be the best potential employers, and focus your targeted mail effort on them, tailoring your letters to their individual needs. Then you can do a mass mailing to hundreds of other companies—those that interest you to a lesser degree.

By combining methods, you maximize your chances of receiving the reply you want: *I want to meet you in person.*

Following is the information you'll need to proceed on both fronts. First, a look at the targeted direct-mail campaign—a step-by-step explanation of how to make this method work as well as possible. Second, resume blitzing—how to make a mass mailing generate as many positive responses as possible.

A TARGETED DIRECT-MAIL CAMPAIGN

▶ **A targeted direct-mail campaign involves three steps: selecting target companies; writing a strong sales letter to them; and following up by telephone.**

It is set up just like a public relations campaign—you research the market and choose the best recipients for your sales message; you make your pitch on paper; then you follow up to find out if the pitch worked—and to do a last-minute pitch when possible.

Each step is an integral part of the process. Too little focus on any of them, and the entire approach will fall apart.

▶ **Step 1 is straightforward—you simply put together a mailing list of target companies. The key is to make your selections judiciously.**

The targeted direct-mail approach takes more time and effort than the resume blitz, so think strategically. Choose companies that seem to have the most employment potential. If you want, include your "dream companies," those that most interest you, even if they're not the best prospects.

Some tips on putting together a mailing list:

- *To come up with a strong list of likely employment prospects, you'll have to rely on research and networking.*

    Follow the methods outlined in Chapter 2, "Research," to pinpoint these companies. For example, read trade journals to get a bead on companies that are expanding, introducing new products, shifting managements, and the like. Talk to colleagues or employees of companies that interest you to learn more about prospects. You might call some companies to get further information. Also, pay attention to industry trends—which sectors are good bets? Which aren't? Are certain geographic regions stronger than others?

- *Be selective . . . but not overly so.*

    In the past, people recommended choosing a select list of only 15 or so companies. The reasoning? The more precisely targeted your list, the more precisely targeted your letter.

    That worked in the past, but it doesn't today, and not for the over-40 job hunter. It's a simple rule of thumb: As mentioned before, the more letters you send out, the more potential "yeses."

    So choose as many companies as you can—keeping in mind, of course, that you will be researching each choice to devise the best written approach and, later, calling each choice to follow up on your mailing. Given this, make the number manageable. If time and energy permit, select as many as 100 or even 200. If you're pressed for time, select as many as you feel you can handle *well*.

Do remember, however, that as time goes on and rejections mount (as, unfortunately, they will), you can add more companies to your list.

TIP: **If you don't have time to pull together your own list, consider buying one from an appropriate trade publication. In many cases, you can buy lists that are presorted by zip code, or even job title. See page 161 for more information on this.**

- *Always get the name of a specific individual to whom you'll address your letter.*

    This may seem obvious, but a number of people blow their chances by sending letters to "Sales Director," even "To Whom It May Concern." What a waste of time and effort! The general rule: Address your letter to the person who would be your boss, or your prospective boss's boss. (In this case, the idea is that your letter will be kicked down one level to your potential boss—who will be more inclined to think positively of you, since his or her boss already does.) Avoid personnel or human resources departments. You want to make a pitch to the person who would hire you, a line person, not a staff person.

    Even if you've already found names in directories or other sources, always call each company to double-check the name, spelling, exact title, and address. As mentioned before, you can't be too careful. Misspelled names or incorrect titles can ruin the otherwise great impression you may make in your letter.

▶ **Step 2—writing a targeted pitch letter—is where you must pour on all of your sales ability.**

Your goal? To generate enough interest to make a prospective employer want to interview you—even if there's no job currently available.

This isn't an easy task: It requires a focused, strong sales effort —*always addressing the needs of the prospective employer.*

Like other letters you'll write in your job hunt, this one will consist of three parts—an opening, a sales pitch, and a close. But this letter must have an exceptionally strong focus and very pointed sales pitch.

Some specifics on how to proceed:

- *Research each company on your list before you begin writing.*

  To write a strong letter, you must know what each company has been doing recently, any business developments, plans or trends, what type of person they would want to hire, etc.

- *Use your research to set up a needs payoff in the opening paragraph.*

  It's the most effective use of your research—and the best way to target your letter from the outset. Remember: In a needs payoff, you identify a problem or need the prospective employer has—and show that *you* can solve it.

EXAMPLE: According to the July 17 issue of *Stores* magazine, the TJK management team is considering a revamp of the flagship chain's image and merchandising in an effort to grow with the maturing baby-boomer market and, in so doing, turn around sales. Repositioning to grow with a changing market is a challenge—and one that I've handled successfully.

(Note: By referring to a specific article about the company or a recent trend or development, you show the reader immediately that this is a personalized letter, not a form letter.)

TIP: Another opening gambit: Identify a problem the company has, and then outline a specific plan you have to solve it. This shows that you've done your homework, you have ideas, and you can immediately contribute to the company. In the close of your letter, say that you would like to discuss your ideas in more depth. The downside? This takes more effort than other openings.

- *In the second paragraph, move into a hard-hitting sales pitch.*

  As in other cover letters, this is where you back your claim that you are the person they need. Include specific achievements and accomplishments and, as always, be pithy, use action words, use numbers when possible, and so on.

EXAMPLE: I am a turnaround specialist, with seventeen years' experience with specialty chain stores. Most recently, as marketing director for a southeastern chain of women's apparel stores, I devised and oversaw a complete image overhaul—redirecting the merchandise, advertising and marketing, and overall focus from juniors to contemporary misses. Among my specific accomplishments:

- Designed and spearheaded extensive multitiered marketing and promotion campaign—including in-store events, direct mailings, increased advertising presence. Secured publicity through special media events.

- Established new direct-mail division to attract new customers, reinforce new image, and develop new profit center. Prepared catalog, trained sales manager, oversaw setup. Division is now earning $1.2 million.

- Improved margins 9% by redirecting shift in merchandise mix. Shift from low-price to higher-price units resulted in a 23% increase in profitability.

- The bottom line: Last year, same-store sales rose 9%, despite poor economic climate. Total sales were up 14%—five percent more than our regional competitors.

- *Take charge of the follow-up in the close.*
  Restate your ability to contribute to the company, and impress the reader with the strength of your interest. Then ask for an interview—and announce your intention to follow up. Because your letter is unsolicited, it is best to take the matter of setting up an interview into your own hands. If the recipient isn't interested, you'll find out when you call.

EXAMPLE: These are the types of programs—and results—I would like to produce for TJK Stores. I would like to get together with you to discuss your plans and how I can assist you during this exciting transition period. I will call you on Tuesday, January 26, to set up a mutually convenient time to meet.

TIP: Type "Personal," "Confidential," or "Personal and Confidential," on the envelope. This may keep your letter from being opened by a secretary, who may then either file it or route it to personnel. It ups your chances of having the addressee, your prospective employer, open it, read it, and make up his or her own mind about you.

▶ Step 3—telephone follow-up—is *crucial* to your success with this method.

Telephone follow-up more than doubles your chances of a positive reply. It's the same premise that agents and public relations placement specialists use—picking up the phone and following up gives you a final selling opportunity.

Unfortunately, telephone follow-up is also the step that many people omit, forget, or freeze at. It's no wonder—cold-calling a prospective employer and facing possible rejection over the telephone line isn't most people's idea of fun.

But it is vital. If you don't follow up, you drastically cut your chances of success with your mail campaign. You will have wasted a great deal of time and effort.

The solution for those job hunters who aren't phone people? Practice, script cards, and as much confidence as you can muster.

The steps to take:

- *Pull together the key sales points you will want to make*—either on paper or mentally.

    Have a copy of the letter you sent in front of you so you can see exactly what you said and when you sent it. Decide at the outset what sales points you'll emphasize.

TIP: Be sure to choose points that you can *talk* about, not just those that look good on paper. Also be prepared to substantiate or expand upon any aspect of your background that you bring up.

TIP: If it makes you feel more comfortable, jot down your sales points on file cards to use as a mini-script. But *don't* write out an actual script. You will sound like you're reciting a canned spiel—and you may be so dependent upon it that you'll ruin the entire conversation if the person you're calling diverts you from the script.

- *Rehearse the conversation—mentally or out loud.*

    Run through the points you're going to cover, the order in which you'll cover them, and how you'll deal with possible problems or questions. You may want to actually call a friend or colleague to rehearse the conversation in as close an approximation to the real thing as possible.

TIP: As part of your advance preparation, call ahead to double-check the pronunciation of the addressee's name. Mispronouncing it might not ruin your chances, but it will shatter your calm, make you sound like you don't know the person you're calling (which may keep you from being put through), and make you sound generally ill prepared.

- *When you call, ask for the addressee in a calm, authoritative voice.*

    Don't think like a supplicant. Remember: You have something to offer this prospective employer—your expertise. You're not selling something you don't believe in, so act like the winner you are.

You probably will initially speak with a secretary or other assistant—whose job is to screen phone calls. Don't announce that you're a job hunter at the outset. Tell the truth, but not the whole truth—"This is Joe Blake. I told Mr. Ashmead I'd be calling" or "He's expecting my call" are reasonably effective. If pressed, you may be forced to 'fess up—"I sent Mr. Ashmead a letter last week, and I'm calling to discuss it."

TIP: One way of getting around interference-running secretaries and assistants is to try what one job seeker did. When calling to follow up on his mailing, he always said, "I'm calling about the new marketing plans for [whatever new product he had mentioned in his letter]." This was the truth, of course. He *had* said that he had devised a marketing plan for the new product in his mailing. But by phrasing it this way, he came off a shade more official—as someone whom the secretary should know, or, at least, should put through. And he usually did get through to the right people.

TIP: Some people swear by the old rule of thumb—calling when a secretary is less inclined to be in—before 9:00 and after 5:00. At these times, executives are generally at their desks, answering their own phones.

TIP: A few ways of sounding assured and professional—take these hints from telemarketers: (1) Dress professionally even though the person on the other end of the line can't see you. You'll feel more businesslike and polished, which will come across over the phone. (2) Don't smoke, chew gum, drink coffee—anything that the person on the other end might hear. (3) Sit straight, at the edge of your chair. Good posture translates into a good speaking voice. (4) Be sure you are calling from a professional-sounding environment—no television set or radio playing in the background, no street noise, no children playing, nothing that detracts from your professional demeanor.

- *When you've gotten through to the right person, refer to your letter right away.*

  Cut to the chase—and your sales pitch—by referring immediately to the letter you sent and, even better, to the part of your letter that presented your strongest sales point.

EXAMPLE: "Mr. Ashmead? This is Tyler Donne speaking. I wrote to you about the marketing plans I have devised for retail companies. In my letter dated June eighteenth, I mentioned how my plan increased sales by thirty-five percent at the . . ."

If you aren't cut off, refer briefly to the main points of your letter, then move in for the kill—setting an interview date.

EXAMPLE: **"The marketing plans I devised for All-Mart Stores and Acme Inc. would be similar to the kind I could develop for Dawson-Pickett, now that you're involved in a similar turnaround situation. I've already drawn up some ideas. I hope you'll be interested in speaking with me about them and how I could contribute to your company. Are you available for a meeting? Say, next Wednesday at any time? Or would Thursday be better?"**

(Note: This last method is an old hard-sell sales technique, but it's effective—you don't ask anything that can be answered with a yes or a no. Instead, you offer an option. If you feel uncomfortable with this type of approach, though, stick with something softer.)

- *Be prepared for some resistance—even some outright rejection.*

As mentioned before, it's built into the system. So, don't sweat it if the person you call is abrupt, or simply says that he or she has nothing for you. If you're a super-salesperson, you can still try to press on. Some people can turn even a virtual turn-down into an interview. Most people, however, can't. Play it by ear—but don't turn yourself into a pest. You don't know who this person knows, and you don't want word to get out that there's an obnoxious would-be employee bugging people over the phone. Remember, you solicited the company, not vice versa —which means that a negative reply is probably a dead end. But you can sometimes turn one of the two following common *semi-negatives* into a sales opportunity!

1. The person says, "I don't recall your letter." Refresh his or her memory. Briefly refer to one or two specifics from your letter. If this doesn't work, either keep trying to sell yourself over the phone or offer to send another letter.

2. The person says, "I haven't gotten to the letter yet." Offer to call back at a later date—and get a specific time. If you suspect the person is lying or doesn't know where your letter is, offer to send another letter.

▶ **One final word on direct-mail campaigns: Expect rejections— but start questioning your approach if you get *only* rejections.**

Yes, rejections are a given with this method. But each rejection should bring you closer to a yes. If you get consistent, across-the-board rejections and no invitations to interview at all, start re-thinking your approach. Ask yourself: Have you picked the wrong companies—that is, complete long shots that have few or no opportunities? Is your letter targeted as precisely as possible? Are you directing your letter to the right person? Have a colleague or friend review your campaign with you so you can get a more objective viewpoint.

SAMPLE DIRECT-MAIL LETTER

122 Washington Ave.
Savannah, GA 31405

September 10, 1993

Mr. Brian Marshall
General Manager
TJK Stores, Inc.
7 TJK Drive
Boston, MA 02105

Dear Mr. Marshall:

According to the July 17th issue of *Stores* magazine, the TJK management team is considering a revamp of the flagship chain's image and merchandising in an effort to grow with the maturing baby-boomer market and, in so doing, turn around sales. Repositioning to grow with a changing market is a challenge—and one that I've handled successfully.

I am a turnaround specialist, with seventeen years' experience with specialty chain stores. Most recently, as marketing director for a southeastern chain of women's apparel stores, I devised and oversaw a complete image overhaul—redirecting the merchandise, advertising and marketing, and overall focus from juniors to contemporary misses. Among my specific accomplishments:

- Designed and spearheaded extensive multitiered marketing and promotion campaign—including in-store events, direct mailings, increased advertising presence. Secured publicity through special media events.

- Established new direct-mail division to attract new customers, reinforce new image, and develop new profit center. Prepared catalog, trained sales manager, oversaw setup. Division is now earning $1.2 million.

- Improved margins 9% by redirecting shift in merchandise mix. Shift from low-price to higher-price units resulted in a 23% increase in profitability.

- The bottom line: Last year, same-store sales rose 9%, despite poor economic climate. Total sales were up 14%—5% more than our regional competitors.

These are the types of programs—and results—I would like to produce for TJK Stores. I would like to get together with you to discuss your plans and how I can assist you during this exciting transition period. I will call you on Tuesday, January 26, to set up a mutually convenient time to meet.

Sincerely,

Donna Johnson

RESUME BLITZING: A VARIATION OF THE DIRECT-MAIL APPROACH

▶ **Resume blitzing is direct mail with a scattershot approach.**

As such, it's automatically less targeted and usually less effective. The big plus with a resume blitz: You can approach a larger number of companies and increase the pool of possible "yeses." The drawback, as mentioned before, is the inability to target your mailing to specific companies.

To make your mailing effective, you must target your letter to the industry and your job objective instead. The focus is still on the needs of the prospective employer, but in a more general way. Essentially, you are telling them that your background suits the job you're after—and may match their needs.

▶ **As with the targeted direct-mail campaign, you begin by selecting a list of companies.**

In this case, you *shouldn't* be overly selective. This is a numbers game, remember? As such, you want to reach as many companies as possible.

Some ideas on putting together an extensive, effective mailing list:

- *Think creatively.*

    That is, don't think only Fortune 500 companies. Small and mid-sized companies are great prospects. Similarly, consider sending your mailing to companies in industries related to your current or most recent one. Don't rule out subsidiaries and branches of bigger companies, even different *departments* within the same large company.

- *Use directories or CD-ROMs to pull together a list of companies that meet your criteria*—geographic location, type of company, company size, etc.

    You can use your public library, corporate library, or home computer to generate a mailing list. See Chapter 2 for detailed information.

- *If you want to save time and effort (and don't mind an extra expense), you can buy a mailing list.*

Your best bet for an industry-specific mailing list is a trade publication list. Most major trades sell lists of their subscribers and can sort them according to company type, location, job title, etc. The result? As focused a list as you want. For example, you can get a list of sales directors of sporting goods companies with earnings in excess of $5 million, located in the metropolitan New York area, or of all executives in sporting goods companies nationwide. The drawback, of course, is the cost. There are many other sources of mailing lists, as well. For more information, check:

SOURCE: *Direct-Mail Lists Rates & Data,* Standard Rate & Data Service, Inc., 3004 Glenview Rd.,Wilmette, IL 60091. Tel.: 708-256-6067.

SOURCE: *Mailing List Companies and Categories Directory,* Enterprise Publishers, 3809 Hudee Dr., Mitchellville, MD 20721-2432. Tel.: 301-464-2110. Includes listings on over 2,000 mailing list companies.

SOURCE: *Mailing Lists Directory,* American Business Directories, Inc., 5711 S. Eighty-sixth Circle, Omaha, NE 68127. Tel.: 402-593-4600. Includes listings on over 2,500 available mailing lists.

SOURCE: *National Directory of Mailing Lists,* Oxbridge Communications, Inc., 150 Fifth Ave., New York, NY 10011. Tel.: 212-741-0231.

▶ The next step: Writing a strong broadcast letter.

The letter you write for a resume blitz is typically called a broadcast letter, because that's just what it does—broadcasts your availability to a wide number of potential employers.

Obviously, the companies you are contacting don't necessarily have any openings at all. So your main goal in writing this type of cover letter is to tout yourself as an achiever who has produced strong results in the past and could do it again for the recipient if he or she has something available. Remember—if there's nothing available, you won't get a call. It's that simple. You don't follow up (the number of letters you're mailing rules that out). It's up to your letter—and luck.

Some guidelines:

- *Make your letter look as personalized as possible.*

    Don't advertise the fact that you're sending the same letter to hundreds of companies. Make each letter look like the only one. A computer-generated letter is your best bet—a basic mail merge program makes it easy to change the address and salutation on each letter. *Don't* send photocopies—it's an immediate turnoff.

- *Your opening paragraph should be as focused as possible—on the industry, or on your job objective.*

    You can't make your letter company specific, but you can play to the reader's interest by focusing on industry trends, especially how they relate to your job objective. Then cut straight to your qualifications.

- *As always, follow up with a sales pitch in which you play up strong achievements that relate to your job objective.*

    The rules that apply to all other letters also apply here: Be brief, use active words, highlight specific examples from your background that show what you've accomplished for past employers, etc.

- *End with a simple close in which you restate your interest and ask for an interview.*

    Nothing clever needed here, just a simple "I would like to meet with you to discuss the contributions I could make to your company. [To make the letter appear more personalized, if you've composed it on a computer put in a merge code here and insert the company's name.] I hope to hear from you in the near future."

SAMPLE RESUME BLITZ LETTER

Ms. Georgia Pendleton
President
TeleCom, Inc.
777 Wilshire Boulevard
Los Angeles, CA 90017

Dear Ms. Pendleton:

As the role of information systems enters the corporate mainstream, professionals are needed who can fulfill the technical requirements and, at the same time, communicate effectively with nontechnical employees. I have the background and the ability to do both.

With a bottom-line orientation and nineteen years of hands-on experience in system analysis, programming, computer operations, project planning, and applications definition and specification, I have a track record of successes:

• As systems manager for a leading telecommunications company, manage all MIS communications, hardware, and software. Design and oversee all special-systems projects and regular-systems operations.

• Designed and oversaw development of automated documentation system. Resulted in company savings of over $350K in paper and printing costs.

• Strong working knowledge of DEC, UNIX, and C, among others.

In addition, I have the managerial skills and background necessary to both implement the systems I have designed and to supervise teams of employees. More specifically, I:

• Currently supervise staff of 120, including technical employees (programmers, analysts, project managers, etc.) and nontechnical (writers, marketers, etc.)

• Instituted open communications and team approach between end users and systems designers. Result: improved morale, work environment, and system quality.

• Devised and oversaw employee-training curriculum. One specialized program provided intensive training for 200 new systems administrators for only $350K.

I would like the opportunity to apply my skills in both the technical and managerial areas to a market leader such as your company. I hope to hear from you in the near future.

Sincerely,

WANT ADS

▶ **They're not your best bet, but you'd be foolish to disregard want ads entirely.**

It's true: Most jobs are never listed in the classifieds. In fact, only about 15% of all job openings are advertised.

Even so, it would be a mistake to completely ignore want ads. Companies *do* place ads for legitimate job openings. You never know when you'll run across one describing a position that suits you. And if you have the qualifications—and know how to best answer the ad, a want ad can lead to an interview. A long shot? Yes. Impossible? Definitely not.

Worth your time? Certainly. (Especially since you're probably reading the want ads anyway.)

Some guidelines on how to find want ads that may pan out:

- *Always check classifieds in the trade publications that serve your industry.* These often provide the best job leads, since they target your field of interest. Also look out for special-focus issues that concentrate on a particular area within an industry and may include classifieds that are also more targeted.

- *Check the major daily newspapers in your area or in the regions that interest you.* Best day: Sunday. And keep an eye out for special advertising inserts on one employment area (health care, engineering, etc.) or on careers in general. To find out if any such sections are planned, call the paper's advertising department.

- *Two more standard sources of classifieds, especially for general management jobs:* the *Wall Street Journal* and *National Business Employment Weekly* (which compiles the *Journal*'s want ads, including those from regional editions).

- *The worst days for want ads—that is, the days that usually have the fewest ads—are Monday and Friday.* Best, as mentioned before, is Sunday.

- *It may sound obvious, but don't forget to look for ads in areas of the paper* other *than the classified section.* For example, in the Sunday *New York Times*, advertisements for educational and health positions run in the "Week in Review" section, and a wide range of others run in the "Business" section.

- *Check under a variety of job titles, not just the one you want.* You may find appropriate listings in several places—even in seemingly unrelated fields. For example, a marketing position at a chemicals company may be listed under sales or marketing—but it also may be under "Chemicals." In addition, companies sometimes list more than one job in a single ad, and the lead job title may have nothing to do with the other jobs listed.

- *Also be on the lookout for ads for jobs a level above you.* In many cases, when upper-level people are hired, they bring on new employees.

- *Some rules of thumb as to which ads to answer:* If there's an employer's name listed in an ad that interests you, always answer it. If it's an ad listed by an employment agency or recruiter, answer it if the job seems right for you—but recognize that the job may not actually be available and that the agency or firm generally won't be the sole agent seeking candidates for the position. In addition, some agencies (typically the less scrupulous ones) use ads touting fictional jobs, or positions that they probably won't fill, to get more resumes for later referrals. (This isn't necessarily bad—you may eventually end up being referred for another job.) If it's a blind ad, one in which only a box number appears, proceed with caution. In some cases, companies place ads when there are no openings to get a taste of who's out there. Another warning about blind ads—if you're very unlucky, you may wind up sending a resume to your current employer . . . and could then need a new job more than ever. However, if a blind ad truly intrigues you, and you feel you have little to lose, go ahead and answer it.

TIP: If you see a blind ad that interests you, but want to find out who placed it *before* replying, you can use an outplacement firm to reply to the ad. The firm's letter to the box number states that they have a client who would be right for the job, includes some information about your background—without mentioning your name—and explains that there is no fee for the company if they're interested in you (since the outplacement firm is your agent, not theirs). If the company is interested in you, they reply to the outplacement firm, which then contacts you.

▶ **An important fact about want ads: Not only are few openings ever listed, those that are usually generate huge responses.**

In a tough market, it isn't unusual for one ad in a major paper to get over 1,000 replies.

This is why it's important for you to make your letter stand out from the hundreds of others.

To begin with, follow the same basic rules that you would in any other letter in your job hunt: Use action words, cite specific examples from your background that demonstrate your qualifications, use numbers and percentages when possible, and so forth.

Here are some more specific hints on making your response to a want ad as strong and salable as possible:

- *Be as specific as possible in the salutation.*

    If the ad gives you the title of the person to send your resume to, use that title. Even better, call the company, ask the receptionist for the name of the person in that position, and address the letter to him or her. (Note: This may be risky if the ad specifically says not to call the company.)

    If you're answering a blind ad, one in which you are directed to reply to a box number rather than a company or title—then you have two choices. Either go for the basic "To Whom It May Concern" or bypass a salutation completely and just write "To: Box 1234."

    In either case, never, never, *never* opt for "Dear Sir or Madam," "Gentlemen," or (if there's any question about the sex of the recipient) "Dear Sir," or "Dear Ms."

TIP: If the ad lists a personnel director as the contact to whom to reply, you may be better off bypassing personnel. Instead, find out (through networking or a simple phone call to the company) the name of the person to whom you would report if you had the job. (But *don't* leave your name when you do this.) Then send your targeted direct-mail letter and resume to that person—without mentioning the ad. This way, you're going directly to the person who would hire you, and your letter won't be lost among the hundreds of others sitting on the personnel director's desk.

- *Open strongly and cut right to the chase.*

    Remember, the person reading your letter has hundreds of others to read. Do him or her a favor and get to the point quickly. In other words, state clearly up front that you're responding to an ad, and that you believe you have the qualifications described in the ad. Summarize your experience and qualifications, then go into more detail in the second paragraph, outlining specific achievements and accomplishments that prove you're qualified for the job.

- *Always mention the title of the job you are interested in.*

    It sounds obvious, but many job seekers don't do this. Instead they just say they're replying to the ad of August 14 and go into their sales pitch. Remember: The company may have run more than one ad. Don't make the person reading your letter have to work to figure out what you're applying for. Spell it out at the top, either with a line after the salutation, such as "Subject: Director, Management Information Systems position advertised in the August 14 *Bugle*" or in the text of your letter such as "The Director of Management Information Systems position described in your advertisement of August 14. . . ."

- *If the ad asks you to send a resume with your letter, always send one.*

    In this case, your letter is more of a cover letter and should stress the highlights of your background, especially those that show you're the right person for the job.

    If the ad doesn't ask for a resume, send a more detailed letter, which can stand in for your resume. Again, you should list the aspects of your background that meet the requirements of the job, and also include more general information, such as past employment history, education (when appropriate), and the like. For pointers, see "Resume Letters" on page 140.

- *Read the ad carefully for clues on how to convince the recipient that you fit the position described.*

    The words used in an ad can give you tips on how to sell yourself into an interview. First of all, read for general style. Does the writing seem informal or formal? Write your letter accordingly, matching your style to that of the ad. Second, pay attention to the words used to describe the job and the ideal candidate. Does the ad call the company "an aggressive leader" and mention a need for people with "new ideas and energy"? Paint yourself as a dynamic innovator with a strong track record of achievements. On the other hand, does the ad call for "a well-rounded individual" to work in an atmosphere marked by "stability" and "a tradition of excellence"? In this case, stress your own stability by presenting yourself as a solid, reliable employee with team-playing skills.

- *Be sure you address each of the main requirements listed in the ad.*

  Each requirement listed in the ad should be addressed by giving an example from your background that shows you meet it, preferably in your second paragraph. You may want to use bullets to set off each point.

TIP: **Strike the same notes that are in the ad by rephrasing it in your letter. In this way, you ensure that you've stressed the right points, without directly copying the wording in the ad. For example, if the ad calls for "an experienced, innovative, achievement-oriented manager," explain that you're "a forward-thinking manager with a proved record who can produce results," and follow up with specific examples.**

If the ad is more general, and tells you little about the job other than the title, opt for a more general letter that stresses your strengths and points out specific examples of accomplishments and achievements that add up to a picture of you as a qualified candidate.

▶ **One last note on want ads: The following tactical tips may help you turn the odds in your favor.**

- *Never answer an ad on the same day it appeared.*

  Wait a few days before responding to a want ad. The reasoning? Most people send in their letters and resumes the same day or the day after—which means the prospective employer is inundated with responses. By waiting a few days, you can make your response stand out—and get more attention.

TIP: **The best time to answer an ad you see in Sunday's paper is the *following* Sunday. Don't be nervous about waiting. Odds are heavily in your favor that the job will remain open—and your letter will be noticed because you waited.**

- *Pay attention to older want ads as well as current ones.*

  Go to the library and check the ads in back issues of trade journals or newspapers, from as far as several weeks back. In many cases, the positions advertised may still be open. Why not try your chances if you find an ad that interests you? If the job is still open, your response will stand out more, since you're replying well after the rush.

- *A last resort idea: if you haven't received a reply within two weeks, follow up.*

     Call if you have the company name and contact; write if it was a blind ad, and include another copy of your resume. In both cases, remind the employer of your application, your qualifications, and your interest. It may be that you still won't get a bite, but it can't hurt to try again.

SAMPLE WANT AD REPLY LETTER (RESUME REQUIRED)

THE AD: CREDIT MANAGER—National manufacturer/distributor seeks experienced manager with analytical ability to review and evaluate financial status of major national accounts to support credit policies and ensure sales profitability. This position requires a candidate to possess exceptional credit/financial skills and be able to assist staff by taking an active role in the account-reconciliation process. Ten years' experience and computer literacy required. Consumer products background a plus. Submit resume and salary history to: F5555 TIMES 10108

THOMAS C. LUKENS
55 West 14th Street
New York, NY 10011

January 29, 1993

SUBJECT: Credit Manager position advertised in the January 24 *New York Times*

The position described in your advertisement and my background mesh perfectly.

As you'll note upon reviewing the enclosed resume, I have fifteen years' experience in the field and have spent the last seven years at a major consumer electronics firm. My working philosophy is a simple one: I believe that all cash due is collectible. Through close attention to detail, quick decision-making ability, and effective problem-solving techniques, I have a history of shortening payout terms and increasing profitability while maintaining strong customer relationships with major national chain stores, among others. Among my recent accomplishments:

• turned sales to cash in 30 days or less by decreasing collection turns from 90 days to an average of 37

• devised alternative financing arrangements with key customers to maintain relationship, resulting in increased sales of 17%

• generated new sales by establishing direct communications between credit and sales through collections.

I am convinced that I could be an asset to your company and would like to discuss my background with you in greater depth. I hope to hear from you soon.

Sincerely,

SAMPLE WANT AD RESPONSE LETTER (NO RESUME REQUIRED)

THE AD: EXECUTIVE ADMINISTRATIVE ASSISTANT
Join an expanding, prestigious investment bank. Requirements include high flexibility to meet challenges with a personal approach, top-notch communication skills, ability to prioritize and work well under pressure. Interact with top bank officers. A minimum of ten years' office management experience and excellent computer skills essential. Reply F5555 TIMES 10108

SYLVIA L. PARKER
524 Garden Street
Hoboken, NJ 07030
201-555-1111

The Executive Administrative Assistant position described in your ad in the January 24 *New York Times* sounds like a job custom-made for me.

For the past eleven years, I have been executive assistant to the president of Manley Brothers, a small brokerage house. This position entails a wide range of responsibilities—including serving as liaison between the president and other officers, as office manager and as administrative assistant. I have day-to-day contact with our clients, who are chiefly pension fund managers for several large corporations, and handle all my own correspondence, as well as that of the president.

Having final responsibility for all administrative duties—including overseeing a clerical staff of five and generally ensuring that the office runs smoothly—has taught me to make decisions quickly and efficiently. In addition, by working in a fast-paced environment, I have developed the ability to switch gears swiftly, matching my actions to the needs of the moment.

I have a bachelor's degree in Business Administration from Fordham University. My hands-on computer knowledge includes experience using WordPerfect 5.1 and several other word-processing programs in both DOS and Windows versions, spreadsheet programs, including Lotus 123, and specific financial programs.

Working as an executive assistant at Manley Brothers has been fulfilling, but it is time for a change and a move to a larger and more stimulating environment. This is what drew me to the position you described. I would like to interview with you for the Executive Administrative Assistant position, and I look forward to hearing from you soon.

Sincerely,

EXECUTIVE RECRUITERS

▶ **Many over-40 job hunters have been or will be contacted by an executive recruiter at some point in their job hunt.**

Once you've reached a certain level in your career, executive recruiters usually seek you out. The clear benefit to this, of course, is that recruiters do the work for you—they find out about the job opening, send your resume, etc.

However, there are a number of factors that can make a great difference in how much—or how little—recruiters actually further your job hunt.

Most important, keep in mind that recruiters aren't in business to get you a job—they're interested in finding an employee for a company. It's a crucial difference: You're not the client, prospective employers are. Executive recruiters maintain a pool of potential candidates from which to supply their clients with possible employees. The key, then, is ensuring that you are in that pool.

Before you can know the best way to get a recruiter interested in you, you need to understand the basics of the recruitment process.

▶ **To begin with, there are two different types of recruiters, each representing about 50% of the total business: contingency search firms and retainer search firms.**

Contingency search firms work on a commission basis—they are paid only when they refer a candidate who is hired by the client company. Their focus: a less targeted, more scattershot approach, in which they actively solicit both resumes from potential job candidates and, even more important for them, job listings from potential employers. In other words, their emphasis isn't on a perfect fit (as with the other type of search firm) but on a numbers game. The more resumes they can get out there and the more job openings they can try to fit, the more money they earn. Most employment agencies also operate in this way. Contingency search firms tend to specialize in lower-level and middle-level managerial positions, as well as technical and other non-managerial positions, in a salary range of $35,000 to $75,000.

What does this mean in terms of your job hunt? If you agree to be represented by a contingency firm, your resume will probably be widely distributed to employers with job openings that fit your background in any way. This can be good or bad. On the plus side, you're getting exposure to many potential employers. But on the negative side, you risk being overexposed—and you may actually be cutting *back* on your number of potential employers, by having your resume sent to (and possibly rejected by) companies you could have contacted on your own. Remember—the companies that the contingency firm is sending your resume to will have to pay a fee (usually about one-third of the job's annual salary) if they hire you. So, once you begin dealing with a contingency recruiter, you add a sign-up cost to yourself. Once the recruiter sends your resume to a company, the additional cost to that company will apply even if, later on, you solicit it yourself.

The best way to fit a contingency recruiter in your job hunt: Given this downside, most of you are probably best off using contingency recruiters only when you're sure that there is a legitimate job opening, and the company with the opening is one that you haven't already solicited on your own. However, there is one important caveat—if you're in non-managerial work (a lawyer, a broker or trader, etc.), you may have to deal with contingency recruiters, since few retainer recruiters handle non-managerial openings.

Some guidelines to follow should you decide to work with a contingency recruiter or employment agency:

- *If you are interested in a particular job that the recruiter or agency has notified you of but* don't *want your resume being given to any and every other employer with a job opening, be clear at the outset.* Put *in writing* that you want to restrict the firm's actions to one particular search.

- *Don't decide to pull a fast one and pursue a job opening on your own once a recruiter has notified you of it.* Not only is this unethical, it is also usually a losing proposition. Once an opening is put up for recruiters, most employers don't pay attention to over-the-transom resumes.

- *If you're using an industry-specific recruiting firm, find out the names of the companies it usually works with, whether it has successfully placed other candidates with backgrounds similar to yours, the types of jobs it usually handles, etc.* You want a good fit between your needs and their experience.

- *Always remember that contingency recruiters and agencies usually don't have exclusives on any job openings.* If you're working with more than one recruiter or agency, your resume may end up being sent to the same prospective employer by different firms. Not the best impression. To avoid this, don't allow recruiters to send out your resume without first notifying you of the company and position. Then, if you know that one firm has already sent in your resume for consideration, you can be sure that no other firm also sends it.

- *If things don't seem to be working out—the job openings aren't right for you, you're not getting leads, and so on—simply dissolve the agreement* by notifying the firm that you no longer wish to be represented by them. Again, put it in writing to make your wishes perfectly clear.

- *Finally, be careful.* While they are a minority, there are unethical or fraudulent contingency firms and agencies. To be sure you're not getting taken for a ride, avoid any hard-sell tactics—recruiters who push for you to let them represent you or try to convince you to sign a contract with them immediately. If you do choose to be represented by a contingency firm or agency, read any contract you're given carefully. Be on the lookout for hidden costs (charges for resume services, counseling sessions, etc.). You're best off seeking this type of assistance, should you want it, elsewhere.

TIP: Be especially wary of agencies that charge an up-front or sign-on fee. These so-called employment agencies (often called advance-fee agencies) are less employment agencies than career services firms—and usually rather poor ones at that. Typically, you sign up with one of these "agencies," pay a fee (which can range from $1,500 to well over $25,000), then receive such things as computer print-outs of company names and addresses (often outdated—some even defunct), form cover letters, dubious resume services, and counseling from unqualified staffers. Tip-offs that you're dealing with this type of firm include pressure to sign a contract, required payment before they perform any services, excessive or glib guarantees such as unusually high placement success rates, and promises of employment in a short period of time—six weeks or the like. If you do fall into the hands of one of these agencies, write a letter of complaint to your state Office of Consumer Protection, outlining the situation. Also notify the U.S. Federal Trade Commission—Attn: Correspondence Division, 6th and Pennsylvania Ave., NW Washington, DC 20580.

▶ **The second type of search firm: Retainer search firms, while usually slower in landing you interviews and less prolific in terms of number of prospective openings you hear about through them, are often the better choice for over-40 job hunters.**

Retainer firms, as the name denotes, are paid a set retainer to find candidates for a client company. These firms are paid regardless of the success of their search. Their focus: finding the right person to fit the very specific needs of a company. Usually when people speak of recruiters or headhunters, they're thinking of retainer firms. This is the type of recruiter you'll typically come across in your job hunt, particularly if you're at the executive level. Retainer firms usually recruit people for middle- and upper-level executive positions, and (less often) senior technical positions, with salaries from $65,000 up.

What does this mean in terms of your job hunt? First of all, the process of learning about prospective job openings is slower, and the number of openings you are recommended for lower, than with a contingency firm. The reason is simple—there must be a perfect (or near-perfect) fit between your background and the qualifications cited by the company seeking an employee before you even get an interview. When contacted by a retainer firm, you have reason to be cautiously upbeat—because the firm has heard of a legitimate job opening for which you appear to fit the bill. On the downside: Because a retainer firm usually has a longstanding relationship with a number of companies, it can't solicit candidates from any of those companies. In other words, if your current employer uses a firm, that firm won't recommend you for jobs. Another negative—you won't be considered for more than one position at a time.

The best way to fit a retainer firm in your job hunt: Once you're contacted by a retainer search firm about a specific job, your best bet is to go along with the search. It costs you nothing; you probably can't contact the target company on your own (if they've already contracted—and paid—a search firm, chances are they don't want to see their money wasted and will look only at candidates referred by the firm); and more. *The bottom line?* If you are contacted by a retainer search firm about a position, it certainly can't hurt to pursue the opportunity. In addition, you may get recruiters interested enough in you that they'll contact you about future job openings, even if the first one doesn't work out.

Read on for tips and hints on how to work with recruiters when they contact you, and how to get them interested in you if they're *not* already calling. Because retainer search firms are the better choice for most over-40 job hunters, the following information concerns them rather than contingency firms. However, whenever appropriate, we've included information on dealing with contingency firms as well.

THE TWO DIFFERENT TYPES OF SEARCH FIRMS

Contingency Search Firms	Retainer Search Firms
Are paid on a commission basis—receive a fee only when their candidate is hired.	Are paid on a retainer basis—receive a fee regardless of the success of their candidates.
Handle lower- and mid-level managerial and technical jobs.	Usually handle upper-level jobs only.
Usually specialize in one or more industries.	Usually no industry specialization—but typically concentrate on managerial positions only.
Can recruit from any company.	Cannot seek candidates from companies they are contracted by.
Usually distribute your resume widely.	Recommend you only for jobs in which you match the employer's needs.

▶ **First, a quick rundown of the executive recruiting process.**

It's a simple and clear-cut process. The first step for recruiters is analyzing the client's needs and determining the qualifications that potential candidates should meet. Second, recruiters check their resume files, data bases, and the like for candidates that fit the profile. They may also check directories, call people for referrals, check the profiles of past candidates, etc. A typical search will result in over 75 potential candidates.

Next, recruiters contact this first pool of candidates to better determine how well each meets the client's criteria. Candidates who seem to fit the bill are usually invited for a screening interview, in which the recruiter decides whether or not each one would be right for the job. The candidates who seem most qualified are sent to meet with the client company; typically only three to five people reach this step. Each candidate usually first meets with the recruiter for general preparation and briefing—a discussion of the position, the company and its corporate culture, the candidate's background, interview questions to expect, and the like. After this, each candidate interviews at the prospective employer and is "debriefed" by the recruiter after the interview.

Pretty basic, right? Of course, the trick is being one of the people who is initially contacted by a recruiter. And this often requires a bit of work on your part.

▶ **There are a number of steps you can take to increase your chances of being noticed by recruiters.**

The best way of attracting the notice of an executive recruiter? Being employed. Right—it's somewhat of a catch-22, but it's a fact. If you're in a job similar to the ones that recruiters try to fill, they will see you as a prime prospect.

Given this, if you are currently employed, you should begin developing relationships with recruiters *before* you actively job hunt. Talk to recruiters who call you. Keep their names, numbers, and even a few notes about the positions they called you about in your Rolodex.

Some other tips:

- *Position yourself as an information source.* Again, this is a step to take before you're actively job hunting. Try to help the recruiters who call you by suggesting names of possible candidates, information about your industry or company, etc.

- *Join trade associations or other professional groups.* Recruiters often call associations for leads on prospective candidates—by being a member, you increase your chances of being referred to a recruiter. (A plus: Associations also offer great networking opportunities.)

TIP: If possible, become an officer in the association or in other organizations. This way, you're perceived as a leader, you automatically have a higher profile, and—most important—you set yourself up to be referred to recruiters. How? Often recruiters call up trade associations to get leads on potential candidates. If you're an officer of the group, people will automatically remember you. You're no longer just another face in the crowd.

- *Give yourself a higher profile*—by writing articles or books, giving lectures or seminars, getting involved in community activities, being interviewed for magazine or newspaper articles—anything that would make your name stand out and be picked up by a recruiter.

- *If you were contacted by recruiters in the past—when you weren't looking for a job—get back in touch with them now* and explain your changed situation. Chances are if they felt you were a potential candidate in the past, they may feel the same way now, and keep your resume on file should any opening that matches your background come up.

- *Contact colleagues or others who have worked with executive recruiters* —and ask them to suggest you when they're approached by recruiters for names of possible candidates.

▶ **Sometimes the direct approach is the best—contacting recruiters on your own.**

Face it. You can't keep waiting and hoping. At a certain point, you should take the matter into your own hands and try to solicit recruiters yourself.

The first step is choosing the recruiters you intend to approach. Some basic guidelines:

- *Get suggestions from friends and colleagues.* This can be the best source of information, as colleagues and friends who have worked with recruiters will give you an honest, objective assessment.

- *Check directories for names of recruiters.* These usually also give you their specialties, names of key personnel, and brief descriptions.

SOURCE: For listings of executive recruiters, check one of these two directories:

Directory of Executive Recruiters
Kennedy Publications
Templeton Road
Fitzwilliam, NH 03447
603-585-2200

This directory ($39.95 in 1992) is your best bet for a comprehensive listing of executive recruiters nationwide.

Membership Directory

Association of Executive Search Consultants
30 Rockefeller Plaza
New York, NY 10012
212-949-9556

This is a low-cost listing of the association's member firms (roughly 70), including their specialties, if any.

TIP: Many associations or industry directories include listings of recruiters that specialize in the industry.

- *Don't feel it's necessary to limit your letter-writing campaign to only one or two search firms.* Frankly, there's no need. Because retained search firms don't send your resume out to dozens of employers, you don't have to worry about oversaturating the market. Why not increase your chances of having a recruiter call you? Write to as many as you like.

- *Address your letter to the recruiter who handles your field.* To find out who that person is, just call the firm and ask. With smaller firms, you may wind up sending your letter and resume to the general manager; but with larger firms, it's always best to make your initial approach to the recruiter who handles the type of job openings you're interested in.

▶ **To contact recruiters on your own, write a basic cover letter—with certain alterations.**

Top executive recruiters receive over 10,000 unsolicited resumes a year. Clearly, you're up against a great deal of competition. The way to come out on top? Frankly, it takes some luck and good timing. For example, you happen to send in your letter at the same time that a recruiter is given a search assignment that fits your background.

But you can also make yourself more attractive to recruiters by putting together a strong letter and resume.

Generally, the rules that apply to a typical cover letter apply to a letter to a recruiter: It should emphasize your strongest points, demonstrate your abilities, and close with a quick summary and a request for a meeting.

There are, however, certain aspects of this letter that will differ: Most important, this letter should not be a hype-y teaser of a letter, enticing a recruiter to want to learn more about you. Instead it should clearly spell out your qualifications. Your goal is to show the recruiter that you have a strong background, one that may fit the criteria of the firm's clients.

Some guidelines:

- *Include everything a recruiter needs to know about you to eventually sell you to his or her clients.* Don't make recruiters work: Lay everything out clearly and concisely. Spell out why you are the type of candidate the firm could recommend to its clients. Be focused and thorough. Avoid catchy openings, clever phrases, and cutesy comments.

- *Be sure to include the following information:*
  —Your current employment status: Don't be concerned that the recruiter will contact your employer.
  —Your job objective: Be as specific as possible. Your resume probably doesn't make this clear, and it's important that the recruiter know where you want to be headed.
  —Your salary history and requirements: It's best to give this information so the recruiter can immediately see if you fit the parameters of the openings he or she is working on. At some point or another, you'll have to divulge this information, so why not at the outset?
  —Your willingness to relocate: This can be a big help in getting recruiters interested in you. Again, spell it out clearly, naming the regions in which you are willing to work.

- *Include anything you think might sell you*—remember, headhunters search for people who meet very specific criteria. Often your best chance of making a match with a job opening is by having the unique combination of skills and experience a company is looking for. Given this, mention fluency in a foreign language and other potentially salable skills in your letter.

- *Keep the letter's look basic*—absolutely no colored paper, untraditional typefaces, or unconventional mailing methods (in a tube, pizza box, etc.). You do want your letter to stand out from the thousands of others the firm receives, but this is the wrong way to stand out.

- *Include a resume if you're actively seeking work.* If you are contacting recruiters because you are unemployed, fear you may soon fall victim to a downsizing, or are otherwise involved in an active job hunt, always include a resume with your letter. It's a signal that you are eager to hear about suitable openings. If, on the other hand, you are content with your current job and are just testing the waters in case a dream job falls in your lap, then a resume isn't needed.

- *Once you've done your mailing to recruiters, sit back and wait.* By all means, do *not* call to follow up and try to sell yourself over the phone. You'll be contacted by the recruiter if there's an opening you fit. If there isn't, you gain nothing by trying to force your way into the recruiter's office.

- *If after a long time—four months or so—you've still heard nothing, try again.* Re-send your letter (updated to include any new projects you've worked on, new title you've received, etc.) and resume to the recruiters who haven't contacted you. Perhaps this time they'll have a position that matches your qualifications. By re-contacting recruiters under the pretext of giving them new information, you don't come across as pushy or desperate.

▶ **In some cases—usually if you're already employed—you'll get a phone call from an executive recruiter without having done anything.**

Obviously, this is the best situation you can hope for. You're sitting at your desk and out of the blue comes a call from a recruiter who has a job opening he or she thinks you'd be perfect for.

In this case, your chief concern should be the legitimacy of the call. If you're unfamiliar with the caller's firm, the first step to take is to determine whether it is a contingency or retainer firm. Simply ask—does the firm have an exclusive contract with the hiring company? If it doesn't, it's a contingency firm, and your best bet, as mentioned before, is to continue only if the recruiter has in mind a specific job at a specific *named* company. If it's a retainer firm, you're in luck. Proceed with (relative) confidence.

If you have any doubts at all, don't be afraid to ask questions.

Legitimate recruiters won't be put off. If you don't know the firm, ask *(tactfully)* about it: its specialties (if any), how long it has been in business, how it got your name, and so on.

TIP: **If you're still skeptical, tell the recruiter you'll call back and then check the firm out by calling the Association of Executive Search Consultants and seeing if it's a member, or by looking it up in the *Directory of Executive Recruiters* (available at most libraries). Once you're satisfied, you can proceed.**

▶ **Naturally, there is a right way and a wrong way to proceed when a recruiter contacts you, whether as a result of your efforts or in an unsolicited approach.**

Here's a quick rundown of what to expect and what to do when you're approached by a recruiter.

- *During the initial phone conversation, the recruiter will give you some general information on the position to gauge your interest.* Expect to learn what type of position it is, the title, general duties, etc. But don't be surprised if the recruiter doesn't mention the company name yet. Generally, you'll get only a thumbnail sketch of the client at this point—its industry, size, location, and so on.

TIP: **If you're busy, have a colleague in your office and can't speak freely, or for any other reason don't want to take the call, simply ask the recruiter if you can call back later. You'll make a better impression when you're relaxed.**

- *Ask questions if you want more information.* Don't be pushy or overly concerned about minor points, but do feel free to ask about salary if you'd like, or about other aspects of the position. But be careful not to seem too focused on the money, nor expect to get detailed information. You'll learn the details when and if you have a screening interview with the recruiter.

- An important point to keep in mind: *Just because a recruiter calls you doesn't mean you've made the cut of candidates that will be sent to the employer.* The battle's not over once you're contacted. The recruiter is fishing to discover whether you actually have the qualifications for the job opening or not. Unfortunately, if you don't, there's not much you can do about it. If the recruiter doesn't think you meet his client's needs, don't waste time trying to convince him.

- *Expect to be asked a number of general questions to determine if you're right for the position.* Questions about your background, your current job, past successes and achievements, even your salary, are designed to help the recruiter decide whether you fit the needs of the client.

- If the recruiter thinks you may be right for the position after the first telephone call, *expect to be invited for a screening interview.* An hour to an hour and a half is a typical length of time that you will spend chatting with the recruiter. But always remember— this really is a *job interview.* The recruiter is representing the company.

TIP: When invited for an interview, bring along a copy of your resume even if you've already sent one to the recruiter. Recruiters often misplace resumes. It's best to be prepared.

- *During your interview with a recruiter, be prepared to sell yourself as you would in a regular job interview.* A quick rundown of interview dos and don'ts: **Do** be ready to sell yourself by telling the recruiter about specific accomplishments from your past employment history. **Do** back up every claim on your resume—or in your conversation—with examples of actual achievements. **Don't** bad-mouth your current employer or any previous one. **Do** dress conservatively, show up on time, and generally make the best impression you can. (For more detailed tips, see "Interviewing," page 194.)

- *Ask questions during your interview.* This is a great way to demonstrate your interest in the position or client. Most recruiters say this is something they're impressed by—it shows both your enthusiasm and your desire to succeed. Moreover, it adds to your knowledge about the prospective position, which will enable you to sell yourself better if and when you meet the prospective employer. Ask about the corporate culture, where the company is headed, financial information, or anything that will help you decide whether you're interested. Always find out why there is a job opening—was the previous person laid off? Fired? Promoted?

- *Without appearing mercenary or pushy, be candid about your require-ments for a job,* from compensation to responsibilities. This infor-mation will help the recruiter determine whether you're suitable for the opening. Remember, in the long run you gain nothing by withholding information.

- *Be aware of certain characteristics that executive recruiters look for in a potential candidate.* Among the qualities most recruiters said they look for (in a December 1991 survey cited in *HR Magazine*) are professionalism; good manners; good verbal and written com-munications skills; the ability to follow through; punctuality; prompt returning of phone calls; being well prepared. As for the automatic turnoffs: being pushy, not listening well, inflexi-bility, and, most important, too great a focus on money and too little on the position itself.

- *After interviewing with a recruiter, you don't have to follow up as you would with an employer.* In other words, don't send a meaningless "Thanks so much for taking the time to meet with me" letter. You'll come off as desperate, and not much else. Write a letter only if you want to add something about your background that wasn't covered in the meeting.

- *If the recruiter decides you're right for the opening, you'll go on to interview with the prospective employer.* During this next phase of the search, you'll move on to interviews at the company that is looking to hire someone. The recruiter will brief you before you're interviewed—then it's up to you to sell yourself during the interview. If all goes well, the client will notify the recruiter that you're being considered for the job.

- *Don't be blinded by flattery or relief that you're being considered for a position.* Yes, it's great if you make the first cut. But if the job doesn't seem right for you, you may be better off telling the recruiter to drop you from the search. Remember—the re-cruiter won't recommend you for another position while you're in the running for one job opening. By dropping out of con-tention for a job that doesn't really interest you, you're freeing yourself up in case a better opening comes along. This will also be more fair to the recruiter—he or she won't waste valuable time presenting you to a client whose job you're actually not considering.

- *If you don't hear from the recruiter after you've interviewed with the client, feel free to call back after a few days have passed.* It won't hurt to restate your genuine interest in the job and find out, if possible, what the status of the search is. Is the company interviewing more people? You may still be up for the position; it may just be a matter of time.

- *If the company doesn't turn out to be interested in you, try to maintain ties with the recruiter.* Other positions may open up that you'd be perfect for. Now that you have established a relationship with the recruiter, keep it strong. Your best bet? Being an information source for the recruiter. Refer him or her to other potential candidates.

SOURCE: The preceding section is a brief overview of executive recruitment. For an in-depth discussion of how to get a recruiter interested in you, how they work, how best to work with them, etc., one book is highly recommended: ***How to Get a Headhunter to Call*** by Howard S. Freeman (New York: Wiley, 1986, 1989). This $12.95 paperback offers a wealth of valuable information about the entire executive recruitment process.

ON-LINE CAREER SERVICES: COMPUTER JOB SEARCHES

▶ **A more recent tactic: going on-line for job leads.**

The jury is still out whether going on-line works. But at certain points in your job hunt, you can't afford to close off any possible avenue, and may want to consider using your computer to try to nail down a job opportunity.

Here's how it works: There are two basic types of computerized job databanks, both of which operate on very simple premises. Most commonly used by job hunters are resume banks; the major database vendors (Prodigy, DIALOG, CompuServe, etc.) offer this service, as do other companies. A resume bank is a collection of resumes sent or modemed in by job seekers. Once you know the procedure, all you have to do is send your resume via modem to the resume bank. Companies and executive recruiters that subscribe to the resume listing service key in the criteria for positions they need to fill. If you meet the criteria, your resume is called up—and you may be called in for an interview.

The second type of job databank lists job openings. These tend to be more specialized, often focusing on high-tech careers. Again, some of the major computer on-line service companies offer these, as do career sections of libraries, college placement offices (which often allow alumni access to their computer services), etc.

For listings of the major on-line service companies (that is, companies that will provide you with access to numerous databases), see pages 57–59.

Some of the leading computer databases:

SOURCE: **Adnet Online,** 5987 E. Seventy-first St., Suite 206, Indianapolis, IN 46220. Tel.: 317-579-6922, 800-682-2901. Includes resumes of approximately 1.5 million professional managerial and technical candidates nationwide; available on PRODIGY.

SOURCE: **Career Network,** 640 N. LaSalle, Suite 560, Chicago, IL 60610. Tel.: 800-229-6499. Offers electronic messaging and bulletin board, which provides information on job fairs, employment opportunities, trends, etc.; Online Job Listing Service, on which employers list job openings; and corporate profiles. An Online Subscription gives you daily access to these services for three months for a one-time fee ($50 in 1992). A Candidate Print Subscription gives you two months of the Alumni Career Network newsletter, which contains job listings ($25 in 1992). Available on PRODIGY.

SOURCE: **Career Placement Registry (CPR).** Tel.: 800-338-3282. Offers two resume banks, one for recent college graduates, the other (CPR/Experienced Personnel) consisting of executives and other professionals with substantial work experience. Accessed by recruiters via DIALOG.

SOURCE: **Connexion.** Tel.: 800-338-3282. An international job-listing database, with listings at all levels and in most fields; accessible via CompuServe.

SOURCE: **Corporate Jobs Outlook!** Tel.: 800-325-8808. On-line text of the newsletter with the same name; covers job opportunities at 500 corporations, including information on salary and benefits, corporate forecasts, industry outlooks, and more. Available on NewsNet and HRIN.

SOURCE: **HRIN: Human Resources Information Network.** Tel.: 800-421-8884. Designed for recruiters and human resources personnel. Includes a general resume database, as well as banks of minority college graduates, military departees, college grads, etc. Also includes a job description database.

SOURCE: Job Market, Inc. Tel.: 801-484-3808. Wide variety of listings.

SOURCE: JobNET. Electronic bulletin board, wide variety of listings and industries; some detailed descriptions of positions and corporate profiles. JobNET has also begun, via cable TV, a series of interactive videos with job descriptions and more.

SOURCE: Prodigy, Prodigy Services Company, 445 Hamilton Ave., White Plains, NY 10601. Tel.: 914-993-8000. Lists Adnet (see above) as well as want ads from *USA Today* and the *National Business Employment Weekly.*

SOURCE: ROC: Resumes on Computer, The Curtis Publishing Company, 1000 Waterway Blvd., Indianapolis, IN 46202. Tel.: 317-636-1000.

SOURCE: Career Expo. Tel.: 513-721-3030. Open-house recruitment; call for locations and details.

SOURCE: Job Bank USA. Tel.: 800-296-1USA. Resume bank covering all business levels.

INTERIM MANAGEMENT: EXECUTIVE TEMPING AND HOW IT WORKS AS A BACK DOOR METHOD TO LANDING AN INTERVIEW

▶ **Executive temping (also called interim management and contract employment) is receiving more and more attention lately.**

It's an employment area that has been growing over the past few years, as companies seek new ways of streamlining and cost cutting. The premise is as obvious as it sounds: Just as companies in the past hired lower-level temporary workers to fill short-term needs, now they are also contracting upper-level temps. Common users of temporary executives include start-up operations that need to staff up quickly, small companies that need high-level assistance but can't afford the long-term cost of adding permanent staff, companies involved in special short-term projects (such as new product or services development) who need employees for the duration of the project only, and companies in need of a stop-gap manager while conducting a search for a permanent employee.

▶ **Temporary work for a company sometimes leads to full-time employment, but it would be unwise to get your hopes up.**

The honest truth: No matter what anyone says, temping your way to a full-time job isn't all that common. According to recent studies, at the most roughly 25% of temporary executives wind up converting a temporary position into a permanent one.

TIP: **To maximize your chances of turning a temporary job into a permanent one, maintain a high profile and let people know that you would consider a permanent job. Although you might be the perfect person for a position, the people who have hired you will consider you only a temporary worker if you let them. Only if you make it clear that you're available on a permanent basis will they see you in a different light.**

Typically, when a company hires a temporary worker, it wants a temporary worker. Its needs won't change just because you prove to be a superior employee.

But that doesn't mean you should write temping off. Aside from the slim chance that a temporary job might develop into a permanent one, there are a number of other good uses of temping in your job hunt.

- *Temping allows you to keep adding to your skills and experience while otherwise unemployed.* Temping can keep you abreast of developments in your field, and help you keep your skills on the cutting edge. In addition, temporary assignments included on your resume help you present yourself as a still-active individual with recent experience. If you're changing careers, accepting temporary assignments in your new career gives you a stronger background and helps you show prospective employers that you are qualified in the new field.

- *If you've recently been fired, taking on temporary assignments can be an ego booster as well as a financial stopgap.* By working as a temp, you keep your cash flow up and, more important, your spirits up. It's a way of maintaining those routines—dressing like a professional, going to an office, chatting with co-workers, etc.—that keep you going.

- *Doing short-term work at a company may give you a leg up on learning about permanent positions that open up.* You may learn about an opening before it's publicly broadcast, and get a jump on other candidates. To this end, it's important to keep your eyes and ears open, listen to office gossip, and watch for any tip-offs that a position may be opening.

- *You can learn inside information about a company (or industry) that will add to your salability.* You can use temping as an opportunity to scout out a company or industry, learn about a corporate culture, and keep abreast of industry developments (which you can later use to determine a job objective). In this case, keep your eyes and ears open to learn as much as possible. The information you gather can be used to help you position yourself in letters, target a direct-mail campaign, and network more effectively. Important to keep in mind—often the information you gather can help sell you to that company's *competitor.*

- *Temping enables you to increase your network of contacts—who may eventually lead you to a job.* This is an important benefit of doing temp work that many people fail to recognize. Remember—the permanent managers at the companies for which you temp can become helpful referrals. They've had an opportunity to see you in action.

▶ **The simplest way to get temporary jobs is the obvious way: by contacting an executive temping agency.**

As of early 1992, there were about 70 firms focused on placing executives in temporary positions. In addition, several large general temporary firms (such as Kelly Services, Inc. and Manpower International) have established programs handling higher-level temporaries. Some firms are industry specific, specializing in areas such as law and health care. Others are function specific, placing accountants or human resources workers, for example. Still others simply specialize in upper-level employees, regardless of field.

SOURCE: For a low-cost (only $10 in 1992) list of executive temp firms, contact *Executive Recruiter News,* at 800-531-0007.

While the process varies somewhat from firm to firm, you can expect to fill out an application detailing your employment history, skills, and so forth. This becomes part of the temp agency's database. Depending upon the particular agency, you may interview with one of their placement specialists at the outset, or (more commonly) you will be interviewed only when an opening that you seem to match comes up.

You can also get temp or contract work assignments on your own by directly contacting companies that could use your services, though this is less commonly done. Generally, it makes sense only if you already have a relationship with a company or its executives.

Some general tips on how to proceed as an executive temp:

- *In-depth experience and a strong track record are a must.* To even be considered at most executive temp agencies, you need a minimum of 10 (although many require 15) years of experience in your field. A clean work record, a history of achievement, and strong skills finish up the package that agencies seek. Just like executive recruiters, they're looking for people with skills that meet the very specific needs of their clients.

TIP: **An asset when trying to land temp assignments: a willingness to relocate for the duration of the assignment.**

- *Typically, when you are hired for a temp assignment, your contract will specify the length of time your assignment will last and the salary you'll receive for that period.* If you're working through an agency, it will negotiate the terms of the contract. An average length of time for an assignment is about six to ten months, though it can be much shorter (a month) or longer (two to three years). Salaries are similarly variable. Often, you'll receive more as a contract worker than the permanent counterpart would—about one and a half times the standard salary. But it's important to remember that the majority of contract workers do not receive benefits.

- *Though most of you will use temping as (appropriately) a temporary measure, remember that it can also be a permanent career.* Many older job hunters (particularly retirees) become career temporaries, taking on successive temporary assignments rather than looking for one permanent position. Keep in mind, though, the downside: While the flexibility of accepting different assignments may be nice, the uncertainty of your work schedule could cause problems. *The bottom line?* If you need stability or financial security, opt for a permanent job.

PART-TIME, CONSULTING, AND VOLUNTEER WORK: A QUICK LOOK AT HOW YOU CAN USE THESE FORMS OF WORK AS A JOB-HUNTING TACTIC

▶ **Part-time jobs, like temporary or contract jobs, are another option to consider as a job-hunting tactic while you're looking for full-time employment.**

Again, this is not a foolproof method of landing a job. You may be able to "grow" your part-time job into a full-time one. But, frankly, it isn't easy. The problem? Most companies that hire part-time employees do so because they *need* part-time employees.

Of course, there are exceptions to the rule; some companies bring people on as part-timers, then—when business improves or they otherwise develop a need for more help—change the job to a full-time one, or move part-timers into full-time positions.

It all depends, as you would guess, on the availability of full-time positions and the general profitability of the company. In tough economic times, the number of part-timers that companies employ usually increases. Moreover, certain kinds of companies and organizations tend to hire more part-timers, including nonprofit organizations, high-tech companies, government (municipal, state, and federal) agencies and departments, and small or start-up businesses.

The rules of thumb when trying to grow your part-time job into a full-time one are similar to those for temping: Express your desire for full-time work; take on extra assignments or projects; broadcast your availability and your skills; keep aware of positions that will be opening up by following company gossip and looking for trends.

Also, as with temp work, a part-time job can help your job hunt in other ways. You may learn about full-time opportunities at a company, gain insights that will help you sell yourself to that company or to a competitor, can meet valuable new colleagues, and can get the inside track to a full-time position.

But there are also a number of negatives to keep in mind: Salaries are often low; and a part-time schedule can cut deeply into time you need to hunt for a full-time job.

The bottom line? Part-time work is a viable option for people who genuinely *want* part-time work—typically retirees, those who need the money, or those who are trying to maintain a relationship with a current employer who would otherwise fire or lay them off. As a job-hunting tactic, however, you may be better off spending the time on a direct-mail campaign than at a part-time job.

▶ **Consulting, while time-consuming, often** *does* **lead to job offers.**

Even so, let's begin with the negatives: The most important one —to successfully turn consulting work into a full-time job, you must first succeed at consulting. A truism? Maybe, but it's important to understand. Consulting is no breeze: It's time-consuming, requires the right frame of mind and certain skills, and more.

For these reasons, unless you can meet the taxing demands of self-employment or have a genuine desire to be self-employed, consulting may be not only a dead end but a real detriment to your job hunt.

However, there is a positive side to consulting *if* you have the skills and wherewithal. The key advantage, of course, is the point mentioned above—that consulting work can and often does lead to regular employment. The reasons? As a consultant, you're hired to fulfill a particular need at a company, whether overseeing a project or analyzing operations. This gives you a bird's-eye view from which you can spot any potential need you could fill as a *full-time employee,* and puts you in a position to present this needs-payoff situation to the prospective employer.

In addition, consulting provides you with many of the same assets as temporary work or part-time work.

- *You'll hear about openings more readily because you're right there.*

- *You have a good opportunity to impress the potential employer with your abilities and energy.*

- *You can get inside information about a company, its competitors, or the industry at large,* and use it in a targeted direct-mail campaign or in other parts of your job hunt.

- *You automatically expand your network of contacts*—any of whom may tip you off to a hot job lead.

For a closer look at consulting, see the section on self-employment options, beginning on page 299.

▶ **Finally, some older job hunters (particularly retirees) turn to volunteering—and some of them convert this work into paid positions.**

Like temping, volunteer work allows you to:

- *Become known and liked by a company*—which may eventually have a regular job opening.

- *Develop more skills to put on your resume* (especially valuable if you have been unemployed for a long period of time).

- *Learn more about a company or an industry* (helpful for career changers or in targeting your job campaign more precisely).

You have two options when it comes to volunteering: going through an established group (three of the best known are listed below) or going solo and volunteering your services to a business you know.

It's often simpler to go through a large group. The organization selects your assignment, often covers your expenses, and so forth. However, when it comes to developing a job lead, you may be better off going it alone.

SOURCE: **International Executive Service Corps (IESC),** PO Box 1005, Stamford, CT 06904. Tel.: 203-967-6000. As volunteers for this group, which has an international focus, over 9,000 executives and managers consult on projects in more than 90 developing countries. Volunteers go abroad to do on-site consulting on projects that generally last from three to five months. IESC picks up living and travel expenses.

SOURCE: **National Executive Search Corps (NESC),** 257 Park Avenue South, New York, NY 10010. Tel.: 212-529-6660. Volunteers for this group consult for non-profit organizations in such areas as fund-raising, marketing, and planning.

SOURCE: **Service Corps of Retired Executives (SCORE),** 1825 Connecticut Ave. NW, Suite 503, Washington, DC 20009. Tel.: 202-653-6279. As the name suggests, this group is for retired executives who want to keep a hand in business. SCORE volunteers counsel small-business owners in various areas. With a Small Business Administration program, SCORE has 387 chapters nationwide—look in your local telephone directory or check with the national headquarters listed above.

7

INTERVIEWING

INTRODUCTION

▶ **Interviewing skills are critical: you can get a job without a resume, but you won't get one without a successful interview.**

Interviews are particularly important now that you're past 40. You're not a kid anymore, you won't be excused for as many mistakes, and the odds are you're facing more competitors than ever before. *Key problem:* It may have been years since you've conducted a job hunt; you may be rusty.

▶ **Interviewing well is a skill that can be learned at any age.**

Some people are natural interviewees—they have an inborn talent for saying the right thing. But if you're qualified for a job, there's no reason why you can't beat the naturals at their own game.

Studies of interviewing techniques show that there are a few things "naturals" do right more consistently than everyone else. And so they get more job offers. This section tells you what those correct techniques are, and how you can integrate them into your own interviews.

GENERAL GUIDELINES

▶ **This chapter goes into detail on how to interview well. But before all that—remember two essentials:**

1. *What's a successful interview? One that ends in a job offer.*
Keep that in mind always: *The basic goal of your job interview is to get a job offer.* Obvious—but under the stress of an interview many forget this. Each of us is a grab-bag of various motivations, personality traits, and emotional needs—all of which gives us different basic goals. Some of us need to be liked, some want to be respected, others want to be understood. At any time, any of these goals can conflict with what should be your primary goal: getting hired.

EXAMPLE: **An unsuccessful applicant we counseled had everything it took to get a job— except for his bad habit of showing interviewers his intelligence by correcting their mistakes. He was usually right, but so what? He ended up subordinating his primary goal of getting a job to his goal of appearing intelligent.**

Such tendencies are not necessarily conscious, but you can and should strive to eradicate them. How? By always keeping in mind throughout your interviews the principal goal of being hired. Always ask yourself: *Is what I'm saying or doing helping me get the job?*
By focusing your mind on this goal, you're halfway to a strong interviewing style already.

2. *Behind every question, no matter what he or she is asking, an interviewer is trying to find out the answers to two basic questions.*
Don't get bogged down in the specifics of an interview question or situation. Whether an interviewer is questioning your reasons for leaving your last job or asking you how you managed your team during a sales drive, he or she is really asking:

1. *Can you do our job better than the other applicants?*

2. *Are you one of us?*

The essence of good interviewing is to answer these questions in everything you say or do during an interview. The rest of this chapter explains how.

BEFORE THE INTERVIEW

Planning and Research

▶ **Don't underestimate pre-interview planning.**

Studies show that the best interviewees are the best prepared. They're less apt to be surprised by tricky or unexpected questions during an interview and more likely to come up with ways of linking themselves to the job at hand. In addition, they're more *confident*.

Good preparation means good research, good timing, practice and some hard work.

▶ **When setting an interview date: timing isn't everything, but good timing helps.**

You don't always have a choice, but if you can, follow these rules of thumb when setting your interview date.

- *Schedule your least important interviews first.* This gives you good practice for the important ones later.

- *Don't be the first person interviewed for a position.* Surveys show that interviewers are more likely to hire applicants they've seen later. If you're given a choice, pick a later date.

- *Schedule interviews in the middle of the week, in the morning or early in the afternoon.* If you can, avoid Mondays and late afternoons, when interviewers are too busy or too tired to be as interested in you as they should be.

▶ **Research the company, the position, the industry, and the interviewers.**

It shouldn't have to be said. But those over 40 or 45 are often just as bad at researching as younger job hunters—and it shows during interviews.

Research is particularly important now that you're older. You're selling hard-won experience and knowledge—you can't sell yourself as a malleable but ignorant youth. If you don't know the position, the industry, the company, and what it takes to do the job superlatively, what advantage can you have over competitors?

▶ **Your pre-interview research goals are to *anticipate* the interview—what they'll ask, what you'll say.**

As you research, jot down questions to ask during the interview —questions that reveal your knowledge of the company and your ability to do the job.

More important, during your research jot down questions the interviewer may ask you and qualities he or she may be looking for.

EXAMPLE: **Your research shows the company is just beginning to emphasize export sales to Korea. You will be ready to highlight any (even minor) Far Eastern export or business experience you have.**

And remember, research can give you a vital "feel" for the corporate culture of the company—a valuable edge during an interview.

▶ **Start researching by focusing on employees within the target company.**

Even during the phone call inviting you to an interview, you should strive to get as much information as you can about the company and the position. What to find out:

- *Major responsibilities of the position*

- *Why there is an opening*

- *The job's location within the company structure* (number and titles of supervisors and subordinates)

- *What skills the company is looking for*

- *Who will interview you* (the president, human resources, both, etc.)

Particularly if the person calling you is a line officer, by chatting briefly about the company you may get an idea of current campaigns and problems, and a sense of what skills it's looking for. *Avoid annoying the caller,* but anything you can obtain may be extremely helpful.

Key problem: Many corporations and interviewers don't want you to have too much information—they're afraid you'll do what you should do, which is to tailor yourself as the perfect candidate.

Solution: Do a little snooping. Call anyone you know within the company or the industry and ask about the position, the corporate culture, company plans, and your own ideas. Talk with competitors, customers, anyone who knows the company. Again, don't be overly pushy—you want these people to be on your side—but any inside information you can get will give you an edge over less persistent competitors for the job.

TIP: **Often, the younger the employee within the target company, the better the information you will obtain. Younger employees tend to be less reticent, more inexperienced in knowing what to say and what not to say. Cultivate lower-level or younger contacts.**

▶ **Go back over your library research.**

Now is when your library research pays off. (For more on how to research effectively, see Chapter 2.) Reread your research notes with an eye to your upcoming interview.

Key: Now that you know something of the position, see if you need to fill in the gaps in your knowledge.

▶ **Once you have a strong idea of what the company is like and what the position entails, jot down a brief selling paper on why you're the person for the job.**

Analyze your background in relation to the position and what you think the company is looking for. Look for key selling points—and points that may disqualify you. Ask yourself:

• *Do I really fit?* If you see potential problems, *now* is the time to find ways around them.

- *What are my key selling points for this job?* Think about the skills that will sell you best, and ways of presenting them. Think of problems the company has and why you could solve them.

- *What are my key weaknesses?* How do I downplay them?

- *Is there anything I've forgotten that might be useful?* Put everything together in a few paragraphs, and practice going over your background and key selling points in a ten-minute summation.

▶ **Think about or even jot down the questions you think will probably be asked—and work on effective answers.**

Read pages 222–37 for our listing of typical interview questions, and note the most likely of these, as well as questions you've determined through your own research. Then start planning how you'll answer them. Read pages 222–37 for our suggestions, but formulate your *own* answers in your own words.

The best method: use a single note card for each question; write down the question, then mentally answer it. As you do so, jot down key words or ideas. Don't write out, and don't memorize, entire texts —just a few key words and concepts that will spark a spontaneous-sounding answer to each question.

▶ **Rehearse so that you can cover *all* your major selling points.**

But *don't* memorize a fixed speech and lose your flexibility and naturalness. Nothing is as bad as a canned interview spiel.

As you practice, flip through the note cards until you no longer need them and are able to answer each question succinctly and effectively. Remember, keep it brief—about a minute or two for each answer. *A good method:* have a friend or your spouse act as the interviewer.

Now go back and think out every reason why you should get this job. Check to make certain every reason you come up with is covered in a question and an answer.

That's it. The heart of a prepared, strong interviewing style. You should have an answer to virtually everything you'll be asked.

TIP: Videotape practice interviews, with a spouse or friend playing the interviewer. Analyze your mistakes and strong points, and do it once more. Warning: Do this only if you're the type who doesn't cringe when you hear a tape recording of yourself; you may undermine your natural confidence.

TIP: Take the note cards with you on your interview. You can go over your major points beforehand or between interviews.

▶ **Don't forget to reread your resume and analyze ways to defend it or strengthen it during the interview.**

Do you really *know* what's on your resume? Many job hunters fail to reread it carefully once they've written it. Remember: You probably wrote it *before* you knew much about the company where you'll be interviewing. Now is the time to analyze it in light of your new knowledge about the company—and to think about how an interviewer might use it.

If you spot holes or potential problems, prepare now to explain them during the interview.

▶ **After every interview, analyze your successes and weaknesses.**

Learn from your mistakes. Studies have shown that applicants who analyze their mistakes become better interviewers. Ask yourself how you can improve upon what you did for the next time. And then practice again.

Mental Preparation

▶ **Work on developing a confident interviewing style.**

Confidence is contagious. Interviewers like—and are much more apt to hire—applicants who appear sure of themselves. But confidence can be hard to conjure up, especially if you're over 40 and out of work. Here are a few ideas and tricks from those who've had the same experience. *The key idea:* creating new habits. Instead of fear, you focus on something else.

- *Don't think beyond the interview.* Don't worry about what will happen next; keep your mind on the interview itself.

- *Stop yourself from thinking "what if."* When you start thinking things like "What if I can't answer that correctly," recognize the "what if" pattern, stop, and think of something positive and concrete—such as which facts will best answer the question.

- *Try an old sales technique—count rejections.* It can be tough after 15 —or 50—interviews with no call-backs. To take the sting out, find out how many rejections others in the same boat have had (or just pick a high number), and set this number as a long-term goal of rejections you must collect before you can get a job. Think of each "no" as getting you closer to that ultimate "yes."

- *See each interview as a learning experience.* People learn best from failure—or so virtually every successful person has said. Think of each interview as the ultimate MBA—you're learning, the street-wise way, what it takes to get a job.

- *The next one could be the one.* This is a good habit to get into— remember that the very next interview could be *the* most successful interview of your life.

▶ *Visualize* **your performance during the interview** *before* **the interview.**

Various studies have found that successful interviewers (as well as successful speakers, executives, actors, etc.) frequently use mental imagery. Constantly visualizing yourself as a success tends to be a self-fulfilling prophecy.

What to do: In your free time, imagine yourself going to the interview, greeting the interviewer, answering and asking questions confidently and effectively. For nervous interviewers, here's a more formal way of visualizing:

- *Breathe deeply,* eyes closed, until you feel relaxed.

- With your eyes still closed, *picture the day of the interview,* beginning with waking up and on through going to the interviewer's company.

- *Picture yourself greeting the interviewer confidently*—take pride in your calm and cool introduction to the interviewer.

- *Now picture yourself answering questions effectively.* Go through each question, each answer in your head. Notice how the interviewer is reacting positively to your replies.

- *Close the interview;* watch the interviewer express interest in seeing you again.

- *Open your eyes.*

- *Repeat this exercise* several times a week.

Other Preparations

▶ **Make certain you've got the right clothes for the interview well before the date approaches.**

The key idea: Wear neutral clothing in keeping with the position and the company.

Don't slavishly follow narrow rules from job books. Yes, for most jobs a dark blue pinstriped suit for men is just right. But it may be out of place for a position as a "creative" at an ad agency—and may pinpoint you as not "one of us." Only *you* know—or can find out—the standard dress in your industry or target company.

But these rules generally hold:

- *Dress so that the interviewer will focus on your qualifications, not your clothes.* This means no ornate jewelry, sloppiness, boyish or girlish clothing, low-cut necklines, bow ties, etc.

- *Err on the side of conservatism.* It's better to be a little dull than a little flashy. Even if the company is on the cutting edge in the arts or fashion, employees often dress more conservatively.

- *Always double-check yourself with a critical eye before going on an interview.* Trained interviewers will spot, for example, scuffed shoes, and question your attention to detail.

TIP: **Particularly if you've been laid off recently, make sure your suits fit well. It's common during the stress of unemployment to eat more and gain weight, especially if you're over 40. Even a small weight gain (one you might not even notice) will show when you put on your suit. And even a slightly tight suit looks sloppy and unprosperous, and can be a turnoff to employers.**

A few general tips on how to age-proof your appearance:

- *Don't dress too youthfully.* Paradoxically, overly youthful clothing highlights your age.

- *Soft colors around the face tend to ease the look of wrinkles and lines.*

- *If you use hair dye, make certain that it looks natural.* Get a second, *honest* opinion. Overly dark hair dye telegraphs a message: I've got gray hair underneath.

- *A slight bronze tint to the face makes you look younger.* If you're concerned about skin damage from the sun, use a little bronzer, but blend well.

▶ **Do a dry run to the target company a few days before the interview.**

You know the feeling—that mad dash, half an hour late, only to find a street closed or a wrong address. The only way out: Go there a day early, and *anticipate* any problems with parking, transportation, etc. For out-of-town appointments, get to the hotel early enough to take a cab to the target company and scout it out. Then go back to the hotel. You'll get to bed earlier, and wake up rested and alert the next day.

Just Before the Interview

▶ **Pack your briefcase with extra resumes and appropriate reading material.**

Bring the *Wall Street Journal* or, better yet, a trade journal for the industry. While you're waiting for the interview, you may chance upon something timely and useful. Also bring:

- *A current list of references* (names, addresses, phone numbers). Don't offer them—but if you're asked, you'll be ready.

- *Any selling "props"* (special plans or programs you've drawn up, spec work, etc.).

▶ **Arrive early.**

Allow for the unforeseen: Leave for the interview an hour early. You can always spend half an hour in a coffee shop. Get to the interviewer's office a few minutes before the appointment.

▶ **Be pleasant to secretaries and receptionists.**

It's common courtesy. But more importantly for your purpose: you also don't know the power structure in your target corporation —and some secretaries are very important. Many job hunters have failed to get a job because a trusted secretary nixed them. In the interviewer's mind: *If you can't be pleasant to my secretary, how will you be with customers?*

TIP: Be friendly, but be careful not to be patronizing or a pest. The overbearingly friendly applicant has become a new cliché.

▶ **Watch out for application forms.**

It's the newest trick—asking you to fill out an application form for "insurance purposes" or some other reason. Often, the *real reason* is to find out the truth about your age, health, marital status, or other details you may not wish to reveal during an interview. Or, more legitimately, to fill in the gaps that your resume may disguise. Giving the "wrong" answers may disqualify you before you have a chance to sell yourself.

Best strategy: Look the form over quickly and spot any illegal questions (see page 297). Complete it, putting a dash or N/A in the illegal areas, or ask if you can finish it *after* the interview or the next day. If certain gaps in your employment history show up on the application form, be ready for questions about them during the interview.

DURING THE INTERVIEW

Nonverbal Interviewing

▶ **There are two parts to a job interview—the first one to five minutes and the rest of the interview.**

First impressions count.

In the first four minutes of your interview, according to *Personnel Journal,* virtually 100% of an interviewer's impressions of you are based on nonverbal cues—how you look, how you dress, your demeanor, your perceived age.

These first impressions have a way of sticking. Of course, a good interviewer tries to go beyond a quick first impression—but all too often, during the rest of the interview, he or she is merely adding support to that first impression.

EXAMPLE: **You arrive in scuffed shoes and a rumpled suit. The interviewer mentally pegs you as a slob. All the creative brilliance that you demonstrate so effectively during the interview is interpreted by the interviewer as just another example of what an undisciplined slob you are.**

First impressions are particularly important for older candidates, who might be immediately pegged as "too old," and for upper executive levels and in sales or customer relations positions. But no one gets off scot free. Stories abound of job candidates failing at interviews because their socks didn't cover their calves when they sat, because they looked sloppy, because they had a breezy way of greeting the interviewer, or because they seemed unusually nervous.

Trivial reasons, but reasons you must face and learn from. *This is why you must strive to make the best possible first impression, particularly as you get older.* You may be able to counteract a bad first impression —but it's much, much easier to start off on the right foot.

▶ *Key concept:* **You want to be perceived as an energetic, interesting,** *youthful* **professional.**

Act as you would if you've just been introduced to someone at a party—someone you've never met before, but whom you respect and have wanted to meet. You'd be alert but not anxious, friendly but not cloying, happy but not elated, and confident.

Key: an outgoing, energetic attitude telegraphs youth and vigor.

▶ **Here are the best tips gleaned from experienced job hunters and interviewers on how to create a positive first impression.**

- *Greet the interviewer with a firm (but not bone-crunching), dry hand-shake.* If your hands have a tendency to sweat, arrive early enough to go to the restroom and run hot water over them until they are hot. Then dry them completely. They should remain dry long enough, but just in case, keep a tissue handy to dry them with. Or spritz them with a small sprayer of antiperspirant. When shaking hands, don't pump the interviewer's hand up and down.

- *Smile.* A light smile is psychologically disarming, and sets the tone of the interview as friendly, not adverserial.

- *Maintain a pleasant, strong tone of voice.* This is easy for some, hard for more nervous types. A good idea: Talk with people (a newsstand salesperson, the secretary, etc.) just before your interview to relax your vocal cords.

- *Maintain eye contact.* This doesn't mean staring at the interviewer's eyes, but looking at his or her face, not at the floor. Try focusing on the bridge of the interviewer's nose, which some psychological studies have found to be effective.

- *Make some humanizing opening comment.* You want to establish yourself as a warm *human being* rather than an applicant. Plus, by opening with a pleasant comment, *you* show authority. If it's raining, talk about the rain; if the company has just relocated to a new, plush office, talk about that; if you're here from somewhere else, mention something positive about the town.

  Don't go on and on, unless it is obvious the interviewer wishes to do so. Studies show that normal early interview chit-chat lasts less than five minutes.

- *When offered a seat, try to avoid a sofa, and try to position yourself to the interviewer's left (unless it's clear he's left-handed).* You'll sink awkwardly into a sofa. And if you keep to an interviewer's left, according to some studies, he or she will perceive you more favorably.

▶ **The first minutes are over. Before we get to the meat and potatoes of interviewing, however, consider these tips, based on the latest research, on how to project a confident image during your interview.**

Key point: As you get older, you must project calm but energetic self-confidence to overcome any conscious or subconscious age prejudices on the part of the interviewer. You're not a loser, you're not old, you're not desperate or anxious. You're just more experienced and vital.

But remember: These are just tips. Don't interfere with your own style, or follow them so closely that you walk or sit like a robot going through the correct paces.

- *Keep your arms and legs relaxed.* Crossed arms indicate lower or threatened status. Don't link your arms behind your head, as this signals overagressiveness.

- *Lean forward slightly.* Leaning backward suggests fear.

- *When asked a tough question, don't clasp your hands in front of you (men) or cover your body with your arms (women).* Both unconsciously telegraph fear to the interviewer and may open you up for more probing questions.

- *Position shoulders squarely.* Don't bow your head.

- *Smile, but don't overdo it.* Women in particular have been noted smiling more frequently during interviews. This sometimes signals perceived lesser status.

- *Don't violate the interviewer's personal space.* Usually, people prefer that others maintain a distance of several feet.

- *But take up space yourself.* Weak people tend to cuddle themselves; confident people tend to extend their bodies and fill more space.

- *Avoid choppy or quick movements*—both telegraph anger or nervousness.

The Rest of the Interview: Selling Yourself as a Basic Strategy

▶ **The heart of the interview is your chance to shine. Everything you say should be aimed at selling yourself into a job.**

Every answer should embody certain elements that create a winning impression. Below we've listed the key rules of interviewing, which underlie every answer in every interview for the over-40 job hunter. They are based on interviews and studies of successful job hunters and interviewers.

Read them, then read the sample questions on page 224. *Key:* These rules must become an integral part of you—second nature when you answer an interview question.

▶ **Rule 1:** *Your only job in an interview is to sell yourself into a job.*

As you speak, ask yourself: Is what I'm saying getting me closer to a job offer? We're being repetitive, but it's the best way to sell—keep hammering away at the main point. You've got only an hour or so, so make each word count. Every question deserves a selling answer.

Use a sales technique called the needs payoff, as in your cover letter. Find out what needs the company has, and show how you can fill them. Highlight your skills in a way that shows the interviewer you can solve the company's problems. Constantly emphasize energy, vigor, and action to counteract any age bias and to make it clear that *you* are the person for the job.

EXAMPLE: The interviewer asks, "Can you describe how you get your point across to people of different backgrounds?"

Don't just answer the question, use it to show how good you are: "The best way to get a point across is to *listen* well first—which I found very successful last year, while serving as the head of the only management negotiation team in our industry to successfully avert a threatened strike. Here's what we did." The interviewer not only learns your answer to the question, he or she gets to hear about one of your successes.

▶ **Rule 2:** *Assert yourself during the interview.*

It's a matter of control. Don't take charge overtly—just ensure that you get to make *your* points, and that you're in the best position to make them.

If you're seated eyes to the sun, on a rickety chair, etc., mention this and ask to move to another chair or position.

More important, if you feel, at the end of the interview, an important item has been left out, ask the interviewer if you might add something. If you're asked a question you feel is a waste of time, try a trick politicians use (but do a better job!). Answer the question briefly (you must show respect for the interviewer), then segue into the point *you* want to make.

EXAMPLE: Question: "How do you handle customer relations problems?"

Answer: "We've improved our responsiveness in the past year and reached number one in customer relations. We instituted a new 'customers first' policy that [brief description of the customer relations policy], which leads to what I feel is the key to this program—keeping a management team motivated. I won the company's 'Best Manager of the Year' award last year for my new 'team' approach to my department. That's the real heart of a strong customer relations program."

Here the applicant answers the question, then connects it to his main point—that he is a dynamic manager.

▶ **Rule 3:** *Be yourself.*

Don't be something you aren't or can't be. Of course you should strive to improve your style, take good advice seriously, and alter your approach according to cues from the interviewer. Just don't go overboard and sacrifice your personal style. *Key:* Practice effective interview techniques until they *become* part of your own style.

▶ **Rule 4:** *Organize your answers professionally.*

Begin each answer with a topic sentence that highlights a skill or accomplishment that fits the job and the question, then briefly tell how you did it, keeping in mind the first rule of always selling yourself.

Don't meander. You're trying to sell yourself as a professional, so you must sound organized. Prove you know what you're doing.

EXAMPLE: **Question: "How do you keep track of assignments in your department?"**

Answer: "I've recently instituted a new tracking system, which has been an outstanding success. Using a computerized bulletin board, we're able to coordinate assignments much more effectively, and in fact have raised productivity forty-two percent in the past six months."

The applicant has not only begun answering the question, she has done it in an organized fashion that also shows how competent she is.

TIP: **A good trick is to number ideas or points in your answers—it makes you sound organized and authoritative, and gets the interviewer's attention. For some reason, everyone likes numbers. This is why magazines and newspapers frequently use lists (how many times have you seen things like the "top ten jobs for the 1990s" or the "ten worst hotels"?) Henry Kissinger and many television pundits use this numbering technique. And so did we in this section.**

EXAMPLE: **Question: "What do you consider the key reasons for your success?"**

Answer: "There are three major factors. The first . . ." Just make sure beforehand that you name the right number of points.

▶ **Rule 5:** *Ask questions. Get the interviewer talking.*

Why? For four important reasons:

- *The more the interviewer talks, the more you'll know about the position* (and the personality of the interviewer), and the better you'll be able to tailor yourself to meet the company's needs.

- *To impress the interviewer with your knowledge of the company* by asking smart, informed questions.

- *To establish a dialogue* instead of a grill session.

- *To find out if the position is right for you.*

Rule of thumb: For every two questions the interviewer asks, ask one of your own.

What to ask: What qualifications are you looking for? Why are you looking outside the company? How to ask: if asked about your experiences at XYZ Co., for example, you can counter with your question: "Can you tell me what aspects or skills you're most interested in hearing about?"

TIP: *A good trick for the assertive:* This usually works with line officers, not human relations officers. After the initial chitchat is over, the interviewer will probably signal that it's time to begin by asking a question or saying it's time to start.

You answer: "I'd be glad to, but before we begin, could you tell me a bit more about the skills you're seeking for this position?" Listen, and then tailor yourself to meet those needs.

Also ask questions that highlight your knowledge. *Key point:* Your research should have told you much about the company and the position. If you've jotted down a few questions about the company or industry that show your knowledge and intelligence, you can insert them during the interview.

▶ **Rule 6:** *Summarize.*

Don't let interviewers forget your main points. At the end of your answers, remind them again why they should hire you by reiterating your main selling point. Put a topic sentence at the *end* of an answer, or at the end of a major component of your answer.

EXAMPLE: **"And finally, in 1989, we decreased excess inventory by thirty-four percent. So, as you can see, my introduction and commitment to just-in-time inventory control produced outstanding results at XYZ Corporation, something I'm confident I can repeat here at ABC Company."**

▶ **Rule 7:** *Use concrete terms—numbers, facts, dates, names.*

Interviewers like to hear facts, names, dates, numbers—words they can sink their teeth into. They'll remember *you* if you use them. Use company names (don't say "the firm I previously worked for"), dates, and hard facts. And use numbers. Don't say "I increased sales," say "I increased sales by thirty-four percent in 1991, and by thirty-eight percent in 1992."

EXAMPLE: **"In 1991 I was responsible for a sales staff of ten. My team increased sales by thirty-five percent in the first three quarters, a company record."**

▶ **Rule 8:** *Link yourself and your background to the job.*

Tailor your answers to fit the company and the position to a T. Don't just state what you did; don't just recite your background or accomplishments—show how they can be useful to the company *now*.

What to Do

First of all, research exhaustively. Know the company, the job, and the industry, and think *beforehand* of how your experience can help. Think creatively. The best-qualified candidates don't always get the best offers. Often, it's the most inspired and best-prepared applicants who win—those who can turn even negative questions into positives. In short, *those who can link anything to the job they want.*

EXAMPLE: **Here's a tough one. Question: "I see you've spent most of your time overseas. As you know, our company serves a primarily domestic market."**

Answer: "Exactly. And that's my key *advantage* for this position. You're planning an expansion into five new and different U.S. markets. My international experience has prepared me to effectively introduce new products into diverse environments. Let's take a look at your expansion plans. We're talking about five U.S. markets that are very different in terms of market mixes and subcultures—but I know how to get results in such different markets. For example, I produced fifty-five-percent

. . . Finally, I'd like to add that I was transferred overseas because I led the most successful sales march for XYZ Corporation here in the States, back in Illinois."
A long shot, maybe. But why not try?

▶ **Rule 9:** *Keep your answers short.*

Each answer should last one or two minutes. Long-winded responses bore the interviewer and make *you* sound like a bore. Even worse, while you're babbling, you may find yourself giving away more than you should. Short, concise answers establish you as a professional.

When you're done, stop. If there's a long silence, don't worry. Just ask the interviewer if he or she would like further clarification. If yes, then give another one- or two-minute answer.

▶ **Rule 10:** *Be ready for probing questions.*

Always be ready for a follow-up and then a follow-up after that. For example, after you've explained how you're so skilled at motivating your sales force, be ready for:

1. "How did you do it?"

2. "What were your *worst* problems doing it?"

3. "In terms of that problem you've mentioned, do you think it in any way acts as a detriment to your managerial style?"

Be careful. Follow-up questions are a way of getting behind pat answers and seeing if you really know what you're talking about. They can also be a way of catching you off guard and getting a real answer to a question that's already been asked. For example, questions 2 and 3 above are both asking: "What are your real weaknesses?"

What to Do

Make certain you know the ins and outs of each note-card question and answer (see page 199) thoroughly. Ask yourself practice follow-ups for each question. Get a friend to act as an interviewer and ask probing questions. Go over your career and your past in general to be ready for anything not on your resume. And keep cool. Wait a minute to think before answering.

▶ **Rule 11:** *Don't be glib—give enough information about tough situations to head off the interviewer.*

Here's a trick all experienced interviewees know: They volunteer enough information *up front* when answering a tough question, and thereby avoid tougher, more probing questions later.

The inexperienced interviewee shows in his body language and, more important, in his answer to a question that hits home. For example, to the question "Why did you leave that job?" the inexperienced might answer, "I left for more challenges in another position." Hand goes to mouth, body tenses—and the candidate has *invited* the interviewer to ask why, what do you mean, etc.

A Better Way

Give a few specifics that don't hurt you; don't fidget or change your body language in any way; and watch the interviewer go on to the next question.

▶ **Rule 12:** *Without saying it, prove that you're young and vital.*

Throughout the interview *subtly* show how youthful and vigorous you are. Prove yourself clearly able to handle the stresses of the job you are seeking, in case the interviewer *is* thinking of your age. *The key:* Personalize *you* and *your* youthfulness without overtly drawing attention to your age.

How is this done?

- *Emphasize that you're a cutting-edge person.* Learn and mention examples of modern skills, like computer literacy, knowledge of expert systems, any new developments in your field. You want to prove you haven't been left behind. If you *have,* get back on track by taking courses or reading up *before* your interview.

- *Show you can do the job better than anyone else.* This is really the key to interviewing for everyone; but over-40s may have to be even better. Do more research, and link your past skills to problems you can solve today. Show that you can hit the ground running.

- *Show that you want to spend the rest of your career there.* Even if you're planning to work only a few more years, don't give this away. Besides, maybe you'll change your mind.

- *Don't give away your age.* If you've taken early retirement from your previous employer, for example, don't volunteer the information to your interviewer.

- *Throughout the interview, emphasize high-energy words and actions.* Although a cardinal rule of interviewing is to be yourself, be yourself with extra energy. Create the mental impression of vigorous youth. Use action words—see page 110 for some suggestions.

- *Emphasize what a high-energy, vigorous life you've led, in work and play.* Talk about the challenging fun you had on that last business trip, where you met with fifteen clients in ten days. Slip in a mention of tennis, jogging, hiking, or some other vigorous hobby you have that is clearly identified with youth.

- *If you have to talk about the past, emphasize the* recent *past as much as possible*—especially during small talk about sports, music, or politics. A mistake people often make is to unconsciously mention old books, names, ideas, or metaphors in their conversation, creating in the interviewer a conscious or subconscious perception: This person is *old*.

- *Avoid mentioning tired-sounding habits and attitudes.* Don't talk about sedentary activities like watching TV, and avoid talking about how tired you get after work and the like.

▶ **Rule 13:** *Don't volunteer your negatives—unless you know they'll find them out.*

Interviews are not confessionals—there's no reason to tell interviewers things they won't find out otherwise. This is *not* to say you should lie, but if you've been ill, for example, why volunteer the information? It can only hurt you.

What about your age?

There are two schools of thought. One is that they'll find out sooner or later—why not face the issue directly? We agree.

Here's our reasoning: On your resume, you should keep your age secret, if possible, to get yourself into the selling situation of an interview. In the interview, however, you have a chance to talk. Take the opportunity to defuse the age problem rather than leaving the interviewer to discover it afterward and automatically disqualify you. For more on how to handle age-related questions, see page 234.

The other school of thought says why remind an interviewer that you're over 40 when he or she might not know it or might not care?

Take your pick. Best bet: Play it by ear in each interview.

▶ **Rule 14:** *Pick up cues from your interviewer.*

Adjust your pitch to your audience. Find out what the interviewer wants to hear—and say it in your own words. *Key: Listen* to the interviewer. Is she conservative or hard-charging, does he seem to like your detailed answers or your theoretical ones, does he like to talk or prefers that you talk?

Watch his or her body language. Good signs: leaning forward, smiling, listening carefully, unfolded arms, hand under chin, taking notes, talking of others in the company, talking of benefits or advantages of working there. Bad signs: hand to mouth, fidgeting, glazed eyes, etc.

If the interviewer seems bored, annoyed, or skeptical, try altering your approach, then reassess the interviewer's signals. Some hints and rules of thumb on taking cues and tailoring your approach:

- *Take a quick look around the office.* This can give you an idea of the interviewer's personality. One caution: don't overdo it; for example, even if you see family photos, avoid praising children. It sounds fake.

- *If you have something in common with the interviewer, bring it up.* Maybe you've worked in the same company in the past, even gone to the same college or business school.

- *Follow the interviewer's lines.* One candidate started going on about his business qualifications. But he soon noticed that the interviewer seemed most interested in his after-hours work as a high school football referee. The rest of the interview was about football—and the applicant, who was only marginally qualified, got the job.

- *Be careful with overly agreeable, encouraging interviewers.* These experts are so encouraging, hanging on your every word, agreeing enthusiastically to everything you say, that you may reveal your weaknesses as you bask in their approval. After you leave, they'll coldbloodedly evaluate you.

- *Key point: Are you interviewing with a line manager or a human resources manager?* Line managers tend to be more solution oriented, so emphasize skills and tough-mindedness with them. Human resources managers often don't know the specifics of the job to the same extent and are more personality oriented, more concerned with candidates who "look good" (so *they* don't look bad if they recommend you). So emphasize to them how you fit in well with the corporate culture, and how your resume and background are just right.

▶ **Rule 15:** *Sound positive and optimistic.*

Companies like young applicants because they're often the most enthusiastic and because they seem to offer great possibilities. You can't change your age but you can offer them everything else, particularly youthful optimism.

Positive attitudes are contagious. In fact, even hard-nosed, "objective" interviewers have been known to hire dynamic, positive people who were totally unqualified. Think of how well you can do if you're optimistic *and* qualified.

Some rules of thumb:

- *Don't sound hesitant.* Don't say "maybe," say yes. If you're not certain about something, don't let the interviewer know it. Believe it or not, one applicant we counseled had passed a battery of interviews for a major Washington organization only to be asked, in closing, how he felt about coming on board. His answer? He felt "a bit ambivalent" about moving his family to a new location. Guess what? He didn't get the job.

- *State your accomplishments authoritatively but don't brag.* Braggarts sound insecure. They're so busy telling everyone how great they are, they don't notice that interviewers are discounting everything they say.

- *Use active words and sentence constructions.* Don't say "I was responsible for the transformation of my department," say "I changed my section into the leader in . . ."

- *Never bad-mouth your previous employer.* Even if the guy was a jerk, think of other plausible (and verifiable) reasons you left, such as a merger, a cost-cutting move, a major policy difference (you wanted to expand the product line, the company wanted to reduce it).

- *Never apologize.* If someone suggests you're too old, don't be meek and "agree" by being defensive. Say "No, I'm more experienced! You want results, and with my dynamic approach to profits you can have them."

▶ **Rule 16:** *Be a team player.*

This is the era of the team: the management team, the worker's team, and so on. Showing you have a team approach to work proves you're a good delegator, a good co-worker, someone who's not afraid to give credit where credit is due. In short, just the kind of person everyone wants to hire.

What to do: Use "we" instead of "I" often; mention or praise the efforts of your employees and co-workers. But don't overdo it—you don't want the interviewer wondering about *your* role in bringing about success.

EXAMPLE: **Question: "How did you handle your inventory shortfall in 1992?"**

Answer: "Extremely well. We confronted the problem head on. I decided to institute a phone program to get into direct contact with suppliers *before* the problem became acute. At a strategy session, a top employee came up with an excellent additional idea to . . ."

Notice how the applicant gives herself credit, but also shows how she was open to group input and, in fact, used and gave credit for an employee's suggestion.

▶ **Rule 17:** *Be reasonable.*

You may be brilliant and unconventional—but corporate or organizational jobs usually go to the less brilliant and more conventional. There are exceptions, but in general, stick to the middle of the road. Don't highlight off-the-wall ideas you've had, off-the-wall hobbies or opinions you hold. And be careful of attempts to draw out more unconventional opinions.

▶ **Rule 18:** *Close the interview by selling yourself.*

Why be shy about your interest in the job?

As the interview winds down, summarize your main selling points. Give the interviewer a reminder of why you're great.

At the end of the interview, if you are interested in the job, *tell* the interviewer. As you do so, summarize the key reasons why you're right for the job. And end by asking to hear by a *specific* date.

EXAMPLE: **"As you can see, I'm very interested in this job, particularly in light of my extensive experience and accomplishments managing widget manufacturers. I know I can help your operation produce the same results. Can I expect to hear from you by Friday of next week?"**

SPECIAL SITUATIONS

Panel Interviews

Normally, the hiring executive and human resources people will be present, as will several employees from the department or section that has the opening. From the corporate standpoint, panel interviews can be useful because they are harder on *you*. The panel covers more points of view, technical experts can be present to fire technical questions at you, and the interviews are fairly good predictors of how well you can handle yourself with the public. Some tips at coming out unscathed:

- *Strive to remain calm and organized.* Easier said than done, but force yourself to keep your cool.

- *Take time before you answer questions.* Often the questions come rapid fire, but this doesn't mean you have to answer accordingly. Pause before answering, or occasionally rephrase the question—this gives you time to think of an answer.

EXAMPLE: Question: "How would you handle the marketing of widgets in New York?"

Answer: "How would I handle the marketing of widgets in New York? . . ."

- *Be prepared for technical questions.* If you find out beforehand that you'll be interviewed by a panel, be especially ready for technical questions. If you're caught by a question you can't answer, say so—don't try to feel your way out. *Key:* These interviews are also testing the way you'd interact with the public, so a bluff may make you look worse.

- *Don't be overly concerned about the "feel" of the interview.* A natural flow may be lost with more people involved. Don't worry about it—concentrate on selling yourself.

- *Don't ignore anybody.* Maintain eye contact with and talk to everybody on the panel. You don't know which interviewer has the decision-making power.

- *Don't be passive.* Many people just react to questions and don't take an active role. If you feel that a key point has not been addressed, bring it up yourself. Ask questions and sell yourself as you would in any interview.

Group Interviews

Being interviewed with a group of other applicants is a common experience for entry-level candidates, but mid-level candidates may also find themselves in this situation at times. For example, the U.S. Department of Commerce uses group interviews for its Foreign Commercial Service. Often, you are given a group exercise, and the entire group must reach a consensus. Evaluators will watch as you and the group debate to reach certain solutions. The key problem with these interviews is that you are competing with those with whom you must agree.

Briefly, what to do:

- *Jump in early.* Assume the role of *moderator* as soon as you can. Open the discussion, suggest an order of presentation, ask others what they think. Instead of overarguing your points, try to mediate among others. Remember: You are being evaluated for leadership, and leadership often comes from not being too aggressive.

- *Offer solutions,* don't impose them. Again, the more of a mediator you are, the better you will do. Remember that the "agenda" you are debating is not important—but *how* you negotiate is.

- *Take the responsibility for closing the meeting.* Very often a timetable is given. Pay attention to your watch, and as the deadline nears, summarize what the group has accomplished and announce its conclusions.

Lunch Interviews

Who likes them? But you know the good news—it usually means you're one of the leading candidates for the job. *Key:* Chances are you've already been evaluated professionally; a lunch usually focuses on the *intangibles,* such as your social behavior. The big question is "Will you fit in with us?"

Below are some tips to help you assure that the answer will be yes.

- *Don't pick the restaurant.* You'll make a bad impression if you pick a restaurant the others dislike.

- *Be a few minutes early.*

- *Order conservatively.* Pick mid-priced dishes; if asked to choose a wine, pick a mid-priced brand. Avoid food that is difficult to eat (lobster, spaghetti, chicken) or will take longer to prepare.

- *Drink alcoholic beverages very lightly—if at all.* Don't be the first to order a drink, but if everyone else is ordering one, consider following suit if you drink socially. *Rationale:* You'll be seen as "one of us." Don't drink more than one—a loose tongue can lose you the job.

- *Let the interviewers take the conversational lead.* In general, this is not the place for a hard sell—but *do* bring up hobbies or experiences that reflect your sterling character and show you'll fit in well.

- *Avoid politics and other controversial topics.* If asked your opinion directly, make an inoffensive, minor point that won't offend anybody.

TIP: **If you want to be sneaky, try to turn the question around so you can find out the interviewer's opinion before expressing your own.** *Danger:* **The interviewer may just be testing you, and others at the table may disagree with your opinion.**

Stress Interviews

These test how tough you are—by asking difficult questions, by asking them in a hostile way, and by putting you in an uncomfortable environment—light in your eyes, sunken sofas, etc.

Key

Behave calmly, coolly, professionally. Don't take things personally and don't react negatively—react *positively* and try to better the situation. For example:

- *If the environment is set up to unnerve you* (light is in your eyes, etc.) politely ask to move your seat.

- *If questions are extremely difficult,* take a minute to formulate good answers.

- *If questions are delivered rapid fire,* ask the interviewer to repeat the question.

- *If the interviewer is actively hostile,* belittling your accomplishments, politely disagree and explain why.

- *Concentrate on selling yourself,* not on criticisms of your record or answers.

- Remember: *You aren't required to sit through abuse.* If you don't like it, wind up the interview and politely take your leave.

Finally, ask yourself: *If this is the way they interview, do I really want to work here?*

8

COMMON INTERVIEW QUESTIONS AND HOW TO ANSWER THEM

INTRODUCTION

▶ **Interviewers in the 1990s are more savvy than ever. Almost all of them have gone beyond the "What are your strengths?" sort of generic question.**

As an over-40 job hunter, you're facing a more sophisticated job market.

Key

Interviewers want to go beyond pat answers to common questions. They assume you've read books, gone on interviews, and rehearsed neat answers. Their job: to get behind those answers. To do this, they've developed various new methods of interviewing and variations on tried-and-true questions. You've probably faced most of these already:

- *Open questions:* "How do you feel about . . ." This gets you talking, and reveals how you think and formulate answers. *Key:* Be organized. Take a minute before answering to organize a coherent answer. For more, see Rule 4 on page 209.

- *"Show me" questions:* "Give me a specific example of how you reprimanded an employee, and tell me what happened afterward. Was your reprimand in keeping with company policy, or did it differ?" In other words, the interviewer is going beyond the general to real-life incidents. *Key idea:* It's easier for applicants to lie (or fudge) generically. The closer you get to things that actually happened, the easier it is for the interviewer to assess your *true* personality and management style.

- *Leading questions:* "So you think XYZ Corporation is well positioned overseas?" This type of question makes the weak-willed agree—and may lose them the job. Don't let the interviewer think you've agreed for the sake of agreeing. If you agree (or think you should agree) give reasons *why.*

- *Probing questions:* Follow-ups allow the interviewer to control the interview and determine the depth of your knowledge and communications ability. For more, see page 212.

- *Mirror probes:* "So you say XYZ Corporation is well poised to expand overseas. Why?" Be careful—this kind of question can catch you if you've made an unsupported statement.

- *Transition questions:* These center on the major transforming events of your life—and seek to detect the "real" person beneath the practiced interviewee. Expect probing questions as to why you switched careers, etc. Emphasize positive movement in your answers—say you made such changes to better your career, and explain why.

- *Group or panel interviewing:* These test how you handle the stresses of being grilled, and give a sense of how you might communicate with the public in the job you're going for. For more, see page 218.

Whatever the questions, interviewers today are more apt to take notes, weigh your deficiencies and your pluses on forms, and try to make a decision in an objective manner.

▶ **But for all this, behind the more sophisticated questions of the 1990s are the same old questions.**

Let's face facts. Interviewers still need to know the same things as before—they still want to know your strengths and weaknesses, your personality type, your skills and how they fit the needs of the company and the job. *The bottom line:* Most "new" questions and "new interviewing techniques" are merely rephrased versions of the old ones. The trick is to:

- Recognize "new" questions for what they are.

- Prepare mental answers *before* you're asked, so you won't be fazed and waste time stumbling around.

COMMON INTERVIEW QUESTIONS—AND HOW TO ANSWER THEM

▶ **Below are the most common questions interviewers are asking today.**

In some cases we've included examples of new variations of the same question. On page 218, we examine some new and different interview *situations,* and offer suggestions on how to best handle these.

▶ **Question 1:** *Tell me a little about yourself (or your background, your work history, your education).*

These are the ultimate open-ended questions. They place the burden on *you.* The interviewer is looking to see:

- How well you organize your answer.

- What you *omit* (he or she probably has your resume, and maybe an application form, to check it against).

- Which skills you highlight (and whether those skills are compatible or necessary for the position at hand).

How to answer
Keep the above points in mind. You should have already prepared a response ahead of time, keeping the points listed above in

mind, you should be ready with it. Nevertheless, take a minute to organize your thoughts. Quickly take into account your perceptions of the interviewer's personality, and adjust your pre-planned answer as seems necessary. *Key:* Establish a pattern in your background, a movement upward to the position you're interviewing for.

- *Open with something that defines you and highlights a skill or trait the company wants.* In general, don't be too blatant: If you open with something like "I'm a born accountant," you sound like a fool who overrehearsed. Work at a subtle, more low-key opening that gives the impression you want them to hear.

EXAMPLE: **Answer for a life-history version: "I was born in Savannah, Georgia, to parents who owned and ran a family store, where I helped out in the summer. I worked my way through college as a door-to-door salesman, earning one hundred percent of my college expenses, and through the University of Georgia Business School, where I won an award for outstanding . . ."**

The applicant is portraying himself as a hard worker in a family of hard workers, a salesman who was *born* selling.

- Briefly *go over your early work history, etc.* Give more details—and selling points—as you get closer to the present.

EXAMPLE: **For an overseas position: "As the youngest bank officer for XYZ Bank in Europe, I had a great deal of customer contact and became fluent in German and French. This came in handy when I was promoted and transferred back to San Francisco in 1975 as vice president, with responsibility for correspondent banking relations in Europe and Asia. During my tenure, we streamlined . . ."**

- *Give names, dates, and* facts. Throughout, briefly mention selling points as adjuncts to your experience. *Key:* You want the interviewer to ask you more about your successes and to see that they fit the company's needs.

EXAMPLE: **"In 1979 a headhunter called, and I was hired by ABC Corporation to revamp their lighting division—in my two years there I increased sales by seventy-five percent and profits by forty-three percent."**

- *Keep it brief.*
- *Summarize* and close on an upbeat note.

EXAMPLE: **"And that brings me up to today. As you can see, my extensive experience and success as a logistics engineer, particularly with cosmetics companies, makes me very enthusiastic about this position."**

▶ **Question 2:** *With whom, when, where, why did you do this?*

These are all follow-up questions—seeking greater *specificity* about your statements.

How to answer

Be ready to give further details, but don't stray far from your main points. Details should support your main premise, that you are the right person for the position. See page 211.

▶ **Question 3:** *What are your greatest weaknesses?*

New versions:

- What areas have you developed the most in the past year?

- If you were offered a free self-improvement course, which one would you take?

- In your last evaluation, where did you rank the lowest? (There is an implied threat here—they may call and ask your references directly or indirectly. The tendency is for the interviewee to give an honest answer. But remember, most employers will *not* reveal very much, so you might be able to get away with fudging.)

- What do friends criticize about your personality?

- What would your subordinates say you need to improve?

How to answer

Pick weaknesses that are not weaknesses in terms of the job you want. Pick a strength carried a bit too far ("I'm a workaholic," etc.). Or *if it seems you can't get away with a more generic answer, pick a weakness that is not central to the job, and mention it in connection with your strengths.* Add that you've been working on improving the weakness, and tell how.

Be ready for follow-up questions, couched in deceptively positive terms: "Let's go a bit further into that weak point—not to assess your weakness, but to assess, in a positive way, how you've successfully addressed the problem." Best way to answer: Tell how you've improved and why it's not really a major problem, and don't dwell on it.

And be careful of questions like the first of the "new versions," which doesn't even sound like a weakness question.

EXAMPLE: **If asked about her last evaluation, a salesperson might say: "My review was high, particularly in sales, where I ranked the highest in the company, but I was a bit lower in attention to detail, something I've worked to correct by keeping a modified sales log for times when I'm on the road. That way I can do the paperwork more easily—and keep concentrating on my main goal of being the most responsive and effective saleswoman in my company."**

(Note: Mention this sort of weakness only if pressed, or if you're concerned they will find this out.)

▶ **Question 4:** *What are your greatest strengths?*

New versions:

- How do your customers (or subordinates or bosses) describe you?

- What do you think accounted for your rapid rise at XYZ Corporation?

- In college, what did your peers (or professors) think of you? (Don't make the mistake of thinking that if you're over 40 this won't be asked or will be seen as superfluous. Many modern interviewers use this sort of question to get at the "real" you.)

How to answer

Before the interview, write down ten of your strengths in order of importance. Memorize them.

When asked this question or a variant, ask yourself: What is this company looking for? A take-charge turnaround specialist? Or a low-key diplomat who can handle cranky customers? Then pick strengths from your list that show you meet the company's needs.

If asked what your strengths *and* weaknesses are, pick four or five strengths and one or two weaknesses. Close and summarize with the strengths.

TIP: Just to throw you off, some trained interviewers also check to see if your strengths are carried too far, and are in fact weaknesses.

▶ Question 5: *What accomplishment are you most proud of?*

How to answer

Ask yourself what your prospective employer most needs in the job. Then answer with an accomplishment that shows you can meet those needs.

EXAMPLE: For a bank now cautiously expanding after a battering during the recession: "I'm most proud of my lending activity in 1989–1990—the year before the recession. I booked a record number of loans, with a default rate of zero. It was due to old-fashioned, hard-nosed banking—getting the good clients not only by attention to detail but by developing relationships with the best businesspeople in each region."

▶ Question 6: *What are your plans for five or ten years from now?*

New versions:

- What are your long-term plans—and what about any off-the-wall dreams?

- If you had your choice of any job at all in the next few years, what would that be?

How to answer

Say you see yourself in the same industry, in a more senior position than the one you're in now. Show a commitment to this job and this industry. Talk about responsibilities, not titles. Don't say, of course, that you see yourself in the boss's shoes.

EXAMPLE: "I expect to still be in financial services, with an expanded client base, developed by selling XYZ financial products."

Be careful: The new version asking for off-the-wall dreams is an attempt to get an answer to the question "Are you *really* committed to this job?" People sometimes fall for it and describe a secret dream to sail the South Seas or open their own business. Over-40s are particularly vulnerable—it's the time of life when most of us think such thoughts. Best answer: You like what you're doing now—otherwise you wouldn't be doing it.

▶ **Question 7:** *Can you describe your high-school/college years?*

What? Yes, questions about your early years have recently become more common for over-40 job hunters. *Key reason:* These were your formative years, and your answer can give the interviewer an idea of your underlying strengths and weaknesses, as well as of the changes in your life.

How to answer

Point out strengths that highlight skills that are needed *today*—and link them to the job at hand. If there are glaring weaknesses *that the interviewer knows about (from an application form, etc.),* point out how you've mastered those earlier problems. *Key:* This all happened years ago, so what you've got to show is how you've grown with the times.

EXAMPLE: "In college, I first learned how to really *convince* people of something. As vice president of our debating society, I learned how to craft a well-organized argument —and learned the joy of winning people over to my side by convincing them rather than arguing. It's a skill that has stood me well in making presentations over the years."

EXAMPLE: "Yes, my early background does show those trouble spots you mentioned, but I think that's the key to my disciplined maturity today—and it's actually helped me to succeed. I learned the consequences of losing one's temper early on—that's why now I'm called in by my company for the toughest labor-management negotiations. They *know* I'll keep things going smoothly and calmly."

▶ **Question 8:** *Describe your (current, past) positions.*

How to answer

Concisely describe your position and your accomplishments, highlighting major successes. Be specific. Talk about skills this company needs. Don't bad-mouth previous employers or subordinates.

EXAMPLE: "I'm the marketing VP for XYZ Bus Tours—in the past two years of my tenure, I've increased sales by fifty-five percent and fifty-seven percent—in a market that saw a decline in bus touring overall. We're now second in the market and working to become first. My marketing team has accomplished all this through our . . ."

▶ **Question 9:** *What outside interests do you have?*

Translation: Are you an active, all-around sort of person who will be an asset to the company?

How to answer

Pick those interests that show vigor, but not excessive vigor. Sports are a natural choice for business, but don't overdo it—something like hang gliding could peg you as a dangerous nut. But squash, tennis, hiking and the like are fine. Golf is *the* sport of business. Clubs, volunteer organizations, and church or synagogue organizations show a strong social interest, and are good choices as well.

Don't ever mention a sport that you don't play. Don't mention political or otherwise controversial activities, unless you're going to work for a political party or lobbying group where it might be appropriate.

Reading, if mentioned in conjunction with a vigorous activity, is also a good choice, but a caveat is in order: "I like to read, but I'm usually so busy I don't get to as much as I'd like." What do you read? Best choices for most jobs: biographies, business best-sellers. Avoid mentioning controversial books.

TIP: *Read and review* a few best-selling business books, biographies, or other best-sellers. Mentally jot down the best aspects of the book, why you liked it, etc. If you're asked what book you've most recently read, or what book has impressed you the most, you'll be ready for the inevitable follow-up: Why?

TIP: Don't get drawn into controversial discussions. If, for example, the interviewer happens to have read the latest biography of Truman, don't go bad-mouthing Republicans even if he or she does. You don't know if he or she is leading you on, or if he or she is a passionate Democrat who works for Republicans.

▶ **Question 10:** *Why do you want to work here?*

How to answer

This is an invitation to sell yourself. Some good directions to take your answer: You wish to work here because the position matches your experience, because the challenges the job offers excite you, because you know you can do the job superlatively well. Give specific examples that support your case.

▶ **Question 11:** *What compensation expectations do you have?*

Try to avoid this question. The interviewer might be fishing for a low-ball answer, and by giving one you can appear desperate. He or she may also be seeking to disqualify you for asking for too much.

If you can't avoid it, seek to delay the answer to the *end* of the interview. *Key:* Salaries are normally set *after* a hiring decision has been made. By delaying, you can impress the interviewer with your skills and accomplishments, and actually obtain a better compensation package.

How to answer

If pressed to answer, put the ball back into the interviewer's court: "What compensation range has your company been considering?" Or try this: "I expect a salary commensurate with my own background and industry levels."

EXAMPLE: **"Salary, though important, was not a prime reason for my choosing to interview here. However, I'm certain after we discuss my qualifications and how I can fit in with the corporation, we'll find a mutually agreeable figure."**

If you still have to name your price

Think back on your research and come up with a middle-salary figure that matches your background and the position. Or, for middle to upper levels, mention major provisions (bonuses, etc.) in keeping with the position and try to put off salary discussion until later.

Rationale

Too low, and you'll look cheap, or at best, you'll get an offer at a low price; too high, and you may be disqualified as overqualified, a "typical older candidate with unrealistic expectations."

▶ **Question 12:** *Describe the people who worked under (over) you.*

Key

This question is trying to get at what kind of person *you* are. When you discuss subordinates or superiors, you will mention those traits that you like, giving the interviewer a very strong idea of your own management style—and how you'll fit in at the company.

How to answer

Know the company, the position, and the interviewer's personality, and adjust accordingly. Pick or emphasize those subordinates and superiors you've had who mesh with your perception of what the company wants. Don't mention negatives.

EXAMPLE: Someone going for a job at an entrepreneurial computer firm that has now hired a professional manager to tighten things up: "My VP was an excellent administrator, a man who understood that attention to costs is essential, particularly in a free-wheeling competitive environment. We worked extremely well together, especially in our joint effort to . . ."

▶ **Question 13:** *Why did you leave that position?*

How to answer

If you were fired, say so. There's no stigma in today's tough business climate, and it's easy for the interviewer to check it out. Why were you fired? *Key:* Reasons should show you are a competent professional. Best answers: A merger forced cutbacks, your section was cut, your section was not expanded as planned.

If you left voluntarily, be specific: Avoid vague statements like "The job lost its challenge, and my skills were not fully utilized." You sound like you're trying to avoid talking about something—or worse, like a liar. And never bad-mouth your previous employer—at worst, say you left due to policy differences.

EXAMPLE: "It was a tough choice, because I was very happy at XYZ Company. But the recession put plans for the expansion of my section into Europe on hold for the foreseeable future. As I had been specifically hired to spearhead the European operation, I felt that, regardless of the company's offer to keep me on in New York, it was better I move."

TIP: Don't volunteer that you took early retirement. What does that say? Maybe you only want this job to fill in the idle hours—you're not *committed.*

▶ **Question 14:** *Why have you changed jobs so frequently?* **or** *Why have you been laid off so frequently?*

This is a tough, negative question, *very* hard to answer.

How to answer

First of all, if you get this question in an early interview, stop and re-assess your resume and see if you can delete or combine any jobs to head off the question. Can you make it appear that some of your experience was in consulting? Work at getting good references who will go to bat all the way for you if the interviewer decides to check up.

In general, assess your background creatively. Were you involved in entrepreneurial firms that folded? Were you in an industry where layoffs are frequent? Or were most of the moves concentrated in a few years after a layoff, when you couldn't find the right job? Or did most of the moves occur when you were younger? All of these are (relatively) reasonable explanations for frequent job changes. Also, ask yourself: Is this really a legitimate question, or is the interviewer trying to see if *I* think it's a problem? By all means, answer positively, not defensively—and play up jobs you've held longest.

EXAMPLE: "As you notice, I spent eight years at XYZ Corporation. After the merger, my specialty was not in demand, and I found myself out of work—until I found the right position at ABC Company, where I spent four years until a merger made my department redundant. But there, just as with the position here, my skills matched the job, and as my references can attest, my performance was outstanding, producing a record sixty-five-percent profit increase."

▶ **Question 15:** *Have you received any other job offers?*

If you have, the best answer is yes—this shows that you're in demand. But add that this is the job you're most interested in.

LOADED QUESTIONS

▶ **This section tells how to deal with the "loaded questions" about your age that come up—as well as questions about other *perceived* negatives.**

Key fact

To many interviewers, older is not better.

Obviously, this is not always true. Chairmen of the board of major corporations are disproportionately in their fifties and sixties —but most of us are not going for those positions. In general, whether we like it or not, interviewers prefer younger candidates. And despite the Americans with Disabilities Act (ADA), interviewers usually prefer candidates with no physical or mental disabilities. In addition, employers prefer applicants who have no ill dependents (insurance problems) and who are not single mothers (and with the childbearing age going up, even over-40 women are not exempt from questions about this).

▶ **In general, here's how to handle an overly personal question that tries to get at areas of your life you'd rather not discuss.**

Although interviewers may not legally question you on your race, national origin, marital status, age, religious beliefs, children, or disabilities (with certain exceptions), this sometimes happens. When confronted with one of these questions, you have two options —you can confront the interviewer, threaten to leave and proceed with a lawsuit, or answer as best you can.

Best bet

Answer it. You're not here to set legal precedents, you're here to get a job.

The best starting approach

Ask "Is this a major concern of yours? If so, why?" The interviewer will answer either no or yes, and explain why he or she is concerned. *Either* way, confront the problem and explain why your qualifications—*what you can do for the company now*—are the critical reason for hiring you.

Below are some loaded questions, with suggestions on how to answer them.

▶ **Loaded Question 1:** *When were you employed at these companies?*

Translation: How old are you anyway? This sometimes is used as a quasi-legal way of finding out your age.

How to answer

In general, don't lie or waffle. Tell the interviewer the dates of employment (he'll be able to find out anyway) and add how your employment history shows dependability, consistency, etc.—and get right back to explaining how your experience can help his company *now.*

▶ **Loaded Question 2:** *Your resume (or background or responsibilities) are extremely impressive; in fact . . .*

Translation: You're overqualified. This is a tough question to counter, because it signals that the interviewer is concerned you might jump ship if another, better opportunity comes by. And the interviewer is probably right.

How to answer

Be up front. Ask if overqualification is a concern, and explain why *this* job is an excellent fit for you and why you see the position as one where you can (and fully intend to) stay and grow. Pull in personal reasons if appropriate—you like the town and intend to stay here for the rest of your life, etc. Explain that you are a task-oriented person who finds *in this position* a unique set of challenges, and go on to explain how your experience can offer various advantages to the company. *Key point:* Experience is at a premium—and you'll take less time to train.

This is a tricky question—be prepared for it beforehand.

▶ **Loaded Question 3:** *Is there any problem with your ability to work overtime?*

Translation: Do you have children who will interfere with your work life? Variations include questions on your availability to work long hours or if you'll need much time off, etc. These tend to be directed at women, and, nowadays, being over 40 doesn't mean you won't be asked.

How to answer

The best answer is simple—no, you don't see any problem with your ability to work overtime. If pressed, you can say something like "I enjoy my time off, but whenever necessary, I'm certainly available for work. I'm very task oriented, and fully understand the need for a strong commitment to my work." Stop. Don't elaborate.

▶ **Loaded Question 4:** *Do you realize we have a very forward-looking corporation here?*

Translation: Sometimes this means "You're too old for us." Variations on this question abound. Sometimes, of course, it means just what it says.

How to answer

Say you're delighted, since that's just the type of company where you thrive. In other words, answer the surface meaning of this question by showing how up to date and modern your career has been. Also, play up your high-energy background. For example: "Excellent. I'm looking for a high-energy, cutting-edge environment. That's where I do my best work. For instance, in my last position I was instrumental in changing our outdated inventory reporting system to a Novell LAN system, which improved efficiency and was a part of our switch to just-in-time production."

▶ **Loaded Question 5:** *How do you feel about working for a younger boss?*

Translation: You won't like taking orders from someone younger than you, right?

How to answer

Obviously, you're expected to say it doesn't bother you a bit ("I can work with anyone in a position of respect and professionalism"). So what you've got to do is go one step further and *prove* you'll have no problems. Briefly highlight instances where you have worked for a younger superior or with younger peers. If you haven't, think about occasions outside the office. Throughout, emphasize your professionalism with examples. Age is not important; what matters is skills.

9

FOLLOWING UP

INTRODUCTION

▶ **Writing a follow-up letter after an interview is more than common courtesy—it's good salesmanship.**

Most people know that they should write a thank-you letter after an interview. But many of them don't maximize the impact this letter can (and should) have.

The key point
Recognize that a follow-up letter is much more than a simple "Thanks for taking the time to meet me." Written correctly, a follow-up letter can:

1. Reinforce the good impression you made in an interview.

2. Bring up sales points that you feel didn't come across strongly enough or that you omitted in the interview.

3. Compensate for any negative impression you may have left.

4. Serve as a general memory tickler so the interviewer remembers you.

HOW TO WRITE A FOLLOW-UP LETTER THAT SELLS YOU . . . SOFTLY

▶ **Always send your follow-up letter no later than a week after your interview.**

Any later, and you appear disinterested, discourteous, or simply less than prompt.

TIP: **Impress the interviewer with your (honest) enthusiasm by writing and sending a letter either the day of or the day after an interview. You don't look desperate. Just interested—and very polite.**

▶ **An important note: This isn't the time for a hard sell.**

You should have done your main selling during the interview. This follow-up letter is exactly what it says—a follow-up to your sales call. As such, it should be a soft sell, a brief reminder of the reasons the interviewer should hire you, or an opportunity to repair any damage done during the interview.

▶ **Keep it short and sweet.**

Reselling yourself doesn't mean going into high gear and inundating the interviewer with a bulk of new information. Stick to three to four paragraphs, one page or less. This is more than enough space in which to (1) remind the prospective employer of your interview, (2) sell yourself one more time, and (3) recap—the three essential sections of a strong follow-up letter.

▶ **Open simply.**

The opening of your letter should be a basic reminder of who you are and when you spoke with the interviewer. This is one case when you don't have to grab the reader's attention. A no-frills "Thanks for interviewing me Thursday, June 14" or "Thank you for considering me for your director of marketing position" is just fine.

TIP: **As always, keep your intended audience in mind and skew your writing style to fit it. Was the interviewer traditional and formal? Write formally. Was she more casual and laid back? Be more informal (but don't overdo it).**

▶ **Restate your interest in the job and move into a soft sales pitch.**

Again, keep it *brief*. This sales portion of the letter shouldn't be heavy, long-winded, or irritating. It should simply remind the interviewer of key points brought up during your interview. An important point: This is *not* the time to come up with a new way of presenting yourself. Instead, use the letter to build on the foundation you established during the interview. The point you should be making in this section: I am the person you should hire.

Some quick tips:

- *Mention or elaborate on several examples of your qualifications* that you brought up during your interview, ideally those the interviewer seemed most impressed by. This should remind the interviewer of the aspects of your background that make you right for the position. If you feel that certain points weren't adequately covered, expand on them here.

- *If you have additional information that will strengthen your case, this is the place to add it.* Mention anything that wasn't covered in the interview that enhances your qualifications. This is especially helpful if you've since learned more about the position or company, and now realize certain things you should emphasize.

TIP: **If you've included a few pieces of new information, use bullets to draw the reader's attention and signal that they are important.**

- *Smooth over a bad interview or eliminate any misconceptions that may have arisen* by countering them with positive sales points in this section. You may want to approach this head on by saying "I know you believe my background is too narrow [broad, unrelated, etc.], but . . ." and follow up with specific examples of why your background actually fits the job in question.

▶ **Close cleanly and concisely.**

Again, keep it short and sweet. In effect, this paragraph should be a repetition of the opening—thank the interviewer for the time spent with you and restate how interested you are in the position.

TIP: **If you're truly aggressive, you may want to set up a reason to contact the interviewer again and say you'll call to arrange the time.**

For example: "Based on our discussion concerning the need for a new streamlined series of human resources training programs, I've begun outlining a series that should work well for AMB. I will give you a call early next week to set up a time when you and I can go over them."

(Note: This can force the interviewer to make a decision more quickly, can bolster a weak interview, or—if the interviewer doesn't strike you as the type to like a hard sell—can lose you the job. Use at your own discretion.)

▶ **As with all other letters you write in your job hunt, content isn't everything—appearance counts too.**

Follow the standard rules of thumb: White, cream, buff, or other neutral stationery; a neatly typed or printed letter; careful double-checking of spelling, including name and address of recipient.

TIP: **If you have Monarch-size stationery—7¼ x 10"—use it for your follow-up letters. It looks sharp, executive-like, and (best of all) prevents you from writing too much.**

SAMPLE FOLLOW-UP LETTER

Mr. Martin Quinn
Executive Vice President, Human Resources
MegaBux Inc.
666 Sixth Ave.
New York, NY 10022

Dear Mr. Quinn:

Thank you for meeting with me today to discuss the Director of Training position. I was especially interested in your comments about the need for expanded employee education in light of MegaBux's recent shift in direction and latest acquisitions.

As I mentioned during our conversation, I have a proven track record in the development and implementation of training programs. Most recently, I designed and oversaw a series of intensive sales training seminars for Alta Industries. The proof of their effectiveness was dramatic—sales increased 23% and the sales staff reported higher morale. This is the type of result I'd like to produce for MegaBux.

There is no doubt in my mind that developing a corporate-wide system of interactive employee education programs for MegaBux would be a rewarding challenge—the type of challenge I know I can meet successfully. Again, many thanks for your time and attention, and I look forward to hearing from you in the near future.

Sincerely,

▶ **In certain cases, you may wind up making a follow-up telephone call.**

No, it's not all that common, and it isn't recommended—except in these circumstances:

- *You've gotten another job offer* and you need to know your status at this company before you make your final decision.

- *You have new, important information to share with the interviewer—* and you want to be sure he or she gets it immediately.

- *Your interview went very badly,* you're virtually sure you've already lost the job, you've heard nothing since you sent your follow-up letter, but you want to make one last-ditch effort to sell the interviewer.

A few tips on the best way of making your follow-up call:

- *Keep it short and to the point.* Answer any questions the person you call might pose *before* he or she has to ask them—by cutting quickly to the chase and explaining who you are, why he or she should know you, and when you were interviewed and for what position.

EXAMPLE: **"Mr. Wallace? This is Daniel Kinney. We met two weeks ago, June fourteenth, to discuss the human resources director opening."**

- *Be straightforward about the reason you're calling—to check up on the status of your candidacy.* Again, you should bring up the subject, not wait for a question. Depending upon the specific circumstances, you might also mention that you've had another offer but are still interested, or tell the person new information that might somehow convince him or her that you should still be in the running, or simply try to close in on an interview.

EXAMPLE: **If you've received another offer or if you want to force the issue by pretending you've received another offer: "I would like to know if you've reached a decision yet on that position. As I mentioned during the interview, I'm very interested in working at Barr Industries, but in the meantime I've received another job offer that I'm considering. Before I make my final decision, I would like to know where I stand with Barr." Or—riskier, but sometimes effective—mention some further** work you've done: "As I'm sure you realize, I'm very interested in the position. Since we met, I've taken the time to draw up several new training programs I think would help streamline the human resources function—and I'd like to go over them with you. When could I come in to discuss them with you?"

- *Be prepared for rejection.* Sorry, but it's true—if you haven't heard from a company, it's usually a bad sign. If you do get a "Sorry, but . . ." answer from the person you call—and if you feel up to it—ask what objections the employer had. You may be able to answer those objections, or at least can guard against the problem arising again with another company. And one final note to keep in mind: Don't get discouraged. Rejections are part of the process that brings you closer to a yes.

10

THE JOB OFFER: ASSESSING THE COMPANY, JOB, AND SALARY/BENEFITS

INTRODUCTION

▶ **You've done it—you've interviewed your way into a job offer. It's time for celebration . . . almost.**

Yes, almost. You should be pleased, but not relaxed. Yet. You have one final hurdle in front of you—assessing the job offer and (probably) negotiating for the terms you want.

Then, and only then, will your job hunt finally be over.

This chapter takes you through the steps you'll take upon receiving a job offer: assessing the company, the position, and the salary and benefits package, then negotiating for the best-possible agreement.

WHEN YOU RECEIVE AN OFFER

▶ **Upon receiving a job offer, your first step is the simplest: Wait.**

It's the obvious rule of thumb: Never accept anything on the spot. The corollary: Never say anything you might later regret—such as "A hundred nine thousand sounds great, but I'll have to think about it" or even a more general "The offer sounds great, but I'll have to think about it." Statements like these can cause you to lose any negotiating ground you might later want.

When you receive a job offer, be enthusiastic (if you are), say you're interested (if you are), then say that you'll get back to them in a day or two.

Sure, especially if you've been unemployed for a while, your first inclination is to say "Hallelujah" and sign on the dotted line. But the consequences can be great—ranging from a lower than normal salary to poor working conditions.

You should be sure you know what you're getting into and how the new job will compare with the one you most recently held or currently hold. Careful assessment is crucial.

▶ **Keep in mind: If you've been working with an executive recruiter, the job-offer situation is slightly different—which means you'll handle it differently.**

Usually you will receive a "feeling-out" job offer first, then a formal one. The recruiter will let you know that the company is interested in making an offer and will tell you what terms it's thinking of—the probable salary, benefits, etc.

There shouldn't be any surprises. The recruiter will have given you a general idea of the job and what it pays at the outset. If you think you deserve more, tell the recruiter. He or she will take it up with the client company. If you're interested, say so, and then the company will make its formal offer to you, usually by phone.

At this point, you have three options: Accept immediately (if the offer is just what you want); think about it and get back to them (but don't make them wait more than a day or two); or, if the offer seems low to you, talk with your recruiter and then the company and try to hammer out a new deal. It's crucial to speak with the recruiter *first*. Then he or she can help in the negotiations and possibly get you the package you want—or advise you that there is no way the company will budge from its offer.

▶ **At this point in your job hunt, you should have a good idea of what you want—and expect—from a job offer.**

This is part of the self-assessment process you probably went through earlier in your job hunt. If you haven't done it already, do it now: Take the time to determine what you want, in terms of salary and compensation, job responsibilities, career track, and the like. Decide what is important to you—and what isn't. Determine which elements of a job agreement you are willing to relinquish (from job title to bonus to executive perks) and those that will be deal breakers, that you can't or won't live without.

The key to this exercise, of course, is clear: If you know precisely what you want, what you're willing to back down on, and what will be a deal breaker, you can readily evaluate the job offer and make a decision that pleases you.

ASSESSING THE JOB OFFER: THE COMPANY AND THE POSITION

▶ **Once you have an idea of what you want, assess the job offer carefully to determine what matches your needs and what doesn't. Your first object of scrutiny: the company.**

Especially in tough economic times, it is vital to look into the stability of your potential employer. Follow the guidelines discussed in Chapter 2, "Research"—read newspaper and magazine articles on the company; check the corporate profile on one of the corporate databases, such as Standard & Poor's; ask your stockbroker for an analysis. Pay special attention to past performance and forecasts for the future. Analyze the company as carefully as you would if you were considering investing in it. Remember—you *are* thinking about an investment, but instead of investing money, you'll be investing yourself. So, be hypercritical.

Your goal? To determine whether the company is on solid financial footing.

TIP: If you're a troubleshooter who is being offered a turnaround position, you will really have to read between the lines. Clearly, the company is currently in less-

than-great shape, but can you see it pulling out of the slough it's in? Focus especially on your job responsibilities—will you be given the support you need to bring about the turnaround? What's the time frame (if any) you'll be given to effect this reversal of fortunes?

In addition, try to get a feel for the corporate culture. Remember, if you accept the position, you'll want to fit into the environment. Read between the lines in articles to get an idea of what it's really like at the company. Get your hands on a company newsletter. Ask to meet the people with whom you'll work. If possible, talk to other employees or ex-employees, as well. Go to the restaurant or bar that employees frequent and listen to conversations or join in. Be up front—you're thinking about joining the company and want to learn as much as you can about it. Most people will be glad to help you out. Again, you're trying to put together as clear a picture of the company as possible. So analyze the *intangibles* as well. It's the combination of concrete elements—the company's goals, its stability, etc.—and the intangibles—the people with whom you'll work, the "feel" of the company—that will contribute to your success there.

TIP: **Also pull together information that can help you in the future—areas of the company that are expanding, new opportunities that appear to be arising. This will give you a leg up in the future. You'll be able to target yourself for a promotion or new position later on down the road.**

The questions to answer as you assess the company:

1. Is the company healthy?
2. Would I fit in at the company?
3. Does the company compare favorably to my current (or most recent) employer?
4. Will working for this company fit in with my goals, both short term and long term?

▶ **Next, take a good hard look at the position itself.**

Oddly, this is one aspect of evaluating a job offer that many people do most perfunctorily—yet, clearly, it's crucial.

To begin with, review the job description carefully. Don't assume you have a complete understanding of the position on your own. Read what, exactly, your responsibilities would be. Look into the career track and review the history of the position—what happened to the person who held it before you? This may help you foresee your fate.

The questions to answer:

1. Will the position fulfill you?

2. Does it meet your needs in terms of promotability?

3. Do you have the characteristics, experience, and skills that will enable you to fulfill the requirements well?

4. Do you feel comfortable with your boss and colleagues?

ASSESSING THE SALARY AND BENEFITS PACKAGE

▶ **This is the area that most people focus on—and rightly so.**

To decide whether the job offer is right for you, you must analyze it in terms of what your current (or most recent) job provided you. In other words, you want to be sure you aren't losing by accepting the new job.

The simplest way of comparing? List your current salary and benefits. Include salary, bonuses, pension plan (including SERPs), company contributions to a 401(k), approximate annualized value of stock options (the average stock value for the past three years or an estimate of future value based on earnings per share), company-paid car, any special insurance coverage (coverage for any special medical condition of you or a family member that goes beyond the usual coverage), life insurance, executive health programs, company car allowance, company-paid memberships (country clubs, etc.). Match this against what you are being offered by your new employer.

It's a simple way of seeing if the new package equals or, ideally, exceeds what you've been getting.

Keep in mind: This is also the time to determine what perks and benefits *aren't* important to you—such niceties as executive dining-room privileges or country-club memberships, perhaps—and which ones are must-haves and, as such, are potential deal-breakers.

▶ **An important general note: When it comes to evaluating your salary-and-benefits package, keep in mind that times have changed. Whereas companies used to be fairly generous, now they are much less so.**

It's a fallout from the restructuring and downsizing companies were forced into because of the poor economic climate. More companies have cut back on medical coverage, retirement plans, and the like. Similarly, there has been an increased emphasis on bonuses and other incentives to replace the old annual merit raise.

So, when you're considering a job offer, it's vital to know what salary and benefits are standard for the industry, what the company policy is, and the like.

Following is a look at the various elements in a salary and benefits package—what is usually offered, less common features that may interest you or may appear in your offer, and so forth.

Salary and Other Financial Compensation

▶ **Salary is a straightforward proposition, on the whole.**

You should have a good idea of whether the salary offered is a fair one. It should meet industry standards for the position. If you're at all unsure what these standards should be, because you've changed careers or industries, check against want ads and articles in trade publications, annual salary surveys published in magazines and newspapers or available through trade and professional organizations, and word of mouth from friends and acquaintances in the field.

Be concerned if the salary you're offered is much higher or lower than that at your last job. Higher, and it may mean the company is trying too hard to seduce you into taking the job. Perhaps no one else will take it (which means something is clearly wrong), or they're trying to compensate for poor working conditions. On the other hand, perhaps you've been underpaid in the past.

Lower, and you may be underselling yourself. Or have your expectations been unrealistic? Or perhaps the benefits and other compensation (bonuses, etc.) make up the difference.

Of course, there are instances when a lower salary is almost a given—you're changing careers, for example, and thus can't get what you've been getting.

▶ **A growing trend: being offered payment outside your base salary.**

In addition to base salary, there are a number of other forms of compensation that are growing in popularity. Many replace the traditional annual raise; others are given to keep base salary lower. The key problem with these alternative forms of compensation is obvious: Unlike a base salary, which is guaranteed, you can't count on incentive-based compensation. More simply put, when the economy or the company suffers—or simply when the company doesn't meet the expectations laid out in its strategic plan—you don't get the bonus or incentive.

However, it's clear that these alternative forms of compensation are here to stay. Already, on the average, executives receive about 40% of their total compensation in the form of bonuses, incentives, and other alternative forms. So it's highly likely you'll run across one or more of these in your job offer (or later on during your tenure with the company).

Among them:

- *Bonuses*—the traditional addition to base salary and one that is used more and more. Once limited to upper management, bonuses are now being offered to middle managers and supervisors as well. Bonus amounts vary widely, as do the conditions under which they're given. Usually, they are given annually, and are tied to how well you (or the department or area you are responsible for) perform. Often they're also tied to how well the company has performed as well—although, if you're a top achiever, bonuses can be quite generous, even in lean times. At the upper level, bonuses typically equal 30 to 40% of base pay (although some industries and companies pay astronomical amounts). At the middle level, it's roughly 20 to 30% of base pay.

TIP: A negotiating rule of thumb: Try to lock in a guaranteed first-year bonus. The reason? Most bonuses are performance based and, because you won't have been at the company long, your new employer won't have much of a chance to see you perform.

- *Sign-on bonuses*—increasingly common as employers try to avoid giving other, more expensive perks. These (also called "one-time" or "special" bonuses) are given, obviously, upon accepting the job. Often they're offered to offset relocation costs. The amount of the bonus can vary widely, but is rarely extremely high.

TIP: **If you want the up-front money (particularly useful if you've been unemployed for a long period), you can often negotiate a fairly generous sign-on bonus as a replacement for other perks (company car, country club, etc.) that would be paid for over a long period of time. The reason? Up-front costs are cheaper for the company.**

- *Stock options/grants*—very popular, these are offered to employees by nearly one-third of all U.S. companies. Most common are stock options, in which you have the option to purchase company stock at a set price. These usually cannot be exercised for a set time period. There are a number of different stock-option arrangements; some companies may offer more than one type. With stock grants, you are given shares of company stock. One variation of a stock grant is a restricted stock grant, under which you receive stock only after a certain time period has passed, or upon meeting certain goals.

- *Stock purchase plans:* These allow you to buy company stock (up to a preset amount) at book value or at a discount. In one variation on this, you buy an amount of stock at market price, and the company then matches your purchase either dollar for dollar or at a percentage thereof, and buys you more stock.

- *"Lightning strike," or instant incentives:* Also in use by nearly one-third of all U.S. companies, these incentives—ranging from cash (a percentage of your salary) to other awards (trips, televisions, etc.)—are given, as the name denotes, out of the blue, for special performance.

- *Gain sharing:* A group bonus plan, under which employees receive a percentage (usually 50%) of a company gain in productivity or savings. This is most common in manufacturing companies, although its use has spread to other areas as well. This type of group bonus plan can also apply to smaller groups —for example, to a small team working on a specific project as a reward for getting it off the ground.

- *Pay-for-quality arrangements:* These are similar to gain-sharing plans in that the reward is tied to company performance. Under pay-for-quality arrangements, management rewards employees for doing better than in the past, for meeting quality goals, etc. The payment may be a bonus or a portion of the base salary, and may be paid on an individual basis or to a group. Expect to see a rise in the use of these arrangements, as American corporations become more quality conscious and seek new ways of tying compensation to quality.

Severance Agreements

▶ **Exit terms (also called severance agreements or packages) are no longer just for the highest-level managers.**

It's a sign of the times. Severance agreements used to be the realm of the high and mighty only, but now they've become a common option for middle managers as well. It makes sense—when you get a job offer these days, you want to be sure that you won't be left high and dry later on down the road, should the new ax fall.

In many cases, your job offer will include a set severance agreement. If you aren't offered one, it's something you should seriously consider asking for. If you work in an industry that has been shaken by rough times, marked by downsizings and the like, negotiating a severance agreement should be a high priority. Even if you're in an industry that has been relatively stable, a good severance agreement makes sense.

What should you look for in a severance package?

- *Salary or severance payment,* ideally paid for a year or more if fired. Obviously you can negotiate for a compromise—one year plus stock options, for example. You can also negotiate the form in which you'll receive your payment—as a lump sum or as a weekly or monthly payment. Opt for a lump sum if you fear for the company's long-term financial stability, or if you want to invest the money to ensure covering financial outlays if you are laid off or fired. More often, however, you are better off asking to receive your severance pay as regular salary. Why? Because usually, receiving continuing salary payments means you'll also still be participating in company retirement plans, and so will continue contributing to a 401(k) or the like. In addition, receiving severance as a salary often means you'll also receive continued insurance coverage for the duration of the severance pay.

- *Continued medical coverage:* Again, coverage for a year or more is optimum.

- *Continued life insurance coverage:* Though it's not as important as the previous two options, this too can save you money in the long run.

TIP: **If negotiating a severance agreement, try for a longer period of severance pay, but agree to have benefits coverage drop upon your taking a new job.**

- *Relocation expenses:* This applies if you have to relocate to take the job. In this case, the company agrees to pay for your move back, should you be fired.

TIP: **A good negotiating stance—if your company bases its severance packages on length of service with the company, ask for terms that match those of an employee your age or one at your job level.**

The following are icing on the cake—items that you may want to consider for your severance package but are not as important:

- *Continued employee discounts on company products:* Some top executives have negotiated for lifetime discounts.

- *Continued free use of the company's product/services for a set period (one to five years typically):* This is an especially good item to consider negotiating for if your prospective employer is in a service industry—airline, hotel, telecommunications. You can save a great deal of money by getting this added to your severance arrangement.

- *Private-school tuition:* If you have children currently attending a private school or, more important, if they would have to attend private school for you to take the job, this makes sense to try for.

Benefits

▶ **Benefits packages (retirement plans, company-sponsored health and life insurance, etc.) usually equal more than 20% of total compensation.**

In other words, you would have to earn over 20% more to get similar health coverage, retirement benefits, and the rest. That translates into quite a large dollar figure. For example, according to a 1992 study done by a Washington, D.C. benefits consulting firm, the Wyatt Company, an employee who earns $75,000 a year would have to make an additional $17,000 to cover his or her company-provided benefits—$5,000 for health coverage alone.

Therefore, it's important to closely analyze the benefits you'll be receiving from a new employer, and weigh them against what you're currently receiving. Do keep in mind, however, that more companies are scaling back benefits these days. In other words, you may not be offered as much as you were in the past. However, you should expect the basics—medical, disability, life, and pension—at the very least.

Benefits packages may be standardized packages with minimal flexibility and negotiability, or cafeteria-style, allowing you to design your own package from a variety of options. In the latter case, you have the flexibility to custom-tailor a package, buy supplemental insurance coverage, elect special perks, and the like. This is usually more popular among employees than the standardized package.

Whichever type of benefits package you are offered, however, it's vital that you think carefully about the worth of what you're getting and whether it meets your needs.

Following are some details about the different types of benefits you may be offered, the features to look for, and what to look out for.

Pensions and Retirement Savings Plans

▶ **For the over-40 job hunter, pensions and other retirement savings plans are a particularly important part of the job offer.**

It's obvious—when you were in your 20s, retirement was something in the almost unforeseeable future. Now that you're over 40, retirement isn't quite as far off. It's important that you understand exactly what you will be getting in terms of a pension and other company plans.

In light of this, do be sure to get specifics about the pension plan and other savings plans you may participate in. Just knowing you'll be getting a 401(k) isn't enough. Ask questions to get a complete picture.

SOURCE: A handy guide to help you understand pension plans in general, and yours in particular, is the American Association for Retired People (AARP)'s *A Guide to Understanding Your Pension Plan.* Write to: AARP Fulfillment Center, 1909 K St. NW, Washington, DC 20049

Here is a brief rundown of the various common retirement and company savings plans, and the pros and cons of each.

- *Defined benefits plans:* A company pension plan under which you receive a *guaranteed* amount of money upon retirement, based upon your years of service, salary level, and other factors. This type of pension plan is declining in use, as many employers opt for the more cost-effective defined contribution plans. According to the Internal Revenue Service, over the past ten years at least 22% of all defined benefits plans have been dropped.

  The upside: You can track the amount you will receive upon retirement, as it doesn't fluctuate according to investments or company profitability. Another big plus: these plans are federally insured; so regardless of what happens to the company or the economy, you will receive a fixed monthly payment from the plan.

  The downside: You usually have no input in this type of plan. Your money is invested by professionals; you can't choose investment vehicles. In addition, these plans are typically not portable—if you change jobs, you usually can't switch your pension over to your new company. Finally, while federal insurance does guarantee you payment, it guarantees only a set amount (only up to $2,250 a month of promised benefits for plans ending in 1991—or $27,000 a year at age 65. Not exactly a fortune.)

- *Defined contribution plans:* Under this type of plan, the company contributes a set amount to the company pension fund in your name (usually a percentage of your salary). In most cases, you can direct the investments—that is, you can choose what your contributions will be invested in. Typical choices include company stock, other stocks or stock funds, fixed income securities, etc. In contrast to a defined benefit plan, the amount you receive upon retirement is not guaranteed. It depends upon a number of variables: how well the fund was invested, the state of the economy, the current value of the investments, etc.

  The upside: Most defined contribution plans are portable—

you can roll them into your new employer's similar plan if you change jobs or into your own IRA.

The downside: As mentioned above, your pension money is only as safe as what it is invested in.

Among the common defined contribution plans offered: profit sharing, 401(k)s, thrift plans, and employee stock ownership plans. These are defined starting below.

- *Cash-balance pension plans:* The newest kid on the block, these plans are a combination of defined benefit and defined contribution plans. With a cash-balance pension plan, each employee has his or her own individual account. The amount in each pension grows over time, based on the percentage of pay, plus annual interest credits.

  The upside: Benefits can build up earlier than with defined benefits plans, but like a defined benefit plan, the amount remains trackable.

- *401(k) plans:* 401(k)s are salary reduction plans—you contribute a portion of your salary up to a set maximum, which changes annually to keep in sync with inflation rates. Under some plans, the employer matches a portion of, or all of, your contribution. (The most common matching amount—50%.) You pay no taxes on either the contributions or the amount earned on them until you withdraw the money (usually at age 59½, upon retirement). In most cases, your company offers you investment options—most commonly offered are stock funds, bond funds, or Guaranteed Investment Contracts (GICs).

TIP: The general rules of thumb where 401(k) investment is concerned—stock funds tend to do better than the other two options in the long term, but are often risky; bond funds are the least risky; and GICs, while safe bets in the past, are riskier because of recent problems with insurance companies.

The upside: You can save in taxes—your employer is usually matching all or part of your contribution, which further increases your nest egg; and you have portability—if you leave this position, you can roll the money into another employer's 401(k) or into an IRA.

The downside: Matching contributions on the part of employers have been dwindling recently—the money in the 401(k) may be primarily yours. In addition, it's vital to realize that the amount you receive is entirely dependent upon two facts: the amount you contribute, and how well that money is invested.

- *Profit-sharing plans:* With these, a company annually contributes a portion of its profits into an employee fund that is invested in one or a number of ways. Often, you can choose the investment options—typical choices include company stock, a diversified stock account, or a fixed income account.

    The upside: This type of plan requires nothing from you— no personal contributions, no salary deferments, nothing. As such, it's a painless way of making money.

    The downside: Nothing major. The one drawback occurs when a profit-sharing plan is your sole pension plan. In this case, as with a defined contribution plan, you won't be able to estimate eventual retirement earnings. In addition, you have no control over the amount you receive—if the company falters, you lose a good portion or all of your retirement nest egg.

- *Thrift plans:* This type of plan (also called a company savings plan) is similar to 401(k)s in its setup. You contribute a percentage of after-tax salary to the plan—usually between 2% and 6%. The company contributes a matching amount, usually from 25% to 50% of your contribution. This money goes into a fund, which is invested, typically, in stock mutual funds. The contribution is not tax deductible, but earnings on the investment are tax deferred. As with other company plans, upon retirement or resignation, you receive your money—in this case, in a lump-sum distribution. Because your contribution was deducted from your after-tax pay, you owe no taxes on the amount. You will, however, owe taxes on the earnings and the employer's contribution.

    The upside: You can make a decent amount, especially if the company matches a healthy percentage. In addition, because earnings are tax deferred, you can avoid a tax bite as you save. Furthermore, you can often borrow from your vested benefits penalty free.

- *Employee Stock Ownership Plans (ESOPs):* Similar to profit-sharing plans, ESOPs provide employees with shares of company stock instead of shares of company profits. Typically, the number of shares received is based upon salary level. Employees commonly receive from 5% to 25% of their annual salary, up to a maximum of $60,000. You usually pay no taxes on the stock you own until you leave the company or sell them.

The upside: Like profit sharing, ESOPs require nothing from you. Depending upon the worth of the company stock, you may accrue a nice sum for doing nothing but working at the company.

The downside: Nothing major, except for the fact that you may lose everything depending upon the volatility of the stock. In other words, ESOPs are a nice benefit, but not to be counted on where retirement planning is concerned.

- *Supplementary Employee Retirement Plans (SERPs):* SERPS are designed to supplement the retirement benefits of higher-paid employees (typically those earning over $200,000). In contrast to a regular pension, in which the company pays pension benefits from a specific fund to which it has been contributing pension money in your name, with a SERP, the company pays your benefits out of its general operating profits. There is no pre-funding. In addition, because a SERP isn't a standard qualified pension plan, you don't get the guarantees you get under other plans— you could lose the entire amount funded by the SERP if the company goes bankrupt or if you leave the company.

The upside: SERPs enable higher-income professionals to receive an amount of pension money *over* the federal cap set on benefits.

The downside: You run the risk of losing the entire amount funded by the SERP if the company goes belly up. In this case, you would have to file a claim like other creditors. Similarly, if the company is taken over, new management technically (and legally) could decide not to pay you.

For this reason, check to see how much of your pension will be funded by a SERP. Then check to see if the company has set up a funding vehicle that will protect you from some of the possible negatives. There are three common ways of doing this: 1) Corporate-owned life insurance (COLI)—while this doesn't protect against creditors' claims or management's refusal to pay benefits, it does set up a reserve against future plan obligations and so offers you some reassurance that your nonqualified pension will indeed be funded. 2) Rabbi trusts—these protect the pension from management changes or takeovers, but don't protect against company bankruptcy. A plus: You won't pay tax on the amount in the plan until you receive the benefits. 3) Secular trusts—less common and more complicated, but growing in popularity, these set up individual employee accounts to completely protect the amount in the plan. The downside? You pay taxes on contributions. Of course, on the flip side, you don't pay taxes upon receiving the funds.

TIP: **Because you are an older job hunter, you have less time to accrue much under a regular pension plan based on years of service. Your best bet is to negotiate a SERP to make up the difference between what you would have received if you had stayed in your old job and the straight pension amount you will get here. One cautionary note—this can be a tough negotiating point as more companies cut back on SERPs.**

- *Excess Retirement Plans (or Restoration Plans):* These plans are similar to SERPs in that benefits paid upon retirement can exceed the federal tax law limits. But, unlike with a SERP, the money is provided under the qualified plan formula.

▶ **As you assess this part of the job offer, do remember that pensions and other retirement plans have been going through some shaky times.**

There has been a good deal of concern about the state of a number of pension plans, and about the stability of the pension system in general. To be frank, the concern is justified to a great degree. For example, in May 1990, the Pension Benefit Guaranty Corporation (PBGC), the federal agency that insures defined benefit plans, reported that the pension funds of 50 leading corporations were *each* at least $440 million short of the money needed to meet their pension obligations.

Add to this the fact that the most popular investment vehicle for 401(k)s, GICs, has run into extremely bad times because of upheaval among insurance companies.

And a final point to add—as companies cut costs, many have done away with pension coverage altogether; others are relying on employee-driven 401(k)s to supply pension money.

The bottom line?

Actually, there are two.

Bottom line 1. If you are at all concerned about the safety of a pension fund, *check it out now!* Not later, after you've accepted the offer. Check the company's annual report or the financial section of the 10k report that is filed with the Securities and Exchange Commission by larger public companies. Or ask for a copy of government Form 5500, which will tell you about the plan's investments, how many investment managers there have been, and so forth. Check what the fund has been invested in, and how well the investments have performed relative to the book value of the fund. Better yet, get an outside pension expert to review the management of the plan.

Bottom line 2. Remember that all the problems with the pension system have resulted in a scale-back of pension coverage, and judge the plan you're being offered on that basis—not according to what you may have been offered years ago. And pay special attention to the other company-sponsored savings plans (ESOPs, thrifts, and so forth). Experts agree that in the future pensions will play a less significant role in retirement funding. Personal savings and investment will fill the gap. This being the case, any savings programs the company offers could turn out to be more important than you think.

Medical Benefits

▶ **Similarly, when assessing your benefits package, recognize that health insurance is no longer the given it once was. There's a very good chance that you won't be offered the tried-and-true, old-fashioned medical indemnity insurance you've always had.**

Faced with rising prices of health care, many employers have changed the coverage they offer. Some have scaled back their coverage, increasing the cost of dependent coverage and cutting retiree coverage. Some are offering new options to standard health insurance. Others are instituting cost-sharing programs, in which you are given a choice of coverage and share the costs with your employer.

Following is a quick rundown of the most common health coverage arrangements and specific features to be on the lookout for. Given the above trends, it is highly probable that you will encounter more than one of these types of health coverage as part of your benefits.

- *A standard health plan* usually has a deductible of $100–$200 and covers 80–85% of your medical expenses, up to a limit (usually between $2,000 and $5,000), after which the plan covers 100% of further medical expenses, up to a lifetime cap. The better plans also cover dental and eye care expenses; the best add in orthodontic and substance-abuse treatment coverage. Some plans offer dependent coverage; others require you to pay extra for this. One important note: particularly when dealing with smaller companies, make sure that existing medical problems will be covered by your new employer's plan. Some plans don't allow this, and you may be left having to pay for your own medical expenses.

TIP: **If you're thinking about early retirement in the future, also look into the company's policy concerning health insurance benefits for retirees. You probably will want to keep employer-provided health insurance if you are planning to retire before you hit 65 (when Medicare coverage begins). Check whether you'll be covered, your spouse or dependents will be covered, you'll be responsible for premiums, co-payments, deductibles, and so on. Along the same lines, you may also want to check to see if the company offers prepaid retirement health coverage. It's a relatively new plan that many companies are introducing to help defray the high costs of health benefits and still enable you to retain employer coverage upon retirement—important if you're not near Medicare age. With prepaid coverage, you make a monthly contribution to the company retirement plan. The amount is usually determined by your age. After a certain period—usually 10 years—you are eligible to receive *full* health benefits upon retirement. (If you leave the company before you retire, you receive the full amount you have contributed plus earned interest.)**

- *A standard health plan restricted by board approval* is the newest variation on the standard health insurance coverage. Essentially everything remains the same as in the past—80% to 85% of your medical expenses are covered once you've reached the deductible—but with one crucial difference: Medical recommendations that you receive are reviewed by a utilization review board. If the board considers any recommendation (from medication to other treatment to hospital stays) unnecessary, you will be covered either minimally or not at all.

- *An HMO (Health Maintenance Organization)* provides medical services to company employees for one set per-patient fee—which is paid by the employer. Regardless of the type of care you need, your employer will pay the same set fee (which is why these plans are usually cheaper to employers than standard health coverage

—as long as the greater percentage of their employees are healthy). Depending upon the specific HMO setup, you usually are covered minimally—or, more often, not at all—if you seek medical services outside the HMO network.

HMOs can be staffed HMOs, in which doctors work in one location and send patients to a restricted list of HMO-network hospitals; IPAs (Individual Practice Associations) in which you choose doctors from a list of HMO members and consult them in their offices, and when necessary are sent to the HMO network hospital(s); and open HMOs (a new variation), in which you can seek treatment outside the HMO network, but pay an additional fee for this flexibility, as well as a deductible.

Services covered by HMOs generally range from office visits to hospitalization to surgery. Some also pay for prescriptions, eyeglasses and contact lenses, and other special health services, although such comprehensive coverage is becoming rarer.

- *A PPO (Preferred Provider Organization)* combines certain aspects of standard insurance coverage with HMOs. Like an HMO, a PPO is a network of doctors and hospitals. However, these networks do not receive a set per-patient fee. Instead, they provide *discounted* health care services to PPO members. You pay for services rendered, but less than you would to a practitioner outside the PPO. Under this type of plan, you usually will receive only limited coverage if you go outside the PPO network.

- *Corporate medical centers* are another growing trend. Companies set up their own medical treatment center (usually on site) to cut costs while still offering medical coverage to their employees. Typically, you are covered by employer health insurance *only* if you seek treatment at the company clinic.

- *Catastrophic coverage* is often offered these days, and, because of its limitations, typically is not the only form of coverage available. As the name denotes, catastrophic coverage is designed to pay medical expenses in the event of a major illness or catastrophic accident. Deductibles are usually very high (over $1,000) and often must be met only through payments made for treatment of a single illness or accident. In other words, you often can't pay toward your deductible with regular office visits or unrelated treatments. The limitations to this type of plan makes it a good choice only for the young and healthy or those covered under a spouse's health plan. The major plus, though—these plans are often offered free of cost.

▶ **You may also be able to get long-term-care insurance through your employer.**

This isn't a common offering yet, but it is something you might check to see if your prospective employer offers. A common arrangement—the company doesn't pay the premiums, but its insurance carrier offers employees the option to pick it up on their own tab. The advantage? Premiums are much lower than if you bought l-t-c insurance on your own.

What to look for in long-term-care insurance is difficult to pinpoint. Costs and coverage vary widely, depending upon the plan. Thus, it's important that you clearly understand what the plan covers and what it doesn't. In some cases, coverage is so incomplete (many plans don't cover such illnesses as Alzheimer's, for example) you will be wasting your money if you pay into it.

SOURCE: For extensive information on long-term-care insurance, as well as other information on retirement planning, see our *The Only Retirement Guide You'll Ever Need* (New York: Poseidon Press, 1991), available at most major bookstores.

▶ **Also be aware of two other health-related benefits that do not involve insurance—medical reimbursement accounts and wellness programs.**

Medical reimbursement accounts are employer-sponsored accounts that can help you defray medical expenses, including your insurance deductible, co-payments, medical-related equipment such as glasses, contact lenses, and orthopedic footwear, by allowing you to pay with pre-tax dollars. You contribute an equal amount from your paycheck throughout the year, usually up to a $2,000 limit, and can use the amount at any time throughout the year—and even withdraw the entire sum. The one catch: accounts run on a calendar year and must be set up in January and closed in December. Any amount you haven't spent by the last day of the year is forfeited.

Wellness programs are another non-insurance health benefit, growing in popularity with employers and employees alike. These are designed to attack potential problems before you have to resort to a doctor or hospital. The programs vary widely from employer to employer, and can include on-site health club facilities, prepaid memberships to health clubs, or even financial incentives for quitting smoking or exercising a certain amount. Many companies now offer stress-reduction and addiction programs, as well. Don't underestimate the value of these programs: certain large corporations estimate that 10% of their employees use the counseling option annually.

Life Insurance

▶ **A common but not crucial part of a benefits package, life insurance shouldn't be a major factor in your evaluation.**

Life insurance coverage provided by an employer is usually minimal—however, you generally have the option to contribute to the insurance to augment coverage. In a typical arrangement, the employer-covered cost of basic life insurance is computed as a percentage of your base salary up to a low maximum. If you choose to buy supplemental coverage, you pay an additional rate, generally a very small percentage of your base salary.

The bottom line where life insurance coverage is concerned? It's a fine benefit, but not one that should make or break the job offer.

Disability Insurance

▶ **Disability insurance is another typical part of a benefits package.**

There are few surprises in the disability insurance employers offer. The typical disability plan pays a percentage of your salary—up to about 60%, up to a set monthly limit of $5,000 to $10,000. Some plans allow you to augment the employer covered amount—for a set contribution, your coverage is increased, but even these plans usually cap at about 70% to 80% of total salary.

Two variables to be aware of: a waiting period before payments start, and the length of benefits coverage (the two most common—coverage until age 65 and lifetime coverage). The better disability plans include a residual benefits clause, which gives you partial benefits for partial injuries, and an inflation protection (or cost-of-living adjustment) clause, which adjusts your benefit to keep in sync with inflation.

THE OVER-40 JOB GUIDE

Other Benefits/Perks

▶ **There are numerous other benefits and perks that may be part of your package, or that you may consider trying for.**

Even the smallest perk can add measurably to the value of your offer. Here's a quick rundown of some of the more popular benefits not already covered. The list is by no means complete or comprehensive, but is intended to give you an idea of what companies today offer—and ideas of what you may want to ask for.

Family leave policy—while companies with over 50 employees must, under recent federal law, offer up to 12 weeks' unpaid leave for medical emergencies or birth or adoption of a child, some companies go a step further and offer *paid* leave, or have policies that cover a longer period of time.

Dependent care benefits—this type of benefit, best for middle-income workers with children, can provide employees with a range of different services. Among the common types of dependent care: dependent care spending accounts, from which employees can pay dependent care expenses with pre-tax dollars (in 1992, up to $2,500 could be placed in the program if an individual tax return was filed; up to $5,000, if a joint return), on-site day care, and tuition reimbursement for dependents.

Adoption benefits—financial assistance to help defray the costs of adopting a child. Among the different arrangements offered (in order of frequency): reimbursement of legal fees, of medical costs for birth mother, of agency/placement fees, and of medical expenses of the child. In most cases, there is a maximum limit on the amount reimbursed (typically ranging from $1,000 to $3,000).

Elder care benefits—services and financial assistance to help those taking care of elderly parents. Benefits vary widely, covering a range including: referral services, senior-citizen care centers, unpaid job leave to care for elderly parents, and seminars. Most commonly offered are information and referral services.

Commuter subsidies—company-subsidized commutation vouchers, tokens, or tickets to defray the cost of traveling to and from work.

Financial counseling (also called pre-retirement)—a growing trend, especially as companies cut back on retirement benefits and employees are forced to make more investment decisions on their own. This benefit sounds better than it usually is. More often than not, the counseling consists of one day of seminars explaining investment basics, how to get the most out of company savings plans, and general financial planning tips.

Executive development programs—a perk given, as the name denotes, to executives only. Generally, the program is designed to polish executives' management skills.

NEGOTIATING YOUR JOB OFFER

▶ **All right. So you've reviewed their offer—and it's not quite what you want. Now it's time to get down to brass tacks.**

It's rare that you'll accept a job offer as is. Usually there is something that you want changed, a perk you want that isn't there, a form of compensation, or a benefit they're not offering.

At this point, you and the prospective employer have to hammer out an agreement that meets both of your needs: one that doesn't overextend the company or alter its set policies, and one that doesn't shortchange you.

To do this, you must size up the situation from your point of view and from theirs, decide what is important to you and what isn't, explain what you want and why, and reach an agreement that gives both of you what you want.

Sounds simple? Well, let's be honest. It isn't. But it isn't impossible, either.

The trick, as with anything else, is knowing the tactics and strategies that get results.

Ten Basic Rules of Negotiation

▶ **Rule 1:** *The most important negotiation rule: Negotiate from strength.*

When are you strongest? When they want you, but they don't *have* you.

In other words, just after you've been offered the job, but before you've accepted it.

This is your window of opportunity in which to negotiate for maximum benefit. Use it.

But first . . .

▶ **Rule 2:** *Know what you want—and are willing to go to the line for.*

Before you begin actual negotiation, set your targets—the salary and compensation you want, the benefits package, and so forth.

Decide which of these are negotiable, and to what extent. Perhaps you will accept a lower base salary if the company raises its sign-on bonus, or will accept a shorter period of severance pay if health insurance coverage is included in the exit terms.

Then decide what the deal breakers will be—the factors that you *must* get in your job offer. The deal breakers may be financially oriented—a salary amount, a package of incentives and bonuses, etc.—or may fall in other areas, such as a car, job title, etc.

TIP: When you decide your negotiating limits, be sure you know what company policy is. In many cases, company policy is written in stone, which will make negotiating futile. For example, you won't gain anything by insisting on a special severance package if the company has set termination policies or if you want different health insurance coverage when the company has only two options available. In cases like this, standing firm won't win you anything. All you will do is set yourself forth as an intractable pain in the neck—not a team player, and (probably) not a new employee any longer, either.

▶ **Rule 3:** *Be realistic.*

This dovetails into Rule 2. While you should negotiate for what you want, be sure that what you want is reasonable and attainable.

This is especially important in a weak economy. You can't automatically expect you'll get the salary and benefits of your dreams. In fact, in tough economic times, you may not get a salary higher than in your last job—or even equal to it.

For example, don't be surprised if the offer on the table provides you with fewer perks and benefits than ones in the past. More companies have been scaling back benefits across the board, so there is a fairly good chance that the offer on the table doesn't match what you've been getting. But you can still negotiate for a better deal. One good bet: Make up for the difference with a sign-on bonus.

▶ **Rule 4:** *Be prepared to back up any of your negotiating points.*

Once you have a clear picture of the ideal job offer, the factors you'll negotiate and the ones you won't, it's time to marshal your arguments.

Effective negotiating demands preparation. When the prospective employer asks "Why?" you must have good reasons. For example, if you feel you're being offered too low a base salary, you should know what the industry standard is, what competitors pay, etc. (You should have found this information already—through reading trade papers, and talking with colleagues, employees, and ex-employees of the company, etc.)

You may also justify your requests by pointing to your current (or most recent) compensation—you've been earning more for the past three years, or you have a company car, or have a more attractive bonus plan. Just don't come on too strong in bringing up the differences between this package and your current one.

Throughout this back-and-forth, it's a good idea to keep your experience in mind, the selling points in your background that convinced the prospective employer to hire you. This can help you remember that you're worth what you're asking for—and that you probably will get if not all, at least some of it. In certain cases, it may also help you back up your requests for more—which leads directly to Rule 5.

▶ **Rule 5:** *Focus on them, not you.*

This is how you can most effectively justify your negotiating points to the employer.

Remember, as in the earlier stages of your job hunt, prospective employers don't care about what you need. They care about themselves—in this instance, about getting you for as little as possible.

Play to their wants and needs. Instead of explaining that you need a higher salary because your oldest son is going to law school or simply because you think you should make more than at your last job, bring up the contributions you can make to the company, extra duties you can do in addition to the basic job description—anything that makes it seem *reasonable* that the company pay more.

Your goal? To convince them that you're worth everything you're asking for.

▶ **Rule 6:** *Be firm, but flexible.*

An oxymoron? Not really. The best negotiators give the people on the other side of the table leeway—a range of options, all of which, or course, are favorable to them.

When negotiating base salary, for example, don't get caught by quoting one figure you must have. This backs you into a corner. If they won't pay up, you might be forced to break the deal. Instead, quote a range—the lower end close to but above the offered amount; the upper end above the amount you actually want. As with other points you negotiate, give the employer a *reason* for this salary range—it's in line with industry standards, you'll be contributing a great deal, as demonstrated by the history of contributions you've made to other companies, and so forth.

▶ **Rule 7: A spin-off of Rule 6:** *Read the employer for clues as to when to push and when to suggest a compromise.*

There is a time to dig your heels in and a time to compromise. And usually you can pick up clues as to which time it is.

First of all, when you prepare for the negotiation, you should have a good idea of what you can actually get and what is more problematic. You should know the company policy on compensation, what other people have gotten, etc.

When you're trying for something problematic, watch and listen to the employer closely. You'll be able to tell when he or she is getting angry or stubborn.

When this happens, back off. Stop pushing. You want to divest the negotiation of emotion. This is business, after all.

Instead of plowing ahead bullheadedly, suggest a compromise (that you've already decided upon, of course), and one that both of you can live with. This way you get what you want and the negotiator doesn't lose face either.

The best example (and a practical one): There usually comes a point when the prospective employer won't go any further in base pay. Instead of hitting your head against a brick wall, insisting that you're worth more, and, in the process (probably), losing the job, offer options. Try to make up the difference between what you think you should get and what they are willing to pay by negotiating extras in other areas, financial (sign-on bonuses, review bonuses, stock options) or non-financial (extra vacation time, first-class travel arrangements, spouse travel expenses, company car).

This way it's a win-win situation—just what a good negotiation should be.

▶ **Rule 8:** *Don't fall into the "can't see the forest for the trees" trap.*

It happens to a number of people. They get stuck on one small perk—a company car, say, or the amount of life insurance coverage —and wind up blowing the entire deal.

Don't let this happen to you. Instead of becoming attached to one perk, look at the entire negotiation objectively. Is a car *really* worth losing the job offer? The answer, of course, is no. The rule of thumb to keep in mind: When negotiating, keep the true value of each benefit and perk in mind. Don't let emotions ride you. Instead, objectively weigh the worth of everything you want.

▶ **Rule 9:** *Stay in control of the situation by taking time.*

Even if everything is going along smoothly, it's still an adversarial relationship. As such, you want to have the upper hand.

Of course, unless you can take or leave this job offer, you really *don't* have the upper hand. But you should still proceed as if you do.

How to do this? Play for time.

Time is your friend in a negotiation—in a number of ways.

First of all, don't give up too much too soon. Instead, take the time to determine what points the negotiator won't give in on and which are open for negotiation.

Second, don't be afraid to take time to think, especially if, in the midst of negotiation, you're offered a compromise that hadn't occurred to you. Don't blunder on without carefully thinking about it. If you're not sure how to react, simply say you'd like to return to the point later. Don't let the negotiator force you into an instant reaction.

Use time to keep the negotiation going at *your* pace; don't allow the employer to rush you. More important, always take the time to *listen*. By listening carefully, you'll know how to proceed, what the employer is willing to concede to you, and what he or she isn't.

TIP: One of the best ways to stay in control: Seize control at the very beginning (politely, of course) by suggesting *when* to start. In other words, you'll usually open negotiations with friendly chitchat. Instead of waiting for the employer to say "Let's begin," jump in with "I'm sure you're as eager as I am to begin." This way it's your game—a psychological edge.

▶ **Rule 10:** *Never let them know what you're* really *thinking*.

An old negotiation rule, but still a vital one.

It's like playing poker—don't expose your hand. If you do, and the negotiator sees which points you'll compromise on and which aren't all that important to you, you've lost any leverage you might have had.

One critical situation in which keeping quiet about what you're thinking can win you important concessions: when the employer feels strongly about a specific point in your contract or offer that you consider a giveaway point. If you don't let him or her know that it's a giveaway, you can use this one issue to negotiate for something you *really* want. This often happens when you've requested something that isn't standard company policy.

Finally—and perhaps most important—don't let them see that you're hungry for this job, even if you are. Be interested, even enthusiastic, but don't let on that you're desperate for one moment. All this does is put a negative spin on negotiations. You become the complete supplicant, willing to do anything for the job—which means you will get little of what you want.

OFFER LETTERS AND EMPLOYMENT CONTRACTS: GETTING THE OFFER IN WRITING

▶ **Once you've reached an agreement, be sure to get an offer letter or a contract.**

The hard-and-fast rule—never quit your current job until you've got an offer letter in your hand.

And, if you're unemployed, still ask for an offer letter or contract. It's rare that a company will renege on an offer. Even so, you're always best off to get it in writing. More important, a letter will set forth the offer clearly. Seeing it in black and white will help you more easily decide whether it's the job for you.

Offer letters are common for middle-level managers. Higher-level managers typically get contracts, which are more specific as to entry and exit terms and compensation.

A good offer letter should include:

- *A complete job description,* including title, in which duties and responsibilities are explained (and, if possible, specifying to whom you'll report and those who will report to you).

- *Your compensation*—salary, bonus, and benefits.

▶ **Contracts, generally offered to upper-level executives and other professionals, are more specific than offer letters.**

They typically include:

- *The term of the contract* (the length of time it is in effect—usually three to five years), including any renewal provisions.

- *Job description*—duties and responsibilities spelled out, including title, the person to whom you'll report, those who will report to you, etc.

- *Termination*—the reasons for which you can be dismissed, the severance package you'll receive (severance pay, continuation of benefits, etc.).

- *Non-compete or confidentiality clauses.*

- *Your compensation*—salary, bonus, and benefits, usually spelled out more specifically than in an offer letter.

Should you get a contract? Whenever it is possible to have one, a contract makes good sense. As you can see, it legally spells out precisely what your job entails, what your compensation is, the reasons you can be dismissed, and so forth. With only rare exceptions, if you're an upper-level executive or professional, you'll be offered a contract. Often, you'll be offered one if you're a mid-level executive as well.

If you are not offered a contract, it's up to you to decide whether or not to ask for one. *The bottom line*—push for one if there is any reason for you to worry about the offer or the length of your tenure. For example, ask for one if the company is known for frequent firings, if it is headed for a merger (or, conversely, going to be acquiring another company), or is in an industry that has been marked by merger and acquisition activity or recent downsizings. In addition, if the company always gives contracts, or if they are typically given at your level in your industry, you should expect one.

If, however, you discover at the outset of your negotiations that a company does not give contracts for some reason, do get an offer letter. There shouldn't be much difficulty. The reason? Offer letters are perceived as less threatening—they do basically the same thing as a contract—that is, outline the basic job agreement. However, if you do decide to go for an offer letter in lieu of a contract, be sure it includes a few lines on severance.

If you are getting a contract, you'll want to negotiate its terms carefully. Here are a few things to watch for in your contract:

- *Be sure that entry and exit terms are clearly spelled out.* Entry terms to try for: sign-on bonuses, performance bonuses (stock options, etc.). Exit terms to try for: severance pay for a year or more, and benefits to continue throughout that period.

- *Try for automatic renewal of the contract, or at least automatic one-year renewal.* This will extend the length of time that the contract covers you, protecting you and the agreement you've hammered out.

- *Make sure the section outlining your job duties and responsibilities is as specific as possible.* Vague phrases can mean your duties change in midstream.

- *In the section explaining why your employer can fire you, again aim for as much specificity as possible.* Usually you'll get a clause saying you can be fired for "cause"—and only sometimes is it defined. Problem: Often, "just cause" is vague, ultimately permitting management to fire you for almost anything. Get "cause" delineated as precisely as possible. Also ask for written warnings, and written notice of the reasons for your firing.

- *Be aware of the "non-compete" clause your employer may insert.* This will state something to the effect that you can't work for a competitor for the term of the contract, and, often, for a number of years after the term. When possible, get this clause stricken; otherwise try to limit its breadth (so it prohibits only full-time work or doesn't apply if you're fired).

11

SPECIAL SITUATIONS: LAYOFFS AND FIRINGS AFTER 40

INTRODUCTION

▶ **When you're laid off or fired, you face a unique set of circumstances.**

Yes, many of the mechanics of your job hunt are the same as those of people who are currently employed. But you have more to cope with than just a job hunt. You'll also be dealing with the emotional side of things—feelings of depression, anger, fear—as well as the practical side—making ends meet without a regular paycheck, collecting and re-investing your pension and 401(k) money, and the like. And, finally, you have to stay motivated enough to keep your job hunt running smoothly even while taking care of the other areas of your life.

This chapter will give you an overview of how to handle these aspects of being unemployed. It includes various tips, techniques, and strategies to help you through this difficult period.

For an in-depth look at being fired or laid off, we recommend one of the many excellent books on the market that focus on this subject. One of our favorites:

SOURCE: ***What Smart People Do When Losing Their Jobs,*** by Kathleen A. Riehle (New York: Wiley, 1991), $10.95. Subjects covered include how to determine if a layoff is in the works, how to cope emotionally, financial planning, and more; highly recommended.

HOW TO TELL WHEN THE AX IS GOING TO FALL: HIDDEN (AND SOME NOT-SO-HIDDEN) SIGNALS THAT CAN TIP YOU OFF

▶ **Preparation can be your best friend—in other words, the earlier you discover that your job is in danger, the more you can do to cushion the blow.**

Often it's not too difficult to realize that there's a good chance you'll soon be unemployed: Your company is going through bad economic times; earnings are down; talk of cutbacks is rampant; industry trends point to continued rough times.

Some other fairly obvious clues that should warn you that you could soon be standing in the unemployment line:

- *Colleagues or the business press are saying that layoffs are imminent.* If you hear gossip or read news in the papers, believe it. Yes, these may be idle rumors, but chances are they're not. Especially if the news hits the papers, odds are layoffs are imminent.

- *Your company institutes a hiring freeze.* An early warning signal of downsizing. When they're having problems and need to keep staffing down, companies often take the first step of not adding new personnel. The next step? Cutting back on existing personnel.

- *Retraining programs begin being offered.* Another early warning signal that your company is trying to control staffing by not adding new staff.

- *Your company begins offering early retirement.* Even if it's not in your department, this clearly points to potential danger. The company is being forced to cut back, and early retirement is usually the precursor to layoffs. Similarly, other cost-cutting measures—pay cuts, benefits cutbacks, and the like—signal that a company is edging toward financial dark times and may be forced to cut staff.

- *Your company merges with or is acquired by another company.* This leads to the much-dreaded "redundancy" syndrome—positions that repeat those in the acquiring or larger company get cut. This is especially dangerous for those in staff instead of line positions.

- *The flip side to the above—your company acquires another or fights off an acquisition bid.* The problem? Excess debt taken on either to acquire a company or fight off an acquisition can send a company into a tailspin, resulting in staff cutbacks.

- *You lose a portion of your duties or an assignment to someone else.* This is often a signal that your days are numbered—that management doesn't expect you to be around to finish a specific assignment, or that someone else is being groomed for your position.

- *You receive a poor performance review, or your duties switch to lower-priority assignments.* Unlike the above examples, this is a signal that affects you personally. If you realize that your assignments are less important or that your performance is slipping (in actuality or in the eyes of your supervisor), the ax might be falling soon.

And some less obvious tip-offs that your job may be in danger:

- *Your boss is fired.* Often this is a signal that there's going to be a housecleaning. Perhaps the entire department will be eliminated, or the new boss will want to bring on his or her own people.

- *You are cut out of the communications loop*—memos aren't routed to you; you're not invited to meetings or lunches and so on. This is a signal that you are no longer part of the power circuit and may soon be cut.

- *You receive most or all communications from your boss in writing, not verbally.* If in the past your boss always spoke to you, but now you're receiving written memos, start worrying. This often is a sign that your boss is beginning to put together a written file on you—to back his or her claim that you should be fired.

- *You lose your office, secretary, etc.* If you begin losing the trappings of power, chances are you'll soon be losing your job as well.

- *Management begins holding a series of theoretically morale-boosting meetings to combat negative rumors.* General meetings in which upper management continues insisting that everything is fine are often a tip-off that everything is far from fine—and that layoffs may be imminent.

- *You're kicked upstairs into a dead-end position or into a struggling department or impossible job.* Either one can mean that upper management plans to get rid of you. In the former case, the employer eventually cuts the position because it isn't needed, leaving you out of a job. In the latter, you're placed in a no-win situation. When you can't turn the department around, you're cut.

▶ **Don't be afraid to make a last-ditch effort to keep your job, even if downsizing seems inevitable.**

Some people are able to stay afloat and keep their jobs even through fairly extensive purges.

First, however, decide whether or not it is worth it to preserve your job. This is especially important if your layoff is a result of company troubles. Is your company beyond hope? Or does the current situation appear to be temporary? Clearly, it's important for you to research the situation as thoroughly as possible and objectively assess the chances for recovery. Look at industry trends, your company's past performance, its balance sheet—anything that can help you determine how well your current employer can weather the storm.

If you decide that you want to try to stay at the company, your next step depends upon the particular situation—whether a layoff is in the air or whether your layoff has already been announced.

In the former case, when your company is going through or has gone through downsizing and you fear you may be next, you can start with an indirect approach. Your goal? To make yourself as valuable to the company as possible; in effect, to make yourself layoff-proof. To do this, take on extra responsibilities. Come up with new proposals, new ways of doing business, or, best of all, ways the company can either save or make money. Be sure everyone knows how much you've contributed to the company—toot your own horn. Network like mad, making sure as many people in the company as possible (particularly the top decision makers) know you.

TIP: **One way of standing out in a company: Organize company events, volunteer for company programs or committees. Be a person, not just a name.**

If you know definitely that you're going to be laid off or have already been told that your days are numbered, opt for a more direct approach. Take the initiative and talk to management—an individual at as high a level as possible, who has the clout to keep you on staff. Go in prepared to explain why you're an asset to the company, using specific examples of how you've contributed. It's crucial to remain calm. When you sound too emotional, you blow your case.

TIP: **If you're sure they can't use you on a full-time, permanent basis, there's still hope. Explain that you're willing to be a consultant or contract employee. It can't hurt to ask—and may help a great deal.**

▶ **Begin anticipating the layoff by making some final preparations for your job hunt.**

Your general goal is to make yourself as employable as possible. As such, take advantage of the fact that you're still employed. Use the time before you are actually laid off or fired to gain as much exposure and experience as possible, as background work for your job hunt.

A few hints on how to proceed while you're still employed:

- *Start pulling together information on your skills, recent accomplishments, assignments, etc.* You'll use this information in your resume, when networking, and in interviews.

- *Strengthen ties with colleagues at your company.* These people will become part of your network when you leave. Be sure they know who you are and what you've done.

- *Read newspapers, business publications, and trade journals more avidly than in the past.* This will give you a head start on your research, tip you off on possible employment prospects, and give you a feel for the job-hunting environment you'll soon be in.

- *Take on new duties, responsibilities, and projects with an eye to building your skills and adding to your salability.* Think ahead. Taking on high visibility and impressive projects will make you more salable on your resume and in interviews.

- *Finally, when it seems inevitable, but before the ax actually falls, start looking for that new job.* It makes sense. Face it, it's still easier to land a new job while you're currently employed. Given this, you would be wise to begin job hunting as soon as rumors of layoffs arise. Begin networking, researching prospective targets for your resume, and the like.

THE PRACTICAL SIDE: PREPARATIONS TO MAKE *BEFORE* YOU'RE LAID OFF OR FIRED (OR AS SOON AFTER AS POSSIBLE)

▶ **Try for a better severance package. Or, if you don't have it, negotiate for severance coverage.**

In some cases, you may be able to convince the company to sweeten your severance. The rule of thumb to judge yours by: A standard package for managers and executives equals one to two weeks of pay per years at the company, typically with a two- to three-month minimum payment regardless of service. The norm in 1992 was one to two years' base salary for high-level executives, six months' to a year for middle level.

Often included in the severance agreement: outplacement services for a period of time (usually ranging from a few months to a year), and health and other insurance coverage continued for the severance pay period.

TIP: **If you have a company car, try to negotiate for the continued use of it during the length of the severance pay period.**

If at all possible, try for six months of pay plus health and other insurance coverage for the same amount of time. But keep in mind that getting management to change the amount of severance pay is a long shot. Many companies have set termination policies—and no amount of negotiation on your part will change those policies.

One area, however, in which you may get results: *how* you receive your severance pay. Depending upon the company, you receive one lump sum payment or continue receiving your salary (on a weekly, biweekly, or monthly basis, according to the usual payment schedule) for a time.

The biggest plus about receiving timed payments of your severance is that often you'll also receive continued insurance coverage and continue to participate in company retirement plans. As such, if the company is in good financial health and you can afford to receive the money as if it were regular salary, negotiate for this type of payment (if you don't already have it).

On the other hand, try to negotiate for a lump sum payment if the company is in poor financial health and in danger of failing, or if you need the cash to meet immediate living expenses.

TIP: **A common scenario: You're promised a sweeter severance deal if you resign, instead of waiting to be fired or laid off. If this happens to you, first figure out what you'll lose in unemployment benefits—does the increased severance make up for the loss? It usually does, as unemployment insurance payments aren't all that high. But if it doesn't, don't resign. Let them fire you.**

One final—and very important—note about your severance arrangement: GET IT IN WRITING!

▶ **Start planning what to do with the money in your company retirement plans.**

Where pension plans, 401(k)s, profit sharing, and the like are concerned, you generally will choose among five options.

1. *Taking a lump sum distribution—that is, cashing out your plans and keeping the money*. In this case, keep in mind that you will owe taxes on the lump sum and will owe a 10% early-withdrawal penalty if you're under age 55 (not 59½, as many think, because you are "separated from service," the IRS term for being fired or resigning). In addition, you'll receive only 80% of the lump sum, as under a new law that went into effect after 1992, 20% of the lump sum is withheld. You may, of course, receive that 20% back in your income tax refund, depending upon your total withholding for the year.

2. *Rolling the money over into a new employer's tax-deferred plan or*

rolling it over into an IRA that you set up. In most cases, you have 60 days to roll over the money from your company retirement plans into your new employer's plan or into an IRA—or, as mentioned above, you'll owe tax on the windfall, plus a 10% early-withdrawal penalty if you're under 55. Again, keep in mind that because this is still technically a lump sum distribution, 20% of the total lump sum due you will be withheld—but if you don't make the rollover within 60 days, you'll owe tax and penalty on 100% of the distribution (yes, even though you aren't getting that money).

TIP: **Keep in mind: If you were a participant in a thrift plan—that is, a plan in which your contribution came from after-tax wages—you will not owe taxes on those after-tax contributions, and you cannot roll that portion of the money over.**

3. *Having your employer arrange a trustee-to-trustee transfer of the money into another retirement plan—an IRA with a bank or brokerage, or your new employer's plan.* Yes, this sounds similar to the above. But there's one crucial difference—with a trustee-to-trustee transfer, the entire lump sum is sheltered; you don't pay the 20% withholding. The problem? Because the withholding law is new, many employers aren't yet equipped to do these transfers.

4. *Withdrawing the money in annuitized amounts.* By setting up a series of annuitized payments based on your life expectancy or the joint life expectancies of you and your designated beneficiary, you are not liable for the 10% early-withdrawal penalty, and you can begin using some of your money.

5. *Leaving your money in your ex-employer's plan for an indefinite period of time.* This option isn't always available; it depends upon the particular plan and employer. It's a good choice if you are pleased with the investment options offered by your ex-employer and if you would rather not be bothered with setting up an IRA and making new choices as to how to invest your retirement money.

Your best bets?

- *If you don't need the money,* have your employer arrange a trustee-to-trustee transfer into an IRA at a bank or brokerage. If your employer isn't able to do this, do the second best thing and set up a segregated IRA—an IRA that is established solely to hold your company retirement money—and roll your money into it. As mentioned before, you have 60 days in which to do this. It saves you both taxes and penalties on the distribution, although not the 20% withholding rate. Another plus: If you're a savvy money manager, you can choose your investment vehicles. Then, when you find a new job, you can roll the money in your IRA into your new company's plans.

TIP: **Don't roll your money into an existing IRA. If you do, you won't be able to roll it over into your new employer's plan later on.**

- *If you do need the money* and you're under age 55 and so eligible for the early-withdrawal penalty, consider setting up a series of periodic withdrawals, as mentioned above. You may discover that you'll get enough of your money to tide you over. The system is fairly basic: First, study actuarial tables to determine what your life expectancy is.

TIP: **Your best bet in figuring out annuitized payments is to use IRS Publication 575— *Pension and Annuity Income*—which includes life expectancy tables.**

Next, amortize your account over your projected life expectancy, using a reasonable rate of interest (usually 6 to 8%). Then set up a payment schedule, giving you a distribution from your retirement plans each year. The rules of thumb to follow in setting up this schedule: (1) Payments must be relatively equal (you can't take a huge sum the first year to tide you over your unemployment, then take minimal amounts thereafter); (2) You must take yearly distributions at the least—more often if you want; (3) You must take payments for at least five years, or until you reach age 59½.

- *If you need more money than can be paid out according to the above,* then cash out part of your plans—as much as you need—and roll the remainder over into an IRA. It's a compromise that might fit the bill—you can meet your immediate financial needs, and still keep some of your retirement funds in a tax-deferred vehicle. The downside, of course, is obvious: You will owe taxes and possibly a penalty on the amount you have withdrawn.

TIP: **In all cases, you would be wise to check with your financial planner or consultant for input as to which option will work best for you. Most major financial services**

companies have computerized programs that will tell you the tax consequences of each different method of receiving your retirement money.

▶ **There are other financial considerations you should take care of as soon as possible.**

Some rules of thumb:

- *Pay back any loans from your company 401(k) plan.* If you don't pay back 401(k) hardship loans within 60 days, you'll owe tax and, in most cases, a 10% early-withdrawal penalty. In a cash crunch and still need the money you borrowed? Consider a home equity loan, and when you land a new job, borrow against your new 401(k) to pay it back.

- *File for unemployment benefits if you're eligible*—and keep abreast of any developments concerning these benefits. If you're unemployed for a long period of time, remember that you may be eligible for emergency unemployment compensation—in 1992, this was an extra 20 or 26 weeks of pay (depending upon your state), once state benefits were exhausted. For specific, up-to-date information on unemployment, call the Office of Program Management for the U.S. Unemployment Service.

- *Weigh the cost of private health insurance against the cost of continuing in your company plan.* Under COBRA, you are entitled to buy into your company medical plan for a period of time (usually 18 months). (Keep in mind that many companies won't remind you of this.) But the cost of your company insurance may be high. Look into alternatives—some trade and professional associations offer group health insurance plans, as do other organizations.

TIP: As mentioned elsewhere in this book, if you have few medical needs, consider opting for a low-cost, high-deductible major medical insurance policy to cover you until you've landed another job. This will take care of your bills if you're hit with a major illness or catastrophic accident, but it won't cost you a high premium.

TIP: While you're still covered by the company plan, take care of any medical needs you have *before* you're laid off—have a checkup, a dental exam, etc.

- *Similarly, check into private disability and life insurance.* Disability insurance will cease upon your leaving the company, but you may be able to convert your coverage. Check with human resources or with the insurance carrier to find out. If you decide to get your own coverage, try to do so before you're unemployed —when rates will be better—and be sure you can claim if you are unemployed. As for life insurance, term life policies generally end with your departure from the company. However, you often have the option of converting your policy into an individual one under the same insurance carrier—but you're usually better off not doing so. Reason? As with medical insurance, costs for these policies are usually higher than those of others that you can find on your own. Shop around for your own coverage. Again, if you belong to a trade or professional association, check to see if they offer any insurance coverage. Rates are often quite good.

- *Identify your financial resources.* Put together a financial asset sheet listing all your available finances—savings accounts, CDs or other bank accounts, securities, cash-value life insurance policies, severance pay, etc. Next, use this information to put together a workable budget. Your best bet? Draw up a budget that will keep you afloat without a job for about 18 months . . . and stick to it!

- *Cut back on expenses NOW,* and not a moment later. Your job hunt may take a long time. So the sooner you start saving money, the better. Lay off credit card usage, disconnect cable TV, start clipping coupons, and do anything else you can to downscale your spending.

- *Remember, many job-hunting expenses are deductible* (as long as you are not switching careers)—so begin keeping records and receipts at the outset of your job hunt. Among the costs you can deduct: the cost of preparing a resume, of traveling to interviews, and of long-distance trips (including lodging and food), if they are taken for job-search reasons.

TIP: To help keep track of your job-hunt expenses (and to prove costs to the IRS should the need arise), enter expenses, interview dates and addresses, etc. in a date book. It's the simplest way of keeping your records straight.

ONCE YOU'RE FIRED: PRACTICAL STEPS TO TAKE IMMEDIATELY AFTER THE AX FALLS

▶ **If you're offered an exit interview, take it.**

But don't, repeat *do not,* begin bad-mouthing your employer during the exit interview. You may be upset, you may have just cause to complain about various aspects of your employment and soon-to-be unemployment, but that doesn't mean you should start venting your spleen.

▶ **Some companies will offer outplacement services—take advantage of them, but don't expect too much.**

Sad but true—even if your company offers you outplacement services, you sometimes won't be able to count on them for a great deal of help. One of the biggest problems? The sheer number of *other* unemployed people requiring help from the outplacement firm. You may find that the typist you were promised also has to type for 50 other people. Or the counselor who was to guide you through your unemployment trauma can't see you for a month.

Even so, if it's offered to you, you would be foolish to write it off completely.

A quick look at what to expect:

- *Depending upon the arrangement made with your company, you may get any or all of the following:* counseling—either group sessions or one-on-one, resume-writing advice; technique workshops (how to interview, etc.); free office space (sometimes including computers and/or private phone lines); access to the firm's job bank or contact lists; job leads; free regular and overnight mail; free long-distance phone calls; secretarial work.

- *In some cases, you may be in a position to choose the outplacement firm yourself.* More companies these days are giving the ex-employee a choice of firms (but still paying the expense). If you find yourself in this situation, be careful. You want to make the best possible choice, even while you're not in the best frame of mind. Generally, you are best off approaching this as you would approach a choice between executive recruiting firms. Assess each firm carefully; ask about its background, experience, client load. Get references. *A key point:* Find out how many clients your counselor currently has. According to experts, the best range is from 10 to 20. Finally, take a look at the office in which you'll work. You will be spending a great deal of time here—if it's too small, poorly equipped, or simply depressing, you won't run your job hunt as well as you should.

- *Some outplacement firms also offer special services for your spouse.* It's increasingly common and can be a great help to you and your family. Typically, the firm offers counseling to your spouse on how to handle your newly unemployed status, both emotionally and financially.

On the down side:

- *Don't count on highly specialized assistance.* Most outplacement firms are generalists—it comes with the territory. Because firms have to help different kinds of people in a wide range of positions, they tend to offer very general assistance.

- *Recognize that many of the standard services may prove to be useless to you.* Expect such services as psychological testing to help you decide what you want to do with your life, basics on resume writing and interview techniques, and the like. Since you are an over-40 job hunter, it's probable you already know these things, but you'll be offered them anyway.

- *Overcrowding can strain the firm's resources.* As mentioned above, you may have to wait for a typist, may be too late to get a cubicle or office, and the like.

On the up side:

- *In an outplacement firm, you'll be with others in your position,* which can be a great emotional boost. You'll be able to share contacts and job leads with other unemployed people, many of whom will be from your ex-company. And it's a help seeing other people landing jobs—which you will.

- *You'll have an office to go to,* which will help you stick to a routine (a definite boon in the initial job-hunting stages). And although the office may be gloomy or cramped, it's always nice to have a private phone line at your disposal instead of relying on your home phone. Similarly, having computers or typists on hand can be a big help.

The final word on outplacement? Try it and then decide whether it will help you or not.

ONCE YOU'RE FIRED: THE PERSONAL SIDE

▶ **Don't ignore the emotional side of being unemployed.**

It's human nature—you're fired and you immediately feel as though you're a failure. Well, you're not.

What you *are* is unemployed, like thousands of others.

Of course, knowing this doesn't make your unemployment any less painful. If you're like most recently unemployed individuals, you're going to be hit with depression, anger, denial—a whole spectrum of intense emotional reactions. It can't be avoided. But there are a number of things you can do to ease the pressure and stress of being laid off or fired.

- *Take it easy for about a week.* You need breathing room and time to collect your thoughts. This may be a good time to get reacquainted with yourself, your hopes for the future, and so forth —especially if you're considering a career change.

- *Acknowledge your emotions—even the most negative of them.* Bottling up your feelings won't help; getting them out will. Recognize that it's normal to be angry at your ex-employer, to feel guilty, and so on.

TIP: **Keep a job-hunting journal. According to a recent study conducted by Southern Methodist University and the outplacement firm Drake Beam Morin, Inc., unemployed professionals who wrote about their job hunts, frustrations, and anger got jobs more frequently and more quickly than those who either wrote nothing or wrote about subjects other than their job hunts.**

- *Share your feelings with your family.* Your family is your greatest source of emotional support. Let them help you by being honest with them and listening to their suggestions.

- *Don't think you're unhirable or in any way stigmatized because you've been fired.* It's such a common condition these days that no one looks down on people who have been fired.

- *Focus on small victories.* Don't concentrate only on the huge goal of landing a job. Focus on smaller ones—writing a new cover letter, calling three new contacts, polishing your resume. Emphasizing short-term goals keeps you constantly successful, which keeps you in a winning frame of mind.

- *Read uplifting books.* It's another way of keeping yourself motivated. Biographies of famous people who surmounted great difficulties (Churchill and Lincoln, for example) can inspire you, guide you, and offer perspective.

- *Don't fall into the sweat-suit trap.* It's all too easy to let yourself sit on the couch and watch television all day. But don't let it happen. Keeping busy will keep you from growing depressed or brooding. Make a list of projects you've been putting off for years—from converting the basement to a family room, to painting the house, to planting a vegetable garden—and start doing them.

- *Similarly, start (or continue) exercising.* Physical activity is an emotion booster. An added plus: looking good will pay off during interviews.

- *Keep up with your social activities.* Don't crawl into a shell because you're unemployed. Stay socially active: see friends, remain a member of community groups, etc. Not only does this help emotionally, it can also present networking opportunities.

- *Call friends—especially those who have been in a similar situation.* This is a good way to combat that isolated feeling you may have, and to get support, encouragement, and perhaps some helpful advice.

- *Try to keep your daily life as normal as possible.* Yes, you should cut back on luxuries, but don't make your life a grim unemployment hell. Go to the movies, have friends over, go out to dinner. People need treats to remain optimistic.

- *Break your identification with your former company*—and focus on your career instead. In other words, don't think of yourself as an ex-Acme employee. Think of yourself as a currently unemployed sales manager. This is often a big step for people who have spent several years at a company, particularly a paternalistic company. But it's a necessary part of breaking the ties with the past and heading into the future.

- *Remember—there is comfort in numbers.* Seek out others in your situation by looking into support groups for the unemployed. Support groups offer you a unique boost, a sense of community. Members of such groups share problems, solutions, tips, and leads with one another. It's a great way to feel less alone and to share the highs and lows of unemployment. Especially helpful for the over-40 job hunter are groups made up of older job hunters, like the Forty Plus groups. (For a complete listing, see Sources, page 312.)

  Use them, but don't get overly attached to support groups. They help you get over the hump and, depending upon the group, can be a real asset in introducing you to job leads and sources. However, they can also become a dangerous crutch, or can focus on the negatives and become an emotional downer instead of a lift.

TIP: To find support groups for the unemployed in your area, check the newspaper index at your local library. Many newspapers run stories on job hunting and include listings of local support groups. Also check community bulletin boards, adult education programs, church listings, Y's, and local colleges.

SOURCE: The *National Business Employment Weekly* (available at most newsstands) often runs listings of support groups. Another source: *The National Self-Help Clearinghouse* offers a list of self-help groups, among them support groups for the unemployed. For a list, send $1 and a stamped, self-addressed envelope to: National Self-Help Clearinghouse, 25 W. Forty-third St., Room 620, New York, NY 10036.

TIP: If your spouse is having trouble coping with your unemployment, be on the lookout for support groups for spouses of the unemployed. In the recent tough economic climate, a number of these groups have emerged, helping spouses deal with the difficulties of their position.

- *If you can't find a support group, start your own.* Put an ad in the paper or on a community bulletin board asking other unemployed over-40s to contact you.

- *If you have the time, do volunteer work.* It's a good way to keep busy, make contributions to the community, and keep your self-esteem up. Plus, in some cases, it may lead to job contacts. For listings of volunteer groups, see "Tactics," pages 192–93.

ONCE YOU'RE FIRED: THE PROFESSIONAL SIDE

▶ **Now to the nuts and bolts—tricks and tips that the unemployed job hunter should know.**

- *Get started.* Yes, you should take about a week to adjust emotionally, but not much longer. Start job hunting soon afterward. It's a help emotionally, plus it gets you right back into the swing of things.

- *Approach your job hunt like a job*—set up a space that will serve as your job-hunting office; get an answering machine so you won't be tied to the phone (remember—job offers tend to come by phone; you don't want to miss a call); if it's financially feasible and if you have children who tie up the phone, consider getting a separate line.

TIP: **If you don't have call-waiting, consider getting it. This way you won't have to worry that an important caller is getting a busy signal while you're on the line with someone else.**

- *Set up a daily schedule.* When you had a job, you had a routine. Establish a new one now. There's nothing more dangerous than letting yourself slide into a routine of sitting around the house doing nothing.

- *Make a set number of phone calls each day,* to build up your network and keep you in touch with the working world. Decide how many calls you want to make each day, and make them. Don't let yourself make excuses. Remember—job hunting is your job now. Just as you wouldn't have let your old job duties go undone, you can't neglect your new ones.

TIP: If you're not a phone person, start the day by calling a friend or colleague to chat. Then ease your way into making your job-hunt-related phone calls.

- *Don't be afraid to admit you were fired to potential employers or networking contacts.* As mentioned before, there's no longer a stigma about being fired. Furthermore, if you try to cover up the truth, people will usually be able to read between the lines and know that you were fired anyway.

- *Keep a job-hunting log,* either in a notebook or on your computer. In it, keep track of progress in every facet of your job hunt—network contacts, when you called them, what they said, companies you've contacted, the dates you sent letters, replies you've received, and so on. This will allow you to see at a glance where your job hunt stands, and is a great way of keeping organized.

- *Check to see what groups may help you in your job hunt.* In addition to support groups (discussed above), many colleges and universities have begun offering assistance, including job leads, job listings in newsletters, and counseling. Also, check into state and local programs.

TIP: Keep your eyes and ears open for special programs to help the unemployed. One good one: Each year the outplacement firm Challenger, Gray & Christmas holds a free national job-search call-in, offering free job-search advice over the phone. Usually the *Wall Street Journal* and other papers run a small news item mentioning the dates (typically the last two business days of the year). Or you can call the firm at 312-332-5790.

- *Leave no networking opportunity unused.* Network wherever you are —in church on Sunday, during intermission at the theater, and so on. Anywhere a group of people is gathered, you should talk about your job hunt. You never know who knows whom, or who has a job lead.

- *Take the time to make yourself more employable.* Take courses, be on the cutting edge of your professional area, learn a language or new computer skills.

- *Don't be ashamed to take a menial or part-time job if you need the money.* If you need to ease your financial burdens, do so—it will make you calmer in the long run. Just don't get so caught up in your part-time or interim job that you neglect your primary work, your job search.

THE THREE RULES OF JOB HUNTING WHILE UNEMPLOYED

▶ **Finally, keep in mind the basic rules of job hunting when you're unemployed.**

▶ **Rule 1:** *Be realistic.*

Accept it. You probably won't find a job tomorrow or even next week. And you might not find the job of your dreams or even a job that's a step up from what you had before you were laid off.

Job hunts take time. As mentioned earlier, the old rule of thumb —one month for every $10,000 earned—doesn't apply anymore. The new rule is that there is no rule. Your job hunt will take as long as it has to.

You also have to recognize that you may not get the job offers you want or think you deserve. In this case, don't get overly depressed. Assess the situation—are you expecting too much? Too much money? Too high a title? You may be aiming too high or targeting yourself incorrectly. Evaluate yourself and your goals objectively—it's the only way you'll break through.

▶ **Rule 2:** *Be flexible.*

This is the perfect time for self-assessment. While you're out of work, you can get in touch with yourself, what you're best at and what you really want to do. This may be the time to change careers or even go it alone in your own business.

So don't be a linear thinker where your career is concerned. In other words, don't assume you should be looking only in the same industry or only for your old position. Be creative. What skills do you have that are transferable? What other areas interest you? Your job hunt may be more successful if you broaden your horizons. (For more, read Chapter 1 on self-assessment.)

And consider being flexible about relocation to increase your employability. Being able to move is a big plus and can multiply your job opportunities.

▶ **Rule 3:** *Keep trying.*

To quote Winston Churchill, "Never give up. Never, never, never, never give up."

You *will* get a job eventually. Believe it.

12

SPECIAL SITUATIONS: AGE DISCRIMINATION

AGE BIAS: WHAT IT IS AND WHAT TO DO ABOUT IT

During some aspect of your job hunt, you may encounter age-related job discrimination and decide enough is enough. You'll sue the bums. In general, your best bet is to focus on getting a job—and not spend valuable time contemplating a lawsuit you may not win. But there are times when legal action is a good idea—and here's how to know when.

▶ **A little legal background: Age-bias cases are decided on the basis of the Age Discrimination in Employment Act (ADEA) of 1967, amended in 1986; the Workers Benefits Protection Act of 1990; and Title VII of the Civil Rights Act of 1964.**

Job-related age discrimination is illegal in most cases. Under the ADEA, if you're an adult between 40 and 70, employers of over-20 workers may not fire, forcibly retire, or refuse to hire you on the basis of your age, with certain exceptions concerning seniority policy and public safety (police, for example, have legal age discrimination) and executive retirement policy (executives can be retired at 65 instead of 70). During the hiring process, employers may not:

1. Ask you your birth date (they may after you have been employed).

2. Ask you your age (other than to determine if you're between 18 and 70—which should be obvious).

3. Make hiring decisions based on your age, in accordance with the above.

Obviously, employers often do just that—but the hard part is proving it. Age bias can be proved via direct evidence, statistical evidence, or circumstantial evidence, such as documentation of preference for younger employees.

The number of age-bias cases is increasing—from 14,500 in 1990 to 17,000 in 1991, with even more in 1992. Most cases never get to court. The Equal Employment Opportunity Commission, the chief federal law enforcement agency concerned with age discrimination, settles most claims out of court—less than 1% of the total number of claims filed end up as full-fledged lawsuits. There is a two-year statute of limitations on age-bias cases.

▶ **To win a case of age discrimination in employment, you'll have to prove:**

1. *You belong to a protected age group.*

2. *You applied for and were qualified for the position in question.* You must make certain you have a full description of the position requirements, and your qualifications.

3. *You weren't hired in spite of your qualifications.* Keep a record of why they said you weren't hired—in cases where words like "overqualified" were used, courts have found for the plaintiffs.

4. *The same position was filled by a younger person.*

▶ **The first steps in any potential legal case are to (1) keep good records; (2) find out whether you have a strong case; and (3) find a good lawyer.**

A good job hunt is a well-organized one—and this goes double if you plan on spending any time in court. Begin by keeping complete and detailed records. Keep a date book handy, and mark down *what* was said, *where, when,* and *how.* Make memoranda of conversations.

But what about the merits of your case? A good way of getting an idea of them is to go to a local 40-plus club (see page 312). This group specializes in helping over-40 job seekers, and has experience in age-related cases. If your case is worthy, a good lawyer is obviously essential, and here, too, the 40-plus club may be able to help you make the right selection. He or she can help you bring your case to court and, more important, settle before a case comes to trial. Over 75% of all age-bias cases (including job discrimination) don't make it to trial—but a good pre-trial settlement can make the matter moot.

Remember, all this must occur within *two years,* according to the statute of limitations. It's no wonder that so few cases make it to court—but as the 1990s progress and as baby-boomers age, some predict that such cases will become far more prominent. Stay tuned.

13

SPECIAL SITUATIONS: SELF-EMPLOYMENT

INTRODUCTION

▶ **Starting your own business can be exhilarating—and daunting.**

There is an enormous amount of legwork to be done *before* you embark upon an entrepreneurial career. As with any career change, initial planning and research pay off. But in many ways starting your own business is very different from any other job or career change: You're on your own, so while the payoff may be larger in terms of autonomy, control, and, sometimes, money, the costs are also larger. With self-employment, as with everything else, there's no such thing as a free lunch . . .

Surveys show that most entrepreneurs entered their fields with a great degree of optimism only to find that:

- It took longer than they expected to make a profit—let alone to make a large profit.

- The work was much harder than they had thought it would be.

- The hours were much longer.

- Being self-employed was lonely.

Did they care? To most of those who succeeded the answer was no—at least not in the long run. The driving need to make it on their own gave them the persistence and strength to ride out the rough periods—and glean the very real rewards of self-employment.

▶ **One more point needs to be made. It may be easier to start out alone when you're 25 or 35, but now that you're over 40 you have some advantages as well, including business acumen, experience, contacts, and street smarts.**

Many people over 40 have made the leap into self-employment and succeeded, and the number is growing. One estimate is that about 20% of all new businesses are launched by those 50 and over. Some are entering self-employment out of neccessity—they're looking at a crowded, tough, and discriminatory job market—but many others are looking at self-employment as a way of enjoying some positive aspects of working that are harder to find at large—or even small—corporations. The self-employed often feel freer, more creative, and more vital than those slogging along in the corporate world. Even if self-employed life is tougher—even if life is *much* tougher (as it so often is)—many self-employed individuals cherish the freedom that comes from not having to follow the often arbitrary rules that govern most corporations. In short, the choice to become self-employed is for many the most positive choice they've made.

This chapter focuses on three avenues of self-employment for those over 40: consulting, starting your own business, and buying a franchise.

ASSESSING THE SELF-EMPLOYMENT OPTION: GENERAL CONSIDERATIONS

▶ **Lifestyle and personality considerations are very important: Self-employment is not just a job, but a way of life.**

Life as a self-employed entrepreneur or consultant is radically different from managerial or corporate life. And often, what appears wonderful on paper is not so wonderful when reality sinks in. *A key question* you must answer: Do you have an entrepreneurial personality—can you survive and thrive during the lonely, tough, sometimes exhilarating, sometimes depressing days ahead? Is your dream of being self-employed just that . . . a dream? Or is it solidly based in reality, a deep-seated desire to make it on your own, which is coupled with the knowledge of what it will take?

Some personal questions to ask yourself:

- *Am I a self-starter?* You won't be able to rely upon others for encouragement, recognition, or, more important, for very much business and technical support beyond the services of an accountant and a lawyer. Initially, at least, *you'll* do the bulk of the marketing, selling, finance, etc., unless you're one of the lucky 0.5% who has sufficient venture capital to hire a team. Even then, as the prime mover behind the business, you'll find yourself doing far more on your own than you would in any corporate position.

- *Am I persistent?* The bottom line in entrepreneurship and self-employment is not giving up, and getting back up after you've failed. Most entrepreneurs are very persistent—their dream sustains them through the inevitable downturns and failures.

- *Am I organized?* Some entrepreneurs aren't, but you'll be ordering supplies, writing and estimating cash flows, keeping detailed tax and personnel records, and more. Even with accountants and lawyers, the amount of paperwork can be overwhelming.

TIP: Several surveys of new entrepreneurs have found that one of the rudest shocks of their new careers was the daunting paperwork required by federal and state governments.

- *Am I disciplined?* Don't underestimate the importance of this question. Many people subconsciously need others to motivate them. Can you force yourself to work well even when you don't want to and nobody's making you?

- *Do I have the energy and time?* If you're over 40, your energy level may be too low, or you may simply value your leisure time too much. As someone who is self-employed you'll have to be ready for many late nights, and you'll probably miss out on vacations, family time, golf or tennis with friends, and so on.

- *Can I handle the risks?* Entrepreneurship is risky—there's no career track, no guaranteed salary, no clear alternative to failure. And failure rates can be high: According to the Small Business Association, 55% of all small businesses fail within the first five years. Think carefully about your attitudes toward risk—can you handle the daily uncertainty, particularly now, when you've got more to lose? Look hard at yourself and ascertain whether you can handle failure.

- *Can I rely upon my family?* Family support in this difficult venture is important. With less time for the family, money plowed back into your business rather than vacations, etc., problems can arise if your family is not supportive.

- *Can I work alone?* Most entrepreneurs start out by themselves or with one or two partners, and such a lifestyle can be very lonely. Don't underestimate this, particularly if you come from a crowded corporate environment where a friendly chat is as near as the company cafeteria.

- *Can I sell?* You can't escape this question. Consultants sell their services; entrepreneurs and franchisees sell products or services. Those who need outside capital must "sell" bankers, friends, or venture capitalists on their business plan. Selling, particularly in start-up environments, is difficult for some. Be certain you have the ability and enthusiasm to sell yourself and your services effectively.

- *Am I ready for the practical aspects of self-employment?* Self-employment entails cutting loose from employer-provided financial assistance. Be prepared to take responsibility for your insurance—health, disability, and life. (See page 285 for some details.) Make certain your financial war chest is sufficiently large—most of the self-employed find that it takes twice as long as they originally projected to make a profit. See page 305 for some financial rules of thumb.

SOURCE: *From Executive to Entrepreneur: Making the Transition,* by Gilbert Zoghlin (Amacom, 1991; $24.95). Includes financial work sheets to help you make a sound decision.

▶ **Before taking the self-employment plunge—do some networking research.**

Visit self-employed people (in your field if you can, although as competitors they may not be as helpful as you wish) and spend some time with them during work. This is the best way to get a real feel for the lifestyle and day-to-day work.

TIP: **Be doubly thorough with businesses that have a high failure rate. Many businesses that sound attractive fall into this category, including restaurants, retail businesses, inns, etc.**

▶ **Research your idea.**

Whether you've decided to become an engineering consultant or to start a puzzle factory, do some initial legwork in the library. Concentrate on the market for your service or product, the ideal locations, the estimated start-up cost, the cost of staying in business. Ask yourself how your product or service differs from others like it. Some questions to answer:

- What exactly is your product or service?

- How does it differ from other products and services like it?

- What and where is your competition? What is their price, their advantage?

- Who are your customers? Give a detailed profile and breakdown.

- Why will they buy your product or service?

- How much will they pay for your product or service?

- How many will buy your product or service?

- How will they find out about your product or service—advertising, PR, word of mouth, etc.? How much will this cost?

SOURCE: *The Small Business Test,* by Colin Ingram (Ten Speed Press, 1990; $8.95). A self-scoring test of your business idea and your personality, which analyzes the viability of both.

Utilize the services of experts as well. One good source of free or inexpensive advice is the Small Business Association, which sponsors a nationwide group of retired executives (not bureaucrats) with experience in all aspects of entrepreneurship. They're volunteers, so the advice you get is unrelated to the selling of any service.

SOURCE: **SCORE (Small Business Association Service Corps of Retired Executives),** 1825 Connecticut Ave. NW, Washington, DC 20009. Tel.: 800-368-5855; or call your local SBA office.

SOURCE: **The Small Business Administration** sells many relevant publications. For a price list, write: SBA Publications List, PO Box 1000, Fort Worth, TX 76119.

SOURCE: **The Small Business Association's Office of Women's Business Ownership** (409 Third St. SW, Sixth Floor, Washington, DC 20416. Tel.: 202-205-6673) offers information on training programs for women.

SOURCE: **American Woman's Economic Development Corporation,** 641 Lexington Ave., New York, NY 10022. Tel.: 212-688-1900. Offers training and counseling; maintains hotline with advice for a fee.

Now consider three skill areas: marketing, financial aspects, and the specific skills required in your planned business. Are you lacking in any of these areas, and if so, is there a way you can improve?

One fact to remember, however. Experts have been wrong before and they're sure to be wrong again. Listen to them—but also to yourself. Experts are great at debunking entrepreneurs—but that's why they're experts and not entrepreneurs.

▶ **Develop a strong business plan.**

To get financing and a good idea of where you plan to go, a business plan is essential. It should include the details of the marketplace you'll be in, the start-up costs, operating costs and expenses, and cash-flow projections. Be tough with yourself—the odds are your business won't make money the first year or so, and few bankers or venture capitalists will believe otherwise.

▶ **The scope of this book prevents complete coverage of self-employment. Here's a summary of the main points to consider and follow.**

Below are rules of thumb for self-employment culled from the best experts of all—those who have done it.

- *Decide if you're psychologically ready for self-employment.* Answer the above questions, and visit self-employed friends and observe their lifestyle. Be prepared for long hours and hard work.

- *Don't count on having much time.* Hopefully, your children are grown, your spouse doesn't need you constantly, and you can devote most of your time to your business.

- *Focus on an idea, service, or product you like and believe in deeply.* If you don't become rich, at least you'll enjoy the work.

- *Get the advice you need from experts.* See the sources above for some help.

- *When in doubt, start small.* Get a feel for things this way. If you're thinking about consulting, moonlight for a while to get the hang of selling your services and get a feel for the market. Consider beginning a home-based business and moving out when the time is right. Forty million Americans currently work out of their homes, and new technologies make it easier than ever to tap into national and world markets from there.

SOURCE: ***Everything You Need to Know About Living and Working Under the Same Roof,*** Paul and Sarah Edwards (NY: J.P. Tarcher, 1990; $14.95).

- *Build a war chest.* Before you take the plunge, get a reserve fund in the bank—preferably six months' or more of living expenses.

- *Put your financial house in order before you begin.* Shop around for the cheapest high-quality insurance you can find, pay down debts (the last thing you need now is high personal debt), prepare a budget, and plan on cutting personal expenses. Check your credit lines.

- *Keep your financial situation under control.* Don't be stingy when it comes to business expenses, but don't waste your money on top-of-the-line ergonomic chairs when what you really need is a top-of-the-line laser printer.

- *Don't take profits in the first years.* Plan on plowing profits back into your business or building a cash reserve to tide you over if the winds change.

- *Don't cut your ties to the past.* Just in case, keep your lines open with old associates from your previous career.

- *Be persistent.* It's never easy, but as one entrepreneur said, "If you really want it, you'll get it."

▶ **Consulting as a self-employment option is increasingly popular.**

Consulting can be a stopgap measure, a way of earning a few dollars, or a full-fledged business. Or it can be a polite euphemism for "unemployed." The key difference lies in your skills and know-how and the marketplace for your services.

Key

Set a game plan for your consulting before you begin. If you intend your self-employment to be merely a stopgap measure, be certain to plan and schedule accordingly—*around* your job hunt. Many older and wiser consultants report that they became so immersed in the business they forgot their primary focus—to get a job. Of course, one major advantage of consulting is that it keeps you plugged into the corporate world, ready and able to spot and act on job opportunities rapidly.

If you're seriously thinking of consulting as a primary business, try to begin networking *before* you leave your job. Gain contacts now —before you need them. And ask yourself:

- *Do I have the mental attributes for a self-employed consultant?* Can you constantly sell and hustle for new jobs—even while you're at work on another?

- *Do I have the necessary skills?* Check with your contacts the market value of your skills. Some in-demand areas: accounting, environmental engineering, health care, security.

- *Do I have the contacts or sales skills to get jobs?* Often, small companies, even mom-and-pop shops, can be good sources of business. Of course, your former employer is the best place to start.

- *Are you ready to set up an office?* Up-front expenses can include computers, new phones, and fax machines. And add the services of an accountant, bookkeeping expenses, etc.

▶ **Franchising is a good option for many, but remember the Latin phrase: Caveat emptor.**

Franchises offer a middle way out for the over-40 manager who wants *some* independence, but also a little hand-holding—either in the form of expertise or in preset mode of doing business.

There are many positive aspects of buying a franchise. Here's a list of some of the advantages many (but not all) franchises offer:

- *The advantages of an established business:* It's often much easier to buy a franchise than start a business from the ground up. Suppliers, marketing, design, national advertising—all may be in place, or at least you'll have benchmarks to compare costs and products.

- *Documented past experience:* Good track records of other franchisees in different locations are no guarantee for your own success, but will at least give you a better idea of what the future may hold. It's often easier to make reasonable cash projections and plan your financial life accordingly.

- *Seminars and help:* Not all franchises offer much of this, but some do, and you'll learn the mechanics of your business from experts in the field, not from generalists.

- *Good will:* Many national franchises have built-in name recognition. Customers may know and like the product or service, without you're having to introduce it—a key advantage in today's crowded marketplace.

▶ **That said, franchises are not the be-all-and-end-all for many.**

Key disadvantage

If you're a truly independent-minded entrepreneur, remember that your independence is severely curtailed in most franchises. A McDonald's franchisee can't decide to independently introduce a soy burger for health food fans, even if the franchise is located in a prime market for such foods. You'll have to go by *their* guidelines, even if you know a better way.

Second, roughly one-third of all franchises fail—to the dismay of the many laid-off managers who have plunked down hard-earned lump sums only to watch the money go down the drain. When you consider that many entrepreneurial businesses have similar failure rates, this number may not seem too high—but then again, you're probably buying a franchise for the added safety.

▶ **What to look for when buying a franchise.**

Again, remember that Latin phrase—caveat emptor: Let the buyer beware. When looking at a franchise or an already existing business, many buyers focus on the business itself and the excitement of it—and fail to look carefully at the financial books, the bottom line, and their own motivation for buying it. In short, they don't do their homework. Some general rules to follow when buying a franchise:

- *Pick a business you like.* Don't waste your time with businesses that don't interest you—you won't *naturally* keep up with trends, etc.

- *Pick a strong franchiser.* A good number of franchisers, particularly small ones, go out of business each year. Investigate the financial strength of your prospective franchiser by taking these five steps.

  1. Check financial disclosure statements filed with the Federal Trade Commission, which will show sales, growth projections, etc.

  2. Call the State Attorney General and the Better Business Bureau to find out if they have any records of complaints outstanding.

  3. The franchiser's offering circular will show the company's financials, as well as lawsuits, bankruptcy filings, etc. Obviously, the latter are bad signs.

  4. Ask your franchiser to introduce you to other franchisees—and ask pointed questions (see below). If the franchiser seems hesitant, be particularly cautious.

5. Hire an accountant or lawyer specializing in franchises to check all of the above with you.

- *Ask questions.* When meeting with your franchiser or other franchisees, ask *specific* business questions: "Are you making a profit?" "What are your problems with sales?" "What are your best-selling and worst-selling products?" Many prospective franchisees focus on the lifestyle and romance of the business, much to their detriment. Also remember that other franchisees may lie—it may be in their best interests to have someone else buy in.

- *Get a clear idea of what the franchiser can do for you.* Some do a lot, others only a little. Get a clear idea of what they can do, and whether it will be of value.

- *Look at the books twice—and then twice again.* Books can be doctored —go over them with your accountant. And don't just analyze the financials, analyze *trends.* Are sales high because of one-time markdowns, what is the average age of inventory, and is the number increasing or decreasing?

- *Study the marketplace: Talk to suppliers and customers.* Your franchiser may not know your specific market well, so you should get to know it by walking around, getting to know prospective customers and suppliers—and competitors. You may find that the franchiser's suggested prices are too high (and hence its profit targets too low), that competition is fierce and undercutting, that good help is hard to come by, etc. Or you may find that everything looks ready to go.

SOURCE: **International Franchise Association,** 1350 New York Ave. NW, Suite 900, Washington DC 20005. Tel.: 202-628-8000.

SOURCE: **Women in Franchising,** 175 W. Jackson Blvd., Suite A-2116, Chicago, IL 60604. Tel.: 800-222-4943.

Sources

Note: For major general directories and more, see listings in Chapter 2, "Research."

American Business Women's Association
9100 Ward Parkway
Kansas City, MO 64114
816-361-6621
Publishes periodical with career advice, etc.

American Management Association
135 W. Fiftieth Street
New York, NY 10020
212-586-8100
The major association for managers. Offers numerous programs, has many offices in the US and worldwide, has information service, bookstore, etc.

Catalyst
250 Park Avenue South
New York, NY 10003
212-777-8900
Promotes change for women in the workplace; offers wide range of career services and information.

National Association for Female Executives
127 W. Twenty-fourth Street, Fourth Floor
New York, NY 10011
212-645-0770
Publishes magazine, offers career workshops, resume guide and writing service, discounts on career books, aptitude testing.

Older Women's League
66 Eleventh Street NW, Suite 700
Washington, DC 20001
202-783-6686
Publishes career information on job discrimination, counseling, etc.

FORTY-PLUS CLUBS

CALIFORNIA

Forty Plus of North America
7440 Lockheed Street
Oakland, CA 94603
415-430-2400

Forty Plus of Southern California
3450 Wilshire Boulevard
Los Angeles, CA 90010
213-388-2301

Orange County Division
23151 Verduga Drive, #114
Laguna Hills, CA 92653
714-581-7990

COLORADO

Forty Plus of Colorado
639 E. Eighteenth Avenue
Denver, CO 80203
303-830-3040

Northern Division
3840 S. Mason Street
Fort Collins, CO 80525
303-223-2470, ext. 261

Southern Division
2555 Airport Road
Colorado Springs, CO 80910
303-473-6220, ext. 271

HAWAII

Forty Plus of Hawaii
126 Queen Street, #227
Honolulu, HI 96813
808-531-0896

ILLINOIS

Forty Plus of Chicago
53 W. Jackson Boulevard
Chicago, IL 60604
312-922-0285

NEW YORK

Forty Plus of Buffalo
701 Seneca Street
Buffalo, NY 14210
716-856-0491

Forty Plus of New York
15 Park Row
New York, NY 10038
212-233-6086

OHIO

Forty Plus of Central Ohio
1700 Arlingate Drive
Columbus, OH 43328
614-275-0040

PENNSYLVANIA

Forty Plus of Philadelphia
1218 Chestnut Street
Philadelphia, PA 19107
215-923-2074

TEXAS

Forty Plus of Dallas
13601 Preston Road, #402
Dallas, TX 75240
214-991-9917

Forty Plus of Houston
935 Westheimer, #205
Houston, TX 77027
713-850-7830

UTAH

Forty Plus of Utah
1234 Main Street
Salt Lake City, UT 84117
801-533-2191

WASHINGTON

Forty Plus of Puget Sound
Northwestern Corporate Park
301 Twentieth Avenue NE, Suite 7-200
Bellevue Avenue NE
Seattle, WA 98005
206-450-0040

WASHINGTON, D.C.

Forty Plus of Greater Washington
1718 P Street NW
Washington, DC 20036
202-387-1562

STATE DIRECTORIES

ALABAMA

Alabama Business Directory
American Business Directories
5711 S. Eighty-sixth Circle
PO Box 27347
Omaha, NE 68127
402-593-4600

Alabama Directory of Mining and Manufacturing, available from:
Harris Publishing Company
2057 Aurora Road
Twinsburg, OH 44087
216-425-9000, 800-888-5900

Alabama Industrial Directory
Alabama Development Office
State Capitol
Montgomery, AL 36130
205-263-0048

Alabama Manufacturers Register
Manufacturers' News, Inc.
1633 Central Street
Evanston, IL 60201
708-864-7000

Southeastern Regional Manufacturers Directory
George D. Hall Company
50 Congress Street
Boston, MA 02109
617-523-3745
(includes Alabama, Georgia, and Mississippi)

ALASKA

Alaska Business Directory
American Business Directories
5711 S. Eighty-sixth Circle
PO Box 27437
Omaha, NE 68127
402-593-4600

ARIZONA

Arizona Business Directory
American Business Directories
5711 S. Eighty-sixth Circle
PO Box 27347
Omaha, NE 68127
402-593-4600

Arizona Industrial Directory
Manufacturers' News, Inc.
1633 Central Street
Evanston, IL 60201
708-864-7000

ARKANSAS

Arkansas Business Directory
American Business Directories
5711 S. Eighty-sixth Circle
PO Box 27347
Omaha, NE 68127
402-593-4600

Directory of Arkansas Manufacturers
Arkansas Industrial Development Foundation
Box 1784
Little Rock, AR 72203
501-371-1121

CALIFORNIA

California Business Directory
American Business Directories
5711 S. Eighty-sixth Circle
PO Box 27347
Omaha, NE 68127
402-593-4600
Two-volume set: North (includes San Francisco area) and South (includes Los Angeles area). Each volume also available singly.

California Manufacturers Register
Database Publishing Co.
523 Superior Avenue
Newport Beach, CA 92663
800-888-8434

San Diego County Business Directory
Database Publishing Co.
523 Superior Avenue
Newport Beach, CA 92663
800-888-8434

Southern California Business Directory and Buyers Guide
Database Publishing Co.
523 Superior Avenue
Newport Beach, CA 92663
800-888-8434

COLORADO

Colorado Business Directory
American Business Directories
5711 S. Eighty-sixth Circle
PO Box 27347
Omaha, NE 68127
402-593-4600

CONNECTICUT

Connecticut Business Directory
American Business Directories
5711 S. Eighty-sixth Circle
PO Box 27347
Omaha, NE 68127
402-593-4600

Connecticut, Rhode Island Directory of Manufacturers
Commerce Register, Inc.
190 Godwin Avenue
Midland Park, NJ 07432
201-445-3000

Connecticut Service Directory
George D. Hall Company
50 Congress Street
Boston, MA 02109
617-523-3745

Directory of Connecticut Manufacturers
George D. Hall Company
50 Congress Street
Boston, MA 02109
617-523-3745

MacRAE's State Industrial Directory
Connecticut-Rhode Island MacRAE's Blue
    Book, Inc.
817 Broadway
New York, NY 10003
212-673-4700
800-MAC-RAES

DELAWARE

**Delaware Directory of Commerce and
    Industry**
Manufacturers' News, Inc.
1633 Central Street
Evanston, IL 60201
708-864-7000

The Delaware Valley Corporate Guide
Corfacts, Inc.
50 Route 9 N.
Morganville, NJ 07751
201-972-2500

**Directory of Central Atlantic States
    Manufacturers**
George D. Hall Company
50 Congress Street
Boston, MA 02109
617-523-3745
(Includes Maryland, Delaware, Virginia, West
    Virginia, North Carolina, and South
    Carolina)

WASHINGTON, D.C.

**Dalton's Baltimore-Washington Metropolitan
    Directory**
Dalton's Directory
410 Lancaster Avenue
Haverford, PA 19041
800-221-1050
215-649-2680

FLORIDA

Florida Business Directory
American Business Directories
5711 S. Eighty-sixth Circle
PO Box 27347
Omaha, NE 68127
402-593-4600

Florida Manufacturers Register
Manufacturers' News, Inc.
1633 Central Street
Evanston, IL 60201
708-864-7000

GEORGIA

Georgia Business Directory
American Business Directories
5711 S. Eighty-sixth Circle
PO Box 27347
Omaha, NE 68127
402-593-4600

Georgia Manufacturers Register
Manufacturers' News, Inc.
1633 Central Street
Evanston, IL 60201
708-864-7000

Georgia Manufacturing Directory
Department of Industry, Trade, and Tourism
Marquis II Tower, Suite 1100
285 Peachtree Center Avenue
Box 56706
Atlanta, GA 30343
404-656-3607

**Southeastern Regional Manufacturers
    Directory**
George D. Hall Company
50 Congress Street
Boston, MA 02109
617-523-3745
(Includes Alabama, Georgia, and Mississippi)

HAWAII

Directory of Manufacturers
Chamber of Commerce of Hawaii
735 Bishop Street
Honolulu, HI 98613
808-531-4111

Hawaii Business Directory
American Business Directories
5711 S. Eighty-sixth Circle
PO Box 27347
Omaha, NE 68127
402-593-4600

IDAHO

Idaho Business Directory
American Business Directories
5711 S. Eighty-sixth Circle
PO Box 27347
Omaha, NE 68127
402-593-4600

Idaho Manufacturing Directory
Center for Business Development and Research
College of Business and Economics
University of Idaho
Moscow, ID 83843
208-885-6611

Inland Northwest Manufacturing Directory
Spokane Area Economic Development Council
N. 221 Well, Suite 310
PO Box 203
Spokane, WA 99210
309-624-9285
(Covers western Montana, northern Idaho and
    Oregon, and eastern Washington)

ILLINOIS

Harris Illinois Industrial Directory
Harris Publishing Company
2057 Aurora Road
Twinsburg, OH 44087
216-425-9000
800-888-5900

Illinois Business Directory
American Business Directories
5711 S. Eighty-sixth Circle
PO Box 27347
Omaha, NE 68127
402-593-4600

Illinois Manufacturers Register
Manufacturers' News, Inc.
1633 Central Street
Evanston, IL 60201
708-864-7000

Illinois Services Register
Manufacturers' News, Inc.
1633 Central Street
Evanston, IL 60201
708-864-7000

INDIANA

Harris Indiana Industrial Directory
Harris Publishing Company
2057 Aurora Road
Twinsburg, OH 44087
216-425-9000
800-888-5900

Indiana Business Directory
American Business Directories
5711 S. Eighty-sixth Circle
PO Box 27347
Omaha, NE 68127
402-593-4600

Indiana Manufacturers Register
Manufacturers' News, Inc.
1633 Central Street
Evanston, IL 60201
708-864-7000

IOWA

Directory of Iowa Manufacturers
Harris Publishing Company
2057 Aurora Road
Twinsburg, OH 44087
216-425-9000
800-888-5900

Iowa Business Directory
American Business Directories
5711 S. Eighty-sixth Circle
PO Box 27347
Omaha, NE 68127
402-593-4600

Iowa Manufacturers Register
Manufacturers' News, Inc.
1633 Central Street
Evanston, IL 60201
708-864-7000

KANSAS

Kansas Business Directory
American Business Directories
5711 S. Eighty-sixth Circle
PO Box 27347
Omaha, NE 68127
402-593-4600

KENTUCKY

Harris Kentucky Industrial Directory
Harris Publishing Company
2057 Aurora Road
Twinsburg, OH 44087
216-425-9000
800-888-5900

Kentucky Business Directory
American Business Directories
5711 S. Eighty-sixth Circle
PO Box 27347
Omaha, NE 68127
402-593-4600

Kentucky Directory of Manufacturers
Department of Business and Industry
Capital Plaza Tower
Frankfort, KY 40601
502-564-4886

Kentucky Manufacturers Register
Manufacturers' News, Inc.
1633 Central Street
Evanston, IL 60201
708-864-7000

LOUISIANA

Directory of Louisiana Manufacturers
Department of Economic Development
Box 94185, Capitol Station
Baton Rouge, LA 70804-9185
504-342-5383

Greater Baton Rouge Manufacturers Directory
Greater Baton Rouge Chamber of Commerce
564 Laurel Street
PO Box 3217
Baton Rouge, LA 70821
504-381-7125

Louisiana Manufacturers Register
Manufacturers' News, Inc.
1633 Central Street
Evanston, IL 60201
708-864-7000

MAINE

Maine, Vermont, New Hampshire Directory of Manufacturers
Commerce Register, Inc.
190 Godwin Avenue
Midland Park, NJ 07432
201-445-3000

MacRAE's State Directories—Maine/New Hampshire/Vermont
MacRAE's Blue Book, Inc.
817 Broadway
New York, NY 10003
212-673-4700
800-MAC-RAES

Maine Business Directory
American Business Directories
5711 S. Eighty-sixth Circle
PO Box 27347
Omaha, NE 68127
402-593-4600

MARYLAND

Dalton's Baltimore-Washington Metropolitan Directory
Dalton's Directory
410 Lancaster Avenue
Haverford, PA 19041
215-649-2680
800-221-1050

Directory of Central Atlantic States Manufacturers
George D. Hall Company
50 Congress Street
Boston, MA 02109
617-523-3745
(Includes Maryland, Delaware, Virginia, West Virginia, North Carolina, and South Carolina)

Harris Directory of Maryland Manufacturers
Harris Publishing Company
2057 Aurora Road
Twinsburg, OH 44087
216-425-9000
800-888-5900

MacRAE's State Directories— Maryland/D.C./Delaware
MacRAE's Blue Book, Inc.
817 Broadway
New York, NY 10003
212-673-4700
800-MAC-RAES

Maryland Business Directory
American Business Directories
5711 S. Eighty-sixth Circle
PO Box 27347
Omaha, NE 68127
402-593-4600

MASSACHUSETTS

Directory of Massachusetts Manufacturers
George D. Hall Company
50 Congress Street
Boston, MA 02109
617-523-3745

Directory of New England Manufacturers
George D. Hall Company
50 Congress Street
Boston, MA 02109
617-523-3745

Massachusetts Business Directory
American Business Directories
5711 S. Eighty-sixth Circle
PO Box 27347
Omaha, NE 68127
402-593-4600

Massachusetts Directory of Manufacturers
Commerce Register, Inc.
190 Godwin Avenue
Midland Park, NJ 07432
201-445-3000

Massachusetts Service Directory
George D. Hall Company
50 Congress Street
Boston, MA 02109
617-523-3745

MICHIGAN

Harris Michigan Industrial Directory
Harris Publishing Company
2057 Aurora Road
Twinsburg, OH 44087
216-425-9000
800-888-5900

Michigan Business Directory
American Business Directories
5711 S. Eighty-sixth Circle
PO Box 27347
Omaha, NE 68127
402-593-4600

Michigan Distributors Directory
Pick Publications, Inc.
28715 Greenfield Road
Southfield, MI 48076
313-443-1799

MINNESOTA

Minnesota Business Directory
American Business Directories
5711 S. Eighty-sixth Circle
PO Box 27347
Omaha, NE 68127
402-593-4600

Minnesota Manufacturers Directory
George D. Hall Company
50 Congress Street
Boston, MA 02109
617-523-3745

Minnesota Manufacturers Register
Manufacturers' News, Inc.
1633 Central Street
Evanston, IL 60201
708-864-7000

MISSISSIPPI

Mississippi Business Directory
American Business Directories
5711 S. Eighty-sixth Circle
PO Box 27347
Omaha, NE 68127
402-593-4600

Southeastern Regional Manufacturers Directory
George D. Hall Company
50 Congress Street
Boston, MA 02109
617-523-3745
(Includes Alabama, Georgia, and Mississippi)

MISSOURI

Harris Missouri Directory of Manufacturers
IDC
(division of Harris Publishing Co.)
2057 Aurora Road
Twinsburg, OH 44087
216-425-9000
800-888-5900

Missouri Business Directory
American Business Directories
5711 S. Eighty-sixth Circle
PO Box 27347
Omaha, NE 68127
402-593-4600

Missouri Manufacturers Register
Manufacturers' News, Inc.
1633 Central Street
Evanston, IL 60201
708-864-7000

MONTANA

Inland Northwest Manufacturing Directory
Spokane Area Economic Development Council
N. 221 Well, Suite 310
Box 203
Spokane, WA 99210
309-624-9285
(Covers western Montana, northern Idaho and Oregon, and eastern Washington)

Montana Business Directory
American Business Directories
5711 S. Eighty-sixth Circle
PO Box 27347
Omaha, NE 68127
402-593-4600

Montana Manufacturers Directory
Montana Department of Commerce
Small Business Development Center
1424 Ninth Avenue
Helena, MT 59620
406-443-3923

NEBRASKA

Directory of Nebraska Manufacturers
Department of Economic Development
Box 94666
Lincoln, NE 68509
402-471-3111

Nebraska Business Directory
American Business Directories
5711 S. Eighty-sixth Circle
PO Box 27347
Omaha, NE 68127
402-593-4600

NEVADA

Nevada Business Directory
American Business Directories
5711 S. Eighty-sixth Circle
PO Box 27347
Omaha, NE 68127
402-593-4600

NEW HAMPSHIRE

Maine, Vermont, New Hampshire Directory of Manufacturers
Commerce Register, Inc.
190 Godwin Avenue
Midland Park, NJ 07432
201-445-3000

New Hampshire Manufacturing Directory
Tower Publishing Co.
36 Diamond Street
PO Box 7720
Portland, ME 04112
207-774-9813
(Also available from:
Manufacturers' News, Inc.
1633 Central Street
Evanston, IL 60201
708-864-8000)

**MacRAE's State Directories—
Maine/New Hampshire/Vermont**
MacRAE's Blue Book, Inc.
817 Broadway
New York, NY 10003
212-673-4700
800-MAC-RAES

New Hampshire Business Directory
American Business Directories
5711 S. Eighty-sixth Circle
PO Box 27347
Omaha, NE 68127
402-593-4600

NEW JERSEY

Business Journal's Directory of Manufacturing
Corfacts—Business Journal of New Jersey
Business Information Division
50 Route 9 N
Morganville, NJ 07751
800-678-2565

New Jersey Business Directory
American Business Directories
5711 S. Eighty-sixth Circle
PO Box 27347
Omaha, NE 68127
402-593-4600

New Jersey Service Directory
George D. Hall Company
50 Congress Street
Boston, MA 02109
617-523-3745

NEW MEXICO

New Mexico Business Directory
American Business Directories
5711 S. Eighty-sixth Circle
PO Box 27347
Omaha, NE 68127
402-593-4600

New Mexico Manufacturing Directory
Economic Development & Tourism Department
1100 St. Francis Drive
Santa Fe, NM 87503
505-827-6217

NEW YORK

Dalton's New York Metropolitan Directory
Dalton's Directory
410 Lancaster Avenue
Haverford, PA 19041
800-221-1050
215-649-2680
(Also includes northern New Jersey)

Greater Buffalo Business Directory
Greater Buffalo Chamber of Commerce
107 Delaware Avenue
Buffalo, NY 14202
716-852-7100

New York Business Directory
American Business Directories
5711 S. Eighty-sixth Circle
PO Box 27347
Omaha, NE 68127
402-593-4600

New York Manufacturers Directory
George D. Hall Company
50 Congress Street
Boston, MA 02109
617-523-3745

**New York Metropolitan Directory of
 Manufacturers**
Commerce Register, Inc.
190 Godwin Avenue
Midland Park, NJ 07432
201-445-3000

New York Upstate Directory of Manufacturers
Commerce Register, Inc.
190 Godwin Avenue
Midland Park, NJ 07432
201-445-3000

NORTH CAROLINA

**Directory of Central Atlantic States
 Manufacturers**
George D. Hall Company
50 Congress Street
Boston, MA 02109
617-523-3745

(Includes Maryland, Delaware, Virginia, West
 Virginia, North Carolina, and South
 Carolina)

Directory of North Carolina Manufacturers
George D. Hall Company
50 Congress Street
Boston, MA 02109
617-523-3745

**MacRAE's State Directories—
 North Carolina/South Carolina/Virginia**
MacRAE's Blue Book, Inc.
817 Broadway
New York, NY 10003
212-673-4700
800-MAC-RAES

North Carolina Business Directory
American Business Directories
5711 S. Eighty-sixth Circle
PO Box 27347
Omaha, NE 68127
402-593-4600

NORTH DAKOTA

Directory of North Dakota Manufacturers
Economic Development Commission
604 E. Boulevard
Bismarck, ND 58505
701-224-2810
(free)

North Dakota Business Directory
American Business Directories
5711 S. Eighty-sixth Circle
PO Box 27347
Omaha, NE 68127
402-593-4600

OHIO

Harris Ohio Industrial Directory
Harris Publishing Company
2057 Aurora Road
Twinsburg, OH 44087
216-425-9000
800-888-5900

Ohio Directory of Manufacturers
Commerce Register, Inc.
190 Godwin Avenue
Midland Park, NJ 07432
201-445-3000

Ohio Manufacturers Register
Manufacturers' News, Inc.
1633 Central Street
Evanston, IL 60201
708-864-7000

Ohio Business Directory
American Business Directories
5711 S. Eighty-sixth Circle
PO Box 27347
Omaha, NE 68127
402-593-4600

OKLAHOMA

Oklahoma Business Directory
American Business Directories
5711 S. Eighty-sixth Circle
PO Box 27347
Omaha, NE 68127
402-593-4600

Oklahoma Directory of Manufacturers
Department of Commerce
PO Box 26980
Oklahoma City, OK 73126

OREGON

Directory of Oregon Manufacturers
Economic Development Department
595 Cottage Street NE
Salem, OR 97310
503-373-1200

Inland Northwest Manufacturing Directory
Spokane Area Economic Development Council
N. 221 Well, Suite 310
PO Box 203
Spokane, WA 99210
309-624-9285

(Covers western Montana, northern Idaho and
   Oregon, and eastern Washington)

Oregon Business Directory
American Business Directories
5711 S. Eighty-sixth Circle
PO Box 27347
Omaha, NE 68127
402-593-4600

PENNSYLVANIA

Dalton's Philadelphia Metropolitan Directory
Dalton's Directory
410 Lancaster Avenue
Haverford, PA 19041
215-649-2680
800-221-1050

Harris Pennsylvania Industrial Directory
Harris Publishing Company
2057 Aurora Road
Twinsburg, OH 44087
216-425-9000
800-888-5900

Pennsylvania Business Directory
American Business Directories
5711 S. Eighty-sixth Circle
PO Box 27347
Omaha, NE 68127
402-593-4600

Pennsylvania Directory of Manufacturers
Commerce Register, Inc.
190 Godwin Avenue
Midland Park, NJ 07432
201-445-3000

Pennsylvania Manufacturers Register
Manufacturers' News, Inc.
1633 Central Street
Evanston, IL 60201
708-864-7000

RHODE ISLAND

Connecticut, Rhode Island Directory of Manufacturers
Commerce Register, Inc.
190 Godwin Avenue
Midland Park, NJ 07432
201-445-3000

MacRAE's State Directories—Massachusetts/Rhode Island
MacRAE's Blue Book, Inc.
817 Broadway
New York, NY 10003
212-673-4700
800-MAC-RAES

Rhode Island Business Directory
American Business Directories
5711 S. Eighty-sixth Circle
PO Box 27347
Omaha, NE 68127
402-593-4600

Rhode Island Directory of Manufacturers
Department of Economic Development
7 Jackson Walkway
Providence, RI 02903
401-227-2601

SOUTH CAROLINA

Directory of Central Atlantic States Manufacturers
George D. Hall Company
50 Congress Street
Boston, MA 02109
617-523-3745
(Includes Maryland, Delaware, Virginia, West Virginia, North Carolina, and South Carolina)

MacRAE's State Directories—North Carolina/South Carolina/Virginia
MacRAE's Blue Book, Inc.
817 Broadway
New York, NY 10003
212-673-4700
800-MAC-RAES

South Carolina Business Directory
American Business Directories
5711 S. Eighty-sixth Circle
PO Box 27347
Omaha, NE 68127
402-593-4600

SOUTH DAKOTA

South Dakota Business Directory
American Business Directories
5711 S. Eighty-sixth Circle
PO Box 27347
Omaha, NE 68127
402-593-4600

South Dakota Manufacturers and Processors Directory
Governor's Office of Economic Development
711 Wells Avenue
Pierre, SD 57501-3369
605-773-5032

TENNESSEE

Tennessee Business Directory
American Business Directories
5711 S. Eighty-sixth Circle
PO Box 27347
Omaha, NE 68127
402-593-4600

TEXAS

Directory of Texas Manufacturers
University of Texas at Austin
Bureau of Business Research
PO Box 7459
Austin, TX 78713
512-471-1616

Texas Business Directory
American Business Directories
5711 S. Eighty-sixth Circle
PO Box 27347
Omaha, NE 68127
402-593-4600

Texas Manufacturers Register
Manufacturers' News, Inc.
1633 Central Street
Evanston, IL 60201
708-864-7000

UTAH

Utah Business Directory
American Business Directories
5711 S. Eighty-sixth Circle
PO Box 27347
Omaha, NE 68127
402-593-4600

Utah Directory of Business and Industry
Department of Employment Security
Division of Economic Development
324 S. State Street, Suite 200
Salt Lake City, UT 84111
801-538-8700

VERMONT

Maine, Vermont, New Hampshire Directory of Manufacturers
Commerce Register, Inc.
190 Godwin Avenue
Midland Park, NJ 07432
201-445-3000

Vermont Business Directory
American Business Directories
5711 S. Eighty-sixth Circle
PO Box 27347
Omaha, NE 68127
402-593-4600

VIRGINIA

Directory of Central Atlantic States Manufacturers
George D. Hall Company
50 Congress Street
Boston, MA 02109
617-523-3745

(Includes Maryland, Delaware, Virginia, West Virginia, North Carolina, and South Carolina)

MacRAE's State Directories—North Carolina/South Carolina/Virginia
MacRAE's Blue Book, Inc.
817 Broadway
New York, NY 10003
212-673-4700
800-MAC-RAES

Virginia Business Directory
American Business Directories
5711 S. Eighty-sixth Circle
PO Box 27347
Omaha, NE 68127
402-593-4600

WASHINGTON

Inland Northwest Manufacturing Directory
Spokane Area Economic Development Council
N. 221 Well, Suite 310
PO Box 203
Spokane, WA 99210
309-624-9285
(Covers western Montana, northern Idaho and Oregon, and eastern Washington)

Washington Business Directory
American Business Directories
5711 S. Eighty-sixth Circle
PO Box 27347
Omaha, NE 68127
402-593-4600

Washington Manufacturers Register
Database Publishing Co.
523 Superior Avenue
Newport Beach, CA 92663
800-888-8434

WEST VIRGINIA

Directory of Central Atlantic States Manufacturers
George D. Hall Company
50 Congress Street
Boston, MA 02109
617-523-3745
(Includes Maryland, Delaware, Virginia, West Virginia, North Carolina, and South Carolina)

Harris West Virginia Manufacturing Directory
Harris Publishing Company
2057 Aurora Road
Twinsburg, OH 44087
216-425-9000
800-888-5900

West Virginia Business Directory
American Business Directories
5711 S. Eighty-sixth Circle
PO Box 27347
Omaha, NE 68127
402-593-4600

West Virginia Manufacturers Register
Manufacturers' News, Inc.
1633 Central Street
Evanston, IL 60201
708-864-7000

WISCONSIN

Classified Directory of Wisconsin Manufacturers
WMC Service Corporation
501 E. Washington Avenue
PO Box 352
Madison, WI 53701-0352
608-258-3400

Wisconsin Business Directory
American Business Directories
5711 S. Eighty-sixth Circle
PO Box 27347
Omaha, NE 68127
402-593-4600

Wisconsin Manufacturers Register
Manufacturers' News, Inc.
1633 Central Street
Evanston, IL 60201
708-864-7000

Wisconsin Services Directory
WMC Service Corporation
501 E. Washington Avenue
PO Box 352
Madison, WI 53701-0352
608-258-3400

WYOMING

Wyoming Business Directory
American Business Directories
5711 S. Eighty-sixth Circle
PO Box 27347
Omaha, NE 68127
402-593-4600

SPECIFIC INDUSTRY DIRECTORIES

ACCOUNTING DIRECTORIES

Accountant's Directory
American Business Directories, Inc.
American Business Information, Inc.
5711 S. Eighty-sixth Circle
PO Box 27347
Omaha, NE 68127
402-593-4600
(broken into 7 parts; cost of entire US directory
   is $3,700; each part is less—for example, the
   Northeast directory of 23,000 addresses is
   $735, or about 3 cents per name)

Firm on Firm Directory
American Institute of Certified Public
   Accountants
Harborside Financial Center
201 Plaza 3
Jersey City, NJ 07311-3881
800-334-6961

**National Directory of Accounting Firms and
   Accountants**
by Thomas M. Bachman
Gale Research
835 Penobscot Building
Detroit, MI 48226-4904
800-877-GALE

ADVERTISING/PUBLIC RELATIONS DIRECTORIES

AAAA Roster and Organization
American Association of Advertising Agencies
666 Third Avenue
New York, NY 10017
212-682-2500

**Macmillan Directory of International
   Advertisers and Agencies**
National Register Publishing Company
3004 Glenview Road
Wilmette, IL 60091
708-441-2210
800-323-6772

**O'Dwyer's Directory of Corporate
   Communications**
271 Madison Avenue
New York, NY 10016
212-679-2471

**O'Dwyers Directory of Public Relations
   Executives**
271 Madison Avenue
New York, NY 10016
212-679-2471

O'Dwyers Directory of Public Relations Firms
271 Madison Avenue
New York, NY 10016
212-679-2471

Standard Directory of Advertising Agencies
National Register Publishing Company
3004 Glenview Road
Wilmette, IL 60091
708-441-2210
800-323-6722

AEROSPACE DIRECTORIES

Aerospace Facts & Figures
Aerospace Industry Association
1250 Eye Street NW
Washington, DC 20005
202-371-8400

ARTS AND DESIGN DIRECTORIES

American Art Directory
R. R. Bowker
121 Chanlon Road
New Providence, NJ 07974
800-521-8110

Creative Black Book
Macmillan Creative Services Group
115 Fifth Avenue
New York, NY 10003
212-254-1330

Design Firm Directory
Wefler & Associates
Box 1167
Evanston, IL 60204
708-475-1866

Graphic Artists Guild Directory
Graphic Artists Guild
11 W. Twentieth Street, Eighth Floor
New York, NY 10011
212-463-7730

Graphic Arts Blue Book
A. F. Lewis and Co., Inc.
79 Madison Avenue
New York, NY 10016
212-679-0770

AUTOMOTIVE INDUSTRY DIRECTORIES

Automotive News Market Data Book
Automotive News
1400 Woodbridge Avenue
Detroit MI 48207
313-446-6000
Annual, special issue of *Automotive News;* in
    addition to statistics, includes extensive
    listings of auto manufacturers, suppliers,
    etc., with addresses and contact names.

Ward's Automotive Yearbook
Ward's Communications, Inc.
28 W. Adams Street
Detroit MI 48226
313-962-4433

BANKING/FINANCE DIRECTORIES

**American Banker Directory of U.S. Banking
    Executives**
American Banker, Inc.
525 W. Forty-second Street
New York, NY 10036
212-563-1900

American Banker Yearbook
American Banker, Inc.
One State Street Plaza
New York, NY 10004
212-943-6700

American Financial Directory
McFadden Business Publications
6195 Crooked Creek Road
Norcross, GA 30092-9986
404-448-1011
800-247-7376

American Savings Directory
McFadden Business Publications
6195 Crooked Creek Road
Norcross, GA 30092-9986
404-448-1011
800-247-7376

**Bankers Monthly Roster of Major Finance
    Companies**
Bankers Monthly
601 Skokie Boulevard
Northbrook, IL 60062
312-498-2500

**Business Week—Top 200 Banking
    Institutions Issue**
McGraw-Hill, Inc.
1221 Avenue of the Americas
New York, NY 10020
212-512-4776

Corporate Finance Sourcebook
National Register Publishing Company
3004 Glenview Road
Wilmette, IL 60091
708-441-2210
800-323-6772

Directory of American Financial Institutions
McFadden Business Publications
6195 Crooked Creek Road
Norcross, GA 30092
404-448-1011

Directory of American Savings & Loan Associations
T. K. Sanderson Organization
200 E. Twenty-fifth Street
Baltimore, MD 21218
301-235-3383

Moody's Bank and Finance Manual
Moody's Investors Service, Inc.
99 Church Street
New York, NY 10007
212-553-0300

Polk's Bank Directory
R. L. Polk & Co.
PO Box 3051000
Nashville, TN 37230-5100
615-889-3350
800-827-2265
(Two different editions: North American and International)

Securities Industry Yearbook
Securities Industry Association
120 Broadway
New York, NY 10271
212-608-1500

BROADCASTING DIRECTORIES

Gale Directory of Publications and Broadcast Media
Gale Research, Inc.
835 Penobscot Building
Detroit, MI 48226-4094
800-877-4253

Standard Rate & Data Service—Spot Radio Rates & Data; Spot Television Rates & Data
3004 Glenview Road
Wilmette, IL 60091
708-256-6067

World Radio TV Handbook
Billboard Publications, Inc.
1515 Broadway
New York, NY 10036
212-764-7300

CHEMICALS INDUSTRY DIRECTORY

Chem Sources—International and **Chem Sources—USA**
Chemical Sources International
PO Box 1824
Clemson, SC 29633
904-673-1241

Chemical Industry Directory
State Mutual Book and Periodical Service
521 Fifth Avenue
New York, NY 10017
212-682-5844

Chemicals Directory
275 Washington
Newton, MA 02158
617-964-3030
(Relatively low-cost—$40 in 1992—making this a good basic source for a resume mailing list)

Directory of Chemical Producers, U.S.A.
Stanford Research Institute International
333 Ravenswood Avenue
Menlo Park, CA 94025
415-859-3627

COMPUTERS/ELECTRONICS DIRECTORIES

Directory of Public High Technology Corporations
American Investor, Inc.
311 Bainbridge Street
Philadelphia, PA 19147
215-925-2761

Directory of Top Computer Executives
Applied Computer Research
PO Box 9280
Phoenix, AZ 85068
602-995-5929

Who's Who in Electronics Regional Source Directory
Harris Publishing Company
2057 Aurora Road
Twinsburg, OH 44087
216-425-9000
800-888-5900

CONSUMER PRODUCTS DIRECTORIES

Appliance Manufacturer Annual Directory
Corcoran Communications, Inc.
29100 Aurora Road, Suite 310
Solon, OH 44139
216-349-3060

Electronic Market Data Book
Electronic Industries Association
2001 Pennsylvania Avenue NW
Washington, DC 20006-1813
202-457-4900

**Household and Personal Products Industry
   Buyers Guide**
Rodman Publishing Corp.
26 Lake Street
Ramsey, NJ 07446
201-825-2552

**Soap/Cosmetics/Chemical Specialties
   Blue Book**
MacNair-Dorland Co.
101 W. Thirty-first Street
New York, NY 10001
212-279-4457

ENERGY DIRECTORIES

**Brown's Directory of North American &
   International Gas Companies**
1 East First Street
Duluth, MN 55802
218-723-9200

Keystone Coal Industry Manual
Maclean Hunter Publishing Co.
29 N. Wacker Drive
Chicago, IL 60606
312-726-2802

Oil & Gas Directory
PO Box 130508
Houston, TX 77219
713-529-8789

Whole World Oil Directory
National Register Publishing Company, Inc.
3004 Glenview Road
Wilmette, IL 60091
708-441-2210
800-323-6772

ENTERTAINMENT DIRECTORIES

Billboard International Buyer's Guide
Billboard Publications, Inc.
1515 Broadway
New York, NY 10036
212-764-7300

Cash Box Annual Worldwide Directory
Cash Box
330 W. Fifty-eighth Street
New York, NY 10019
212-586-2640

International Motion Picture Almanac
Quigley Publishing Co.
159 W. Fifty-third Street
New York, NY 10019
212-247-3100

**Nationwide Music Record Industry Toll-Free
   Directory**
CDE Box 310551
Atlanta, GA 30331
404-344-7621

**On Location: National Film and Videotape
   Production Directory**
6777 Hollywood Boulevard
Los Angeles, CA 90028
213-467-1268

Radio & Records Ratings Report & Directory
Radio and Records, Inc.
1930 Century Park West
Los Angeles, CA 90067
213-553-4330

Recording Engineer/Producer Black Book
Intertec Publishing Corp.
9221 Quivira Road
Overland Park, KS 66215
913-888-4664

FASHION/TEXTILE INDUSTRY DIRECTORIES

AAMA Directory
American Apparel Manufacturers Association
2500 Wilson Boulevard
Arlington, VA 22201
703-524-1864

Apparel Trades Book
Dun & Bradstreet, Inc.
1 Diamond Hill Road
Murray Hill, NJ 07974
201-665-5000

Davison's Textile Blue Book
Davison Publishing Company, Inc.
PO Box 477
Ridgewood, NJ 07451
201-445-3135

The Fashion Guide:
 International Designer Directory
Fairchild Publications
7 E. Twelfth Street
New York, NY 10003
212-630-3880
800-247-6622

The Fashion Resource Directory
Fairchild Publications
7 E. Twelfth Street
New York, NY 10003
212-630-3880
800-247-6622

FOOD AND BEVERAGE INDUSTRY DIRECTORIES

Food Engineering's Directory of U.S. Food
 and Beverage Plants
Chilton Book Co.
Chilton Way
Radnor, PA 19089
215-964-4000

Hereld's 5000: The Directory of Leading U.S.
 Food, Confectionery, Beverage, and
 Petfood Manufacturers
The Hereld Organization
200 Leeder Hill Drive, Suite 341
Hamden, CT 06517
203-281-6766

Jobson's Handbook
Jobson Publishing Corp.
325 Park Avenue South
New York, NY 10010
212-685-4848
(Covers the alcoholic-beverage industry)

Prepared Foods Industry Sourcebook
Prepared Foods
8750 W. Bryn Mawr Avenue
Chicago, IL 60631
312-693-3200

GOVERNMENT DIRECTORIES

Congressional Yellow Book
Monitor Publishing Co.
104 Fifth Avenue, Second Floor
New York, NY 10011
212-627-4140
(Lists members of Congress, committees, etc.)

Federal Career Directory
Superintendent of Documents
Government Printing Office
Washington, DC 20402-9325
202-783-3238
(Order number is 006-000-01339-2; covers
 federal employment)

Federal Personnel Office Directory
Federal Reports, Inc.
1010 Vermont Avenue NW, Suite 408
Washington, DC 20005
202-393-3311 (U.S. government personnel
 offices listed with pertinent information)

Federal Regional Yellow Book
Monitor Publishing Co.
104 Fifth Avenue, Second Floor
New York, NY 10011
212-627-4140
(Lists thousands of local federal offices
nationwide—useful for the non-D.C. federal
job hunter)

Federal Yellow Book
address same as above
(Lists thousands of major employees of the
executive branch)

**FOCIS: The Federal Occupation and Career
Information System**
National Technical Information Service (NTIS)
5285 Port Royal Road
Springfield, VA 22161-0001
703-487-4650
(PC-based interactive expert system that
complements the federal directory; guides
user through hundreds of federal white-
collar positions in hundreds of federal
agencies, with descriptions of type of job,
type of work, address, qualifications, etc.
Current version doesn't include job openings
—future versions may. Cost at time of
writing was $49.95; updated yearly)

State and Regional Associations of the U.S.
Columbia Books
1212 New York Avenue NW, Suite 300
Washington DC 20005
202-898-0662
(Lists most associations state by state and region
by region; useful for the job hunter looking
to contact local affiliates of major associations
to use them to help in job hunt)

Government Job Finder
Planning Communications
7215 Oak Avenue
River Forest, IL 60305
708-366-5200
800-829-5220
(Hundreds of sources, plus evaluations;
affordable and comprehensive; publishes
separate directories for nonprofits and
professionals.)

HEALTH CARE INDUSTRY DIRECTORIES

AHA Guide to the Health Care Field
American Hospital Association
840 N. Lakeshore Drive
Chicago, IL 60611
312-280-6000

Billian's Hospital Blue Book
2100 Powers Ferry Road
Atlanta, GA 30339
404-955-5656
(Affordable price; possibly useful for mailing
lists)

Biotechnology Directory
Stockton Press
15 E. Twenty-sixth Street
New York, NY 10010
212-481-1334

Blue Book Digest of HMOs
National Association of Employers on Health
Care Alternatives
PO Box 220
Key Biscayne, FL 33149
305-361-2810

Dun's Guide to Healthcare Companies
Dun's Marketing Services
3 Sylvan Way
Parsippany, NJ 07054-3896
201-605-6000

Drug Topics Red Book
Medical Economics Co.
5 Paragon Drive
Montvale, NJ 07645
201-358-7200

Hospital Phone Book
Reed Reference Publishing
121 Chanlon Road
New Providence, RI 07974
800-521-8110
(Thousands of numbers, etc., on hospitals
nationwide)

Medical and Health Information Directory
Gale Research Co.
Book Tower
Detroit, MI 48226
313-961-2242
800-223-GALE

U.S. Medical Directory
Reed Reference Publishing
121 Chanlon Road
New Providence, RI 07974
800-521-8110
(Extensive listings of health care facilities and
practitioners)

HOSPITALITY INDUSTRY DIRECTORIES

Chain Restaurant Operators and **High Volume
Independent Restaurants**
Lebhar-Friedman, Inc.
425 Park Avenue
New York, NY 10022
212-371-9400, ext. 306

**Directory of Hotel and Motel Systems Hotel
and Motel Red Book**
American Hotel Association Directory
Corporation
1201 New York Avenue NW
Washington, DC 20005
202-289-3162

Foodservice Industry Directory
National Restaurant Association
1200 Seventeenth Street NW, Suite 800
Washington, DC 20036
800-424-8156

Who's Who in the Lodging Industry
American Hotel and Motel Association
1201 New York Avenue NW
Washington, DC 20005
202-289-3162
(Relatively low-cost annual directory—$39.95
in 1992)

INSURANCE DIRECTORIES

Best's Insurance Reports
Ambest Road
Oldwick, NJ 08858
908-439-2200

Insurance Almanac
Underwriter Printing and Publishing Co.
50 E. Palisade Avenue
Englewood, NJ 07631
201-569-8808
(Lists over 3,000 insurance companies; national,
state, and local insurance associations;
agents; brokers, etc.)

Insurance Field Directories
Insurance Field Company
PO Box 24244
Louisville, KY 40224
502-491-5857
(Directories for 11 different states or regions)

Insurance Phone Book and Directory
U.S. Directory Service
655 NW 128th Street
Miami, FL 33168
305-769-1700

Who's Who in Insurance
Underwriter Printing and Publishing Co.
50 E. Palisade Avenue
Englewood, NJ 07631
201-569-8808
(Lists over 5,000 individuals involved in the
insurance industry, such as officials, brokers,
etc. Includes title, company affiliation, and
address, biographical information, and
more. May be useful to prepare for
interviews.)

METALS AND MINING DIRECTORIES

**Dun's Industrial Guide: The Metalworking
Directory**
Dun and Bradstreet, Inc.
3 Century Drive
Parsippany, NJ 07054-3896
201-455-0900

**Engineering and Mining Journal International
Directory of Mining**
McGraw-Hill, Inc.
1221 Avenue of the Americas
New York, NY 10020
212-512-6158

**Iron and Steel Works Directory of the United
States and Canada**
American Iron and Steel Institute
1000 Sixteenth Street NW
Washington, DC 20036
202-452-7100

PAPER AND FOREST PRODUCTS DIRECTORIES

**Crow's Buyers and Sellers Guide of the Forest
Products Industries**
C. C. Crow Publications
Box 25749
Portland, OR 97225
503-297-1535

Directory of the Forest Products Industry
Miller Freeman Publications, Inc.
PO Box T
Gilroy, CA 95021-9968
408-848-5296

International Pulp and Paper Directory
Miller Freeman Publications, Inc.
PO Box T
Gilroy, CA 95021-9968
408-848-5296

**Lockwood-Post's Directory of the Paper, Pulp,
and Allied Trades**
Miller Freeman Publications, Inc.
PO Box T
Gilroy, CA 95021-9968
408-848-5296

**Walden's ABC Guide and Paper Production
Yearbook**
Walden-Mott Corp.
475 Kinderkamack Road
Oradell, NJ 07649
201-261-2630

PUBLISHING DIRECTORIES

American Book Trade Directory
R. R. Bowker Co.
245 W. Seventeenth Street
New York, NY 10011
212-645-9700
800-521-8110

Bacon's Publicity Checker
Bacon's Publishing Company
332 S. Michigan Avenue, Suite 900
Chicago, IL 60604
312-922-2400
(Lists newspapers and magazines)

Editor & Publisher International Yearbook
Editor & Publisher Company, Inc.
11 W. Nineteenth Street
New York, NY 10011
212-675-4380

Editor & Publisher Market Guide
Editor & Publisher Company, Inc.
11 W. Nineteenth St.
New York, NY 10011
212-675-4380

Gale Directory of Publications and Broadcast Media
Gale Research, Inc.
835 Penobscot Building
Detroit, MI 48226-4094
800-877-4253

Literary Marketplace: The Directory of American Book Publishing and International Literary Marketplace
R. R. Bowker Co.
245 W. Seventeenth Street
New York, NY 10011
212-645-9700
800-521-8110

Magazine Industry Marketplace
R. R. Bowker Company
245 W. Seventeenth Street
New York, NY 10011
212-645-9700

National Directory of Magazines
Oxbridge Communications
150 Fifth Avenue
New York, NY 10011
212-741-0231
800-955-0231

Publishers Directory
Gale Research, Inc.
835 Penobscot Building
Detroit, MI 48226-4094
800-877-4235

Standard Rate & Data Service: Business Publications Rates and Data
Standard Rate & Data Service
3004 Glenview Road
Wilmette, IL 60091
800-323-4588

Ulrich's International Periodicals Directory
R. R. Bowker
PO Box 31
New Providence, NJ 07974-9903
800-521-8100

REAL ESTATE & CONSTRUCTION DIRECTORIES

Blue Book of Major Homebuilders and **Gold Book of Multi-Housing** and **Red Book of Housing Manufacturers**
F. W. Dodge Residential Statistical Services
24 Hartwell Avenue
Lexington, MA 02173
617-860-6821

Executive Guide to Specialists in Industrial and Office Real Estate
Society of Industrial and Office Realtors
777 Fourteenth Street NW
Washington, DC 20005
202-383-1150

National Real Estate Investor Directory
Communications Channels, Inc.
6255 Barfield Road
Atlanta, GA 30328
404-256-9800

The Real Estate Sourcebook
National Register Publishing Company
3004 Glenview Road
Wilmette, IL 60091
708-441-2210
800-323-6772

RETAIL DIRECTORIES

Directory of Consumer Electronics, Photography, and Major Appliance Retailers and Distributors and **Directory of Department Stores** and **Directory of General Merchandise/Variety Chains and Specialty Stores**
Chain Store Guide Information Services
425 Park Avenue
New York, NY 10022
212-371-9400

Fairchild's Financial Manual of Retail Stores
Fairchild Publications
7 E. Twelfth Street
New York, NY 10001
212-244-8780

TELECOMMUNICATIONS DIRECTORIES

Telecommunications Directory
Gale Research, Inc.
835 Penobscot Building
Detroit, MI 48226
800-877-4253

Telephone Engineer & Management Directory
Edgell Communications, Inc.
1 E. First Street
Duluth, MN 55802
218-723-9470
800-346-0085

Telephone Industry Directory and Sourcebook
Phillips Publishing, Inc.
7811 Montrose Road
Potomac, MD 20854
301-340-2100

Telephone Statistics
900 Nineteenth Street NW
Washington, DC 20006-2102
202-835-3100
(Lists top 100 U.S. telephone companies, Class
A & B companies)

TRANSPORTATION DIRECTORIES

Air Freight Directory
Air Cargo, Inc.
1819 Bay Ridge Avenue
Annapolis, MD 21403
301-263-8054

Moody's Transportation Manual
Moody's Investors Service, Inc.
99 Church Street
New York, NY 10007
212-553-0300

National Tank Truck Carrier Directory
2200 Mill Road
Alexandria, VA 22314
703-838-1960

TRAVEL INDUSTRY DIRECTORIES

**Annual Report of the Commuter Regional
    Airline Industry**
Regional Airline Association
1101 Connecticut Avenue NW
Washington, DC 20036
202-857-1170

Aviation and Aerospace White Pages
PO Box 8286
Saddle Brook, NJ 07662
201-794-6725
800-543-6725
(Low-cost directory)

**Official Airline Guide: North American
    Edition** and **Official Airline Guide:
    Worldwide Edition**
Official Airline Guides, Inc.
2000 Clearwater Drive
Oak Brook, IL 60521
312-654-6000
800-323-3537

Travel Industry Personnel Directory
Travel Agent Magazine
825 Seventh Avenue
New York, NY 10019
212-887-1900

Travel Weekly's Work Travel Directory
Travel Weekly
500 Plaza Drive
Secaucus, NJ 07096
201-902-2000

World Aviation Directory
McGraw-Hill
1156 Fifteenth Street
Washington, DC 20005
202-822-4600

UTILITIES DIRECTORIES

American Public Gas Association Directory
American Public Gas Association
PO Box 1426
Vienna, VA 22180
703-281-2910

Directory of Gas Utility Companies
Midwest Oil Register, Inc.
PO Box 7248
Tulsa, OK 74105
918-742-9925

Electrical World Directory of Electric Utilities
McGraw-Hill
1 E. Nineteenth Street
New York, NY 10011
212-337-4068

Moody's Public Utility Manual
Moody's Investors Service, Inc.
99 Church Street
New York, NY 10007
212-553-0300